THE KNOWLEDGE

DAVID KIRBY

Published by Flip Learning

Flip Learning
288 Nimitz Ave
State College, PA 16801

FlipLearning.com

First Flip Learning paperback edition 2021

ISBN-13: 978-1-7355940-2-6

For information about special discounts for bulk purchases,
please contact Flip Learning Sales at sales@fliplearning.com.

Printed in the United States of America

3 5 7 9 10 8 6 4 2

TABLE OF CONTENTS

We're only here for a short while. And I think it's such a lucky accident, having been born, that we're almost obliged to pay attention. In some ways, this is getting far afield. I mean, we are—as far as we know—the only part of the universe that's self-conscious. We could even be the universe's form of consciousness. We might have come along so that the universe could look at itself. I don't know that, but we're made of the same stuff that stars are made of, or that floats around in space. But we're combined in such a way that we can describe what it's like to be alive, to be witnesses. Most of our experience is that of being a witness. We see and hear and smell other things. I think being alive is responding.

—Mark Strand

ABOUT THE AUTHOR

David Kirby's collection *The House on Boulevard St.: New and Selected Poems* was a finalist for the National Book Award in 2007. Kirby is the author of thirty-six books on various topics, including *Little Richard: The Birth of Rock 'n' Roll*, which the *Times Literary Supplement* called "a hymn of praise to the emancipatory power of nonsense" and was named one of *Booklist*'s Top 10 Black History Non-Fiction Books of 2010.

A Johns Hopkins PhD, Kirby teaches at Florida State University, where he has won five major university teaching awards and is the Robert O. Lawton Distinguished Professor of English. Kirby has won fellowships from the Guggenheim Foundation and the National Endowment for the Arts, and recently the Florida Humanities Council presented him with a Lifetime Achievement Award in Writing.

Kirby has what Thomas Jefferson called "a canine appetite for reading" and is a music journalist as well, so his writings are peppered with quotes from science, history, philosophy, and other disciplines in addition to references to music from classical and jazz to R&B and rap.

He lives in Tallahassee with his wife, Barbara Hamby, a poet and fiction writer who also teaches at FSU. Together they edited *Seriously Funny: Poems about Love, Death, Religion, Art, Politics, Sex, and Everything Else*. Kirby's latest poetry collection is *More Than This*.

ABOUT THE AUTHOR

ACKNOWLEDGMENTS

The Knowledge would not exist were it not for Barbara Hamby. Nor would my poems—I'd still write poems if I'd never met Barbara, but they wouldn't be the same poems. When she won a fellowship from the Guggenheim Foundation, a media rep from the university where we both teach called me and said she was writing a press release and wanted to know if I'd married Barbara because she was smart and accomplished. No, I said, I married Barbara because I couldn't keep my hands off her. The media rep says ooo, that's great! So many of the quotes I get are bland—I really like this one!

An hour later, the media rep calls back and says her boss doesn't like my quote, and when I ask why, the rep says it's the hands. So the two of us concocted some milder reason for my attraction to Barbara, but the fact remains that I'm crazy about her. You're holding this copy of *The Knowledge* because you want to know more about poetry. But I'll throw in some romantic advice for free, which is that if you find yourself drawn to someone who does what you do and loves it, and you love her, and she gives every indication of loving you, too, don't just sit there twiddling your thumbs—pop the damned question.

After Barbara, my greatest debt is to my students. Jorge Luis Borges said that surely paradise is a library. I say it's a classroom. When we get up there, students, we'll sit around this big table, and you'll teach me. That's what you've done for decades—why stop now?

I am grateful as well to Allen Woodman of Word Beat Press, publisher of *Diving for Poems*, an early book of mine that I draw on for the first chapter of *The Knowledge*. A number of observations on the connection between poetry and music are from my *Crossroad: Artist, Audience, and the Making of American Music*. Other writings of mine are cited in the Further Reading section, and I am grateful to their publishers, too.

FOREWORD,
OR,
A MISSION FROM GOD

When Jake and Elwood Blues set out to stop a bank from foreclosing on the orphanage where they were raised in *The Blues Brothers*, they face staggering odds, but every time a new obstacle looms, Elwood says stoically, "We're on a mission from God." The film is a musical comedy, so of course the brothers succeed, though they churn out a lot of music and a lot of comedy along the way. To me, that's how we live in this world. We do good work, and along the way, we have as much fun as possible and make sure that others do, too.

Louis Armstrong said that "there are two kinds of music, the good and the bad. I play the good kind." The same is true for poetry. I do my best to write the good kind, and I can show you how to. I've taught thousands of students how to write well. Not all choose to continue as poets, but the ones who do write poems I'd be proud to have written myself. In *The Knowledge*, I will teach you everything I know. I will show you how to write poems that are bright and colorful and engaging and accessible, poems brimming with insight and emotion, ones that not only thrill you as you write them but also make others positively wriggle with joy. I'm on a mission from God.

Poetry is pure excitement for me. That means I get carried away sometimes. When this was just a baby book trying to grow up and become a big one, originally it was called *The Knowledge: Everything You Always Wanted to Know about the High-Stakes, High-Risk, High-Rewards Poetry Game and How to Win It*. But come on—that's twenty words!

So let the present and shorter title of this book be its first lesson, which is that I'm going to show you how to Get It Right: not how to tell the truth or get rich or make other people love you but how, through trial and error and lots of time, to make that perfect (okay, that as-close-to-perfect-as-possible) object, the poem. *The Knowledge* is going to treat every aspect of poetry from its beginning through yesterday, but at every turn, you and I will be working together to find the Goldilocks solution: not the one that's too big or too small but the solution that is just right.

Yes, poetry is a game—for reasons that'll become obvious, if they aren't already, it's the best game you could possibly play—and the good news is that you've already won it. You wouldn't be holding this book unless you've already discovered the joy of playing with words and using them to make a world of your own. So my job isn't to make you a poet. You're a poet already. My job is to show you a slew of techniques and tricks and processes that will make you the best poet you can possibly be.

If that's what you want to be. I tell my students that the best mind you can have is the mind of a poet. Poets are magpies. We pick up shiny objects in our beaks and then fly home and add them to our shiny object collections. Then we put them in a certain order and show early drafts to others and incorporate (or ignore) what they say as we make very different kinds of poems of our finds. But isn't that what a scientist does as they set up an experiment or a lawyer as they prepare an argument for a jury or a chef as they try out a new dish? It's all one mind. I just choose to call it the poet's mind. So you can have a poetic mind and never write a single poem in your life. A lot of my undergraduate students never write another poem after they leave my class, but if they look at the world with a poetic mind for the rest of their lives, I've done my job.

There's nothing special about being a poet. Canadian poet Christian Bök says he knows a lot of poets and that "many are very lazy and very dumb. I always joke with my students that poetry couldn't possibly be as hard as they think it is, because if it were as hard as they thought it was, poets wouldn't do it. Really, they're the laziest, stupidest people I know." Ha, ha! Calm down, Christian—spare my ribs! Really, though, he's right. Poetry is the most democratic of the arts. You have to have cameras and actors and a set to make a movie and brushes and oils and canvas to paint a portrait, but all you need for a poem is a pencil and the back of a takeout menu, so we shouldn't be surprised to find there are people out there who claim they're poets but aren't. That said, if you put some time and effort and training into your poetry, you'll end up not only celebrating the freedom and inventiveness in poems and how that sense of shared play can build community but also connecting through your poems to a larger world of beauty.

I doubt if you have a poster of him up on your dorm room wall, but one of my Elvii is a Russian writer named Varlam Shalamov. Shalamov is chiefly known for *Kolyma Tales*, in which he describes life in the gulag. He was arrested in 1929 for "counterrevolutionary activities" and spent three years in a camp; in 1937, he was arrested again and sentenced to five years in Kolyma in northeastern Siberia. His sentence was extended for additional political crimes, and altogether he spent approximately seventeen years in the camps.

In *Kolyma Tales*, there is no embellishment. The facts themselves are shocking enough. Life in the camp is so primitive that there is neither time nor energy for ideas or even emotions. There is only today, and within this day, the inmates move in robotic exhaustion from one moment to the next.

My favorite story in *Kolyma Tales* is "Cherry Brandy," which relates the death of the poet Osip Mandelstam, who was slightly older than

Shalamov. The point of view is third person, but the action takes place within the poet's fevered mind. Thus the first paragraph begins "the poet was dying" and goes on to say that "the poet had been dying for so long that he no longer understood that he was dying." As in the other *Kolyma Tales*, here the protagonist thinks of the bread he has hidden and how hungry he is. But he thinks of his past life as well and of poetry. Here is what Mandelstam thinks: "Poetry was the lifegiving force by which he had lived. Yes, it had been exactly that way. He had not lived for poetry; he had lived through poetry." And "everything—work, the thud of horses' hoofs, home, birds, rocks, love, the whole world—could be expressed in verse. All life entered easily into verse and made itself comfortably at home there." My buddy and former student, the much-published poet Sandra Simonds, said this recently in a Facebook post: "I feel like when I'm in a poetry writing mode, it's not that I'm really writing any better than in a nonwriting mode but rather anything that I encounter is able to become a part of or enfolded into my poetry very readily."

As Mandelstam takes his final breaths in Shalamov's story, poems come to him as readily as they always did:

> Even now stanzas rose easily, one after the other, in a sort of foreordained but at the same time extraordinary rhythm, although he had not written them down for a long time, and indeed could not write them down. . . . Each word was a piece of the world . . . while the whole world rushed past with the speed of a computer. Everything shouted: "Take me!" "No, me!" There was no need to search, just to reject. It was as if there were two men—one who composed, who spun the wheel, and another who from time to time stopped the machine. And seeing he was two men, the poet understood that he was composing real poetry. And who cared if it was written down or not? Recording and printing was the vanity of vanities. Only that which is born selflessly can be without equal. The best was that which was not written down, which was reacted and disappeared, melted without a trace, and only the creative labor that he sensed and could not possibly confuse with anything else proved that the poem had been realized,

> that beauty had been created. Could he be wrong? Could his creative joy be an error?

The answer to those two questions is a resounding no. Self-doubt is as much a part of writing as it is of life, perhaps especially so when one is leaving life. But poetry knows no limits. It is something we do the way a scientist tries to understand anti-matter or a lawyer works to free an unjustly accused client or a chef noodles around at his stove, trying this ingredient and then that. We all want to be rewarded. But we do what we do first and foremost because the opportunities are boundless and because it gives us pleasure, two criteria that, at their heart, are one.

Listen to what Gustave Flaubert said after writing the passage in *Madame Bovary* where Emma Bovary gallops through the woods with her lover:

> It is a delicious thing to write, to be no longer yourself but to move in an entire universe of your own creating. Today, for instance, as man and woman, both lover and mistress, I rode in a forest on an autumn afternoon under the yellow leaves, and I was also the horses, the leaves, the wind, the words my people uttered, even the red sun that made them almost close their love-drowned eyes.

"Love-drowned eyes": does it get any better than that? In two luscious sentences, Flaubert puts the joy of writing in a nutshell. And while he doesn't say it outright in this passage, he reminds us implicitly that it is our job as writers to not just to feel that joy but pass it on to our readers. I can help you do that.

This book's title derives from something I saw when I lived in London a few years back. In that city, you see women and men on motorbikes with a city atlas bungee'd to the handlebars. These are trainee taxi drivers who are acquiring The Knowledge, an in-depth mastery of every street, alley, mews, court, place, and walk. Once they have their own cabs, it's impossible to stump them: they have The Knowledge.

Similarly, *The Knowledge* is a guide through the byways and arteries of poetry. It is meant to move agilely, to be temporary, provisional, and to give its readers that same outlook. As you turn these pages, expect to travel at different speeds on the different highways and byways. You'll coast at times, lurch forward at others, and sometimes stop dead in your tracks. After all, the city of London is always changing—what do you mean I have to detour? I always go this way! But the Republic of Poetry is always evolving as well. Poetry has changed over the millennia, and so will your poems. Master *The Knowledge*, and you'll be ready for those changes.

So let's get started. Poetry is heightened language. We don't walk around spouting poetic lines, so studying poetry is a little like studying another language, like French, say, or Swahili. In the pages that follow, you'll get basic lessons first, then more complex ones. Some chapters are long, whereas others are just a few pages. If you get tired, pull over. If you get fired up and want to cover more ground in a single day, feel free. There will be sample poems throughout to illustrate the lessons, including poems by great poets past and present, and poems by people just like you. Of the sixty or so poems included here in their entirety, more than half of them are by women, and while you'll encounter some historic names as you make your way through *The Knowledge*—Shakespeare, Keats, Whitman, Dickinson, Frost—you'll also be reading poems by Frannie Choi, Natalie Diaz, Yeney Echevarria, Rita Mookerjee, John Murillo, and many others. Some of these poems are by poets who are still students; I include them so you'll see that if someone your age can write this well, so can you. I've even included a few poems of my own. They're the only poems whose origins and development I can vouch for in any objective way, and I use them to teach lessons I couldn't teach otherwise. There are more great poems out there than I could possibly include, so in addition to whole poems, expect to find snippets of others and sometimes just titles. To keep publishing costs down, a few poems couldn't be reproduced in the text, but in these cases links are provided. Everything's available on the Internet these days, so be sure to chase these poems down as well. It'll be worth it, I guarantee. While you're at it, go to the websites of such services as Poetry Daily, Poem-a-Day, *The Writer's Almanac*, and *Rattle* and subscribe to their daily newsletters. Of these four, you might get the most out of *Rattle*, not just because of the quality of that site's poem picks but also because each daily poem they send out is followed by an insightful comment by that poem's poet as well as links to other similar poems. But no matter where you get your daily poems from, remember that you should always read them aloud. So when the poems show up on your phone first thing every morning and you're living with someone, read those poems to that person as well. Otherwise, mumble.

These chapters are packed with tons of tips and suggestions, some of which will click with you instantly while others will make no sense at all. That's fine. Poems may or may not convey moral messages, but as they are being written, poems are amoral creatures. They're opportunistic. They use whatever tools are handy, often for a purpose for which that tool isn't meant.

My bio note says that I read everything: psychology, neurophysiology, intellectual history, cultural studies, and more. Works from those disciplines will be cited here, as will fiction and movies and music. Most poetry textbooks quote contemporary poets, for the most part, and I do that, too, but I quote Shakespeare as well. When I'm asked who my favorite contemporary American poet is, I always say "Shakespeare." Wait. Shakespeare—American? Sure. Shakespeare thought constantly about the New World. He thought more about America than many Americans do today. You can practically feel him leaning into America in one of the most magical works of literature ever, *The Tempest*.

I spray *The Knowledge* with quotes from and references to all these varied sources for two reasons. The first is that there are basic principles underlying the creation of every human artifact, from cave paintings to opera to the discovery of a new vaccine. The second reason is related to the first, and it's that *The Knowledge* doesn't put poetry on a pedestal and make it an object of worship venerated only by an elite few.

Mikhail Bakhtin says the best writing is "carnivalesque." In the Renaissance, carnival played a central role in the life of all classes, and cities sometimes devoted as much as three months to carnival festivals. According to Bakhtin, carnival is not the province of one sect or class of specialists. Anyone can play. And carnival isn't a spectator sport: you don't watch it, you do it. Carnival is funny, rowdy, anarchic; best of all, it's democratic. Look, the streets are just full of people of every kind. The specialists don't own carnival, and they don't own poetry, either. We all do.

Homer, Dante, Whitman, Emily Dickinson, and many others have taught me that poetry is for everyone. As *The Knowledge* goes along, it'll move in and out of poetry in a way that places it within the very heart of the larger world. Poetry isn't some suburb. It's the city itself, thrumming with life.

And it's precisely life that is missing from a lot of poetry these days. A lot of it is didactic. There's nothing wrong with didacticism, but if I'm going to preach to people, I'm going to reach more of them by writing an editorial for a newspaper or a Facebook post than I am through a poem. A lot of poetry isn't really poetry at all but theory formatted in short stanzas and snapped-off lines. Again, I like theory, too, but if I'm going to write it, I'll do so in essay form.

When I read a poem, I don't want to be lectured. A poem should be as action-packed as those westerns I used to see when I was a farm kid and rode my bike to downtown Baton Rouge and paid a quarter for a ticket at the Paramount or the Ogden or the Hart to watch good guys blazing away at bad ones in a time and place where justice was always hard-won if it was won at all. Poems should be big, which doesn't mean they have to be long: ten well-wrought lines can please and inform you more than many an epic.

In poetry as in every other field, balance is key. Pianist Vladimir Horowitz said that in performance, "three things have to be coordinated, and not one must stick out. Not too much intellect because it can become scholastic. Not too much heart because it can become schmaltz. Not too much technique because you become a mechanic."

Novelist John Barth says about lovemaking that, "on the one hand, heartless ineptitude has its appeal," which would be the bull's way, "and, on the other, so does heartless skill," which is the kind of thing a purely cerebral person would come up with. Therefore "what you want is passionate virtuosity."

Vladimir Horowitz also said "perfection itself is an imperfection."

Ultimately, poems are like people. Or they should be: English poet Adrian Mitchell says that most people ignore poetry because most poetry ignores people. But a poem can be gawky or polished or funny or sad or talky or terse or a hundred other things, and just as we love certain people and are indifferent to others regardless of which of these characteristics they do or don't have, so we begin to doze when we read some poems and jump up as if on fire in the presence of others.

In interviews and appearances, I'm often asked what a young poet should do to prepare for a life in poetry. This is where I'm supposed to say read, read, read, right? To me, that's like telling an athlete to breathe. Besides, you can read the wrong things. Or read them the wrong way: Thomas Hobbes was said to have remarked that "if he had read as much as other men, he should have been as ignorant as they." Leonardo da Vinci's library consisted of only about two hundred books, and he did okay career-wise.

Better, I'd say, to learn to tell a joke. A lot of poetry you see online these days is joyless. It's clotted with Latinate words and is intellectual rather than sensual, as though the poet is trying to prove how smart he is rather than giving the reader something that brims with pleasure. A lot of this kind of writing is really theory disguised as poetry, and since so many of these poets only teach and read each other, the result is a poetry that is 100 percent cerebral. It's like someone describing their dream. It may have meant a lot to them, but you're on the outside of it. Or somebody describing their brother's dream. Or somebody describing a dream their brother had when he was eight.

There's nothing wrong with being cerebral, but if that's all you are, then you're one-dimensional. I want a poetry that's three-, four-, twenty-dimensional. Each of the arts has the capacity to be multidimensional, of course, but poetry does it best.

That's why I say the best thing a budding writer can do is learn to tell a joke. That doesn't mean that your poems have to be funny—far from it. But a poem, like a joke, always works on at least two levels at once. Also, a poem is like a joke in that you either get it or you don't, and that's because the person who tells the joke either tells it right or doesn't. "Stories only happen to people who can tell them," says novelist Allan Gurganus. Whether it's a story or a joke or a poem, that's a skill you can learn with a little practice. Proportion, timing, economy, precision . . . yeah, learn to tell a joke if you want to have a poetic mind. It doesn't mean you have to be funny. People sometimes tell me I write funny poems. Yes, I do. But I don't write only funny poems.

When someone asked James Joyce what he had learned from the Jesuits who taught him at Clongowes College, he said, "I have learnt to arrange things in such a way that they become easy to survey and to judge." Isn't that beautiful? It's also surprising. You'd think Joyce would say he'd learned something visionary or mystical, but no. What he said, in effect, was that he learned to see the world the way poets do.

Oh, and I tell young poets to take care of their bodies. You don't write poems with this mysterious soul of yours. You write them with your body. Do fifteen minutes of exercise every morning, then make a protein shake. If you're of age, drink moderately—I do—but don't drink every day. Get a good night's sleep. Remember, you're not writing for yourself. That's for high schoolers. You're writing for other people. Your readers expect nothing less of you.

Each chapter of *The Knowledge* is going to be packed with tips like these, and after each chapter I'll suggest talking points for you to discuss with others or think about on your own. These may get you started on a poem, but the talking points are really intended to free up your mind and make it stretchy and supple and get you ready to write. In each case, talking points will be suggestions specific to the chapter you've just finished, but you might also simply identify the writing tip in the chapter you find most helpful as well as the one you agree with most. Or disagree with: after all, there are lots of different ways to get from your house to the store and back. The important thing is to keep moving and to end up where you started, though you'll be coming home with more than you had when you left.

And just as there are little quizzes after each unit in a language textbook, there will be one or more prompts after each lesson that are intended to get you going on your own work. Feel free to move the prompts around: if the one you choose after a particular chapter doesn't work for you, go back to a previous prompt or page ahead till you find one that's more useful to you.

And we'll always be reviewing. I do, constantly. My town's not very big, but I can still get lost in its streets if I don't go over them from time to time. Remember what Lil Wayne says: "Repetition is the father of learning. I repeat, repetition is the father of learning." Even after you learn to speak French and Swahili fluently, you'll still be saying "Bonjour!" and "Habari!" every day.

A FEW RULES

If you look at the poems that have been written in the last hundred years, you'll notice not a sameness but an adherence to a few basic rules that have served poets well over the decades. Of course, you'll immediately think of exceptions: "E. E. Cummings didn't do it that way," you'll say, "and he's pretty famous." Right. E. E. Cummings broke most of the rules and triumphed splendidly. Just about everyone else who broke them has failed. Now you could do exactly what he did and become a ninth-rate version of E. E. Cummings, but wouldn't you rather be a first-rate version of yourself?

Most poets of any stature began by mastering the basics and then moving on from there. Allen Ginsberg wrote a lot of postcard-sized lyrics before he started on those sprawling epics that are the reason why we read him today. Each of us wants to write the poetry of the future, but no one has ever broken new ground who hasn't worked first within the poetic tradition. Don't worry about being overwhelmed by that tradition. There's no reason to fear being influenced unduly. If you are capable of developing a strong poetic voice, you will. The tradition won't harm you.

To the contrary, it will give your poem a strength it wouldn't have were you to write it in a vacuum. In "Tradition and the Individual Talent," T. S. Eliot tells us that when real poets emerge, they represent the poetic tradition but in a new and forceful way, so that the poets of the past have to be reread in terms of the genius who has altered them.

That should be the goal of all of us. But first things first, my fellow genii.

1. Write in sentences. Fragments have their place. But a poem made largely or entirely of fragments is not likely to pull together into a coherent whole. Often I'll see a poem that consists of isolated fragments, and among these, there'll be a real zinger or two, an image or phrase that goes straight to the heart. But you want your whole poem to affect your readers, not just part of it.

2. Use concrete language. Include details. Appeal to the senses. There's a poem by Ezra Pound called "There Died a Myriad," which is a savage denunciation of the European powers that fought World War I. In it, Pound doesn't speak out against "a bunch of crummy countries" or "one rotten continent." No, he makes us feel his hatred when he describes that corrupt culture as "an old bitch gone in the teeth."

3. Employ standard usage, at least till you get your footing. Sometimes new poets begin by combining words, coining new words of their own, or devising new spellings for the words we already have. The world is pretty terrific as is. You don't need to slap a coat of paint on it. The real energy in a poem comes from fresh combinations of familiar words and ideas. Say you're looking out a farmhouse window. Is "the winterwind ablowing springward greenly"? Big deal. Look again and you'll see that "the

cows are playing baseball." Congratulations! You're at the start of what could turn out to be a fabulous poem.

Unless you're satirizing them, watch out for archaic forms ("standeth," "o'er"). Similarly, don't use the small "I" unless you're really doing something different with it. It looks like false modesty ("little old humble me"). Besides, so many poets have used it before that it has become a monumental cliché. Don't use ellipses . . . to show you are in a dreamy mood . . . or you'll just irritate your reader. The same goes for exclamation marks! Either the excitement is there or it isn't! You can't create it with punctuation marks! I mean it!

4. At least for now, write free verse, or at least avoid rhymes that force you to sacrifice sense for sound. You don't want to mangle an idea with nursery rhymes. After you've developed your poetic voice, you can use rhyme and other formal techniques to extend it in new directions. I'll show you how. But the rhymes of beginning poets often sound like something along the lines of "I think that I shall never see / A poem as lovely as a tree." Poets who get trapped in tick-tock lines like those sometimes never escape.

5. Title each poem effectively. When a student hands me a good poem with a mediocre title and I point that out, often they look sheepish and say, "I'm not very good with titles." But a title is a line in your poem like any other. If I asked you to pay more attention to the seventeenth line of your poem, would you shrug and say, "I'm never any good with seventeenth lines"? True, good titles are hard to come up with, but look how effective they are. If an elephant took up residence in your backyard, you could write a poem called "The Elephant," but isn't "The Elephant Who Came to Stay" more expressive? If it's one of those elephants from outer space that keep falling from the skies these days, call your poem "The Elephant from Mars." Emily Dickinson didn't title her poems at all, but she

> wasn't planning on publishing them either. But if you were flipping through the table of contents of a magazine or book and saw a poem called "The Elephant from Mars," wouldn't you race to read it? I would.

Are those enough rules for you? How about a poem, then? This is one of my favorite poems to start classes with. "Pangur Bán" is a poem written sometime in the ninth century by an Irish monk. The title is his cat's name, and the poem compares Pangur Bán's mouse hunting to the author's own search for the right word.

Pangur Bán

I and Pangur Bán my cat,
'Tis a like task we are at:
Hunting mice is his delight,
Hunting words I sit all night.

Better far than praise of men
'Tis to sit with book and pen;
Pangur bears me no ill-will,
He too plies his simple skill.

'Tis a merry task to see
At our tasks how glad are we,
When at home we sit and find
Entertainment to our mind.

Oftentimes a mouse will stray
In the hero Pangur's way;
Oftentimes my keen thought set
Takes a meaning in its net.

'Gainst the wall he sets his eye
Full and fierce and sharp and sly;

'Gainst the wall of knowledge I
All my little wisdom try.

When a mouse darts from its den,
O how glad is Pangur then!
O what gladness do I prove
When I solve the doubts I love!

So in peace our task we ply,
Pangur Bán, my cat, and I;
In our arts we find our bliss,
I have mine and he has his.

Practice every day has made
Pangur perfect in his trade;
I get wisdom day and night
Turning darkness into light.

You can draw a dozen lessons from "Pangur Bán," but two stand out to me. The first and more obvious is the emphasis on hard work and meticulousness. It's practice, practice, practice for these two if they are to reap their reward. And what reward is that, you say? Satisfaction in a job well done and done for its sake alone.

That's the second lesson, that "better far than praise of men" is it to feel the joy in having written a good poem. Go to your work as the cat does, says the monk. If he nabs a little squeaker, do you think Pangur Bán expects to hop on a plane to Stockholm and collect the Nobel Prize for Outstanding Achievement in the Field of Mouse Hunting? "In our arts we find our bliss," says our anonymous scribe, and anything else is gravy. Not even gravy, probably, considering the narrow lives monks lived.

Quite a few centuries later, a Croatian-born psychologist named Mihaly Csikszentmihalyi ("mee-hy cheek-sent-me-high-ee") published an influential book called *Flow*. Flow is a state of engagement that a practitioner—painter, composer, athlete, monk, cat—brings to their work, a state so absorbing that time becomes irrelevant and such distractions as hunger and thirst and the need for sleep are forgotten as one surrenders to the pleasure of the task. The big takeaway from *Flow* is that the greatest pleasure in life comes when one receives acclaim for something one has undertaken for its own sake. Yes, work of high quality is often the ultimate outcome of the flow state, but that's a secondary reward. It's extrinsic. The intrinsic reward is the joy one takes in the work itself.

Let's have some fun.

1.1

Here's Some Math for You

Want to write a poem? Here's the formula: b + T = P.

The "b" stands for "beginning" and is lowercase because all beginnings are small. When he wrote the "Ode on a Grecian Urn," Keats didn't say, "I think I'd like to write about art and immortality." He said, "Hey, look at that vase! I'm going to write a poem about it."

The "T" is for "time" and is uppercase because any good poem requires lots of time.

And "P" is for "poem." Or "good poem," really: do you want to write anything less?

That's actually most of this book in seven short sentences. With the b + T = P formula, you can write a whole bunch of poems, and some of them might be pretty decent. But let's see if we can do better than that.

Let's begin by looking at where poems come from, which means a brief excursion into brain physiology. From a poet's viewpoint, of course—don't expect anything technical. And as I say, you wouldn't have to have had this science lesson to write a good poem from time to time. But a career in any field is bound to be plagued with doubt and despair once in a while, and at such moments, it'll be of some comfort to know that at least you're proceeding correctly.

Poetry's not a sprint. It's a distance race. Ludwig Wittgenstein said, "Philosophy is like trying to open a safe with a combination lock: each little adjustment of the dials seems to achieve nothing, and only when everything is in place does the door open." That's true of poetry as well. Any poet worthy of her parchment and quill pens will tell you that some poems take years to write and don't come together until the final moment. Even when things are going well, it's encouraging to know why they're going well. It's also helpful to understand that productivity has its limits: when dry spells come along (and they will, no matter how accomplished you are), it's useful to know that this is natural, too, so you can devote your down time to reading or long walks or charitable works or some other worthwhile activity as you wait for the good times to return. Artistic failure can be caused by many things, but sometimes I wonder if the inability to understand their own minds is the reason behind the self-destructive habits of many in the arts.

FIELD, STEAM ENGINE, COMPUTER, HOTEL, ORANGE, HORSE, CROCODILE

The brain has always been described in terms of the image that dominates the age. Most of human history has been one long agricultural period, so during that time the brain was likened to a farmer's field that might be enriched by wholesome activities and defiled by unsavory practices. Around the time Freud was developing his concept of the subconscious mind, the brain became a steam engine, the dominant image of the Industrial Revolution. Thus, from the psychological point of view, anger and other toxic emotions had to be released—if the operator of the steam engine failed to relieve all that pressure, the engine might explode.

Today we think of the brain as a computer, which is something than can be programmed, and this has changed the way in which we think about the brain's operations. Whereas anger was something that needed to be vented in Freud's day, now we see it as a form of programming and therefore something to be avoided. If not, you'll end up with an angry computer.

My personal image for the brain is that of a hotel. Not a motel, now. Not one of those one-story affairs out on the truck route. No, I'm thinking of a high-rise, a structure with lots of both horizontal and vertical activity. Let's walk through. Some doors are open, others are closed, and a few are ajar, as though someone has stepped out for a minute and will be right back. People arrive and depart, bearing all manner of luggage: a backpack, a seven-piece matched set of suitcases, nothing at all. In this room over here there is passionless sex, in that one heartfelt love. On the floor below, ten or a dozen people are shaking hands because they've just agreed on a business deal. Food and drink are being served in the bar and restaurant. TVs drone in some rooms, and in others people chat quietly or snooze—but in the penthouse, murder! And always someone is cleaning up.

In neurophysiological terms, the image of the hotel with all of its bustle is not a bad one. But let's look a little deeper with the help of not a neuroscientist but a major American poet. Robert Bly is known for his many contributions to the way we think about poetry these days, notably the idea of the "leap" that bridges the gap between conscious and unconscious thought in any great work of art. To Bly's way of thinking, Western religious, intellectual, and literary thought has kept separate the animal and rational ways by which we view the world every day, and so he reveres poets like Federico García Lorca, Chu Yuan, Tomas Tranströmer, and Allen Ginsberg, who use the process of swift allusion to bridge that gap in their writing.

Bly thinks of these writers as "riding dragons." That's an apt image for the dynamics of the writing process, but Bly goes beyond mere metaphor in describing where poems come from. In his essay "Poetry and The Three Brains," Bly points out that, in the proportion of its various parts, the brain is like an orange: the central part is the medulla, a prolongation of the spinal cord, and the outer part is the rind or cortex. (Before we go any further, by the way, let me point out that Bly's essay appeared in 1976. Brain science has come a long way since then. Bly's also a poet. If you have a science question, take it to a scientist.) The cortex itself has three divisions: the archicortex or reptilian brain; the mesocortex or early mammalian brain; and the neocortex or later mammalian brain. These layers are what make the cortex different from other body parts and therefore a lot more interesting. Other body parts changed completely: flippers became arms, for example, and gills turned into lungs. But the cortex just kept adding layers.

According to Bly, each of the three brains has a different function. The reptile brain coldly tends to matters of survival, such as obtaining food. The early mammalian brain is passionate and thus capable of both anger and sexual love. And the later mammalian brain is responsible for higher functions, including contemplation and insight. In other words, the brain is really three brains. To visualize how these three brains work with and against each other, consider the words of physiologist Paul Maclean, who says that "when the psychiatrist bids the patient to lie on a couch, he is asking him to stretch out alongside a horse and a crocodile." That's one crowded piece of furniture, right? No wonder, says Maclean, that "the patient who has personal responsibility for these animals and must serve as their mouthpiece is sometimes accused of being full of resistance and reluctant to talk."

Okay, and now it gets even more complicated. Ready? Here's the thing: in addition to the three cortices, the brain is further divided into left and right hemispheres. You know this already, that there is a left hemisphere concerned with logic and analysis and a right hemisphere that is the seat of intuition and nonverbal perception. Somewhat confusingly, the rational left hemisphere governs the right side of the body, whereas the intuitive right hemisphere controls the left or, as the French would say, "sinister" side, as the French word *sinistre* means "left," leading to a long-lived and baseless suspicion of the left-handed. This doesn't mean that each of us is two persons in one, because the left and right hemispheres do communicate, the dreamy one on the right constantly muttering to the wide-awake left hemisphere mainly by means of a nerve pathway called the corpus callosum.

Had enough brain science? Hang on. We're almost there. The final thing you need to know is that the three cortices are in contact with each other as well. People with poor mental control are prone to emotional problems like paranoia, which stems from unregulated activity in the archicortex—in the absence of real enemies, the reptile brain will invent imaginary ones so that it will have something to conquer.

But the good news is that improved mental control can lead to creativity. Arthur Koestler, whose numerous and varied books are a staggering testament to the powers of the mind, notes that "poetry could . . . be said to achieve a synthesis between the sophisticated reasoning of the neocortex and the more primitive emotional ways of the old brain."

Since we do not spend all day in a single cortex or a single hemisphere of the neocortex but flip back and forth constantly from one to the other, the secret is to be aware of the flips, to bring the deep ancestral images of the reptile brain and the fiery passions of the early mammalian brain up into the well-lit chambers of the new brain. There they can be tested both logically (in the left hemisphere) and intuitively (in the right), examined, sequenced, revised, sent back to their places of origin, if necessary, and retrieved so that the entire process can start all over again.

The result is a poem.

DID SOMEONE SAY VATIC VOICE?

Sappho, Bashō, Alexander Pope, Emily Dickinson, and 95 percent of all the other poets who ever lived never heard the word "neocortex," not once. But each of them had a sense of an inner voice, one that was different from the voice they used to cheer for their favorite sports teams or buy beer. That inner voice is called the vatic voice, and each of us has it. *Vates* is a Greek word that means the inspired poet, the poet speaking the words of a god. To most people, the vatic voice speaks only in dreams. But the vatic voice is also the source of all art, including poetry.

In terms of what you've just read above, the vatic voice is what speaks when energy is transferred from one cortex or hemisphere to another. It's actually possible to trigger that transfer in different ways. Hart Crane listened to the music of Ravel played at high volume to encourage the flow of poetic images. Gertrude Stein is said to have stopped her car dead at Parisian intersections to write as horns blared behind her. Closer to our day, Donald Hall recommends short naps: "There is that wonderful long, delicious slide or drift down heavy air to the bottom of sleep, which you touch only for a moment, and then there is the floating up again, more swiftly, through an incredible world of images, sometimes in bright colors."

If you ask a hundred poets where their poems come from, I bet most of them will champion the value of boredom. One of the greatest poets of our time, Philip Levine, said this in an interview:

> I don't so nearly search for my poems as they find me. I don't run away from them. Which is what I see some people do. I mean, there is no way the poem is going to find you if you're playing ping-pong. Or cha-cha-cha-ing. Chasing girls, or whatever it is that you chase. Perfecting your back stroke. I mean, there's no way. You have to be there. In some state of readiness and hospitality to the fucking muse, you know, who is, after all, only a part of you. You have to let it open the door and come into your brain, into your hand, wherever it comes. And I do a lot of that. I mean I sit lots of hours picking my nose. I don't even pick my nose. I do nothing. I've learned that you have to do nothing. You have to be silent and see if the voice will enter you.

I once asked a group of experienced poets, several of whom had been widely published, how they encouraged their inner voice to speak up. Many of them said that ideas for poems came during classes and lectures, while driving or watching a bad movie. Some students said reading other poets was useful, both in the sense of seeing how they solve problems similar to those of my students but also because often a reader becomes impatient and competitive and says, "I can write a better poem than this." Attending poetry readings can have the same effect. Some students meditated.

If these activities have anything in common, it's that each of them is a way of cultivating boredom. Robert Bly puts it this way in "Poetry and The Three Brains":

> If the body sits in a room for an hour, quietly, doing nothing, the reptile brain becomes increasingly restless. It wants excitement, danger. . . . If the sitter continues the mammal brain quickly becomes restless, too. It wants excitement, confrontations, insults, sexual joy. It now starts to feed in spectacular erotic imagery, of the sort that St. Anthony's sittings were famous for. Yet if the sitter persists in doing nothing, eventually energy has nowhere to go but the new brain.

All the poet has to do then, as Philip Levine says, is be there.

FIRST DRAFTS

By now you've probably figured out that not everything the vatic voice says is worth listening to. Billy Collins says every poem has two subjects, the one you start with and the one you discover as you write. If you're too loyal to the subject you start with and insist on including it, it might end up being a distraction—worse, it could contaminate the finished poem and kill it dead in its tracks. Often I find myself looking at the next-to-last draft of a poem and seeing that my initial subject has to go, that I need to snip it off mercilessly the way the glassblower cuts away her pipe from the object she has just made.

I know, I know. It hurts. You were so excited when you came up with that great idea, certain that the result would be one terrific poem. But what if the poem got better once you've killed your darling? Poems are very personal to those who write them, but they only get that way through a process that is, at least in part, clear-eyed and analytical. Remember, art is a child of both the animal brains and the new brain. Total reliance on instinct is just as fatal as total reliance on logic.

Freud had a wonderful understanding of how artists use the whole brain to create a work that gives the reader pleasure much like that felt by the poet during the act of creation:

> To those who are not artists the gratification that can be drawn from the springs of fantasy is very limited; their inexorable repressions prevent the enjoyment of all but the meager daydreams which can become conscious. A true artist has more at his disposal. First of all he understands how to elaborate his daydreams, so that they lose that personal note which grates upon strange ears and become enjoyable to others; he knows too how to modify them sufficiently so that their origin in prohibited sources is not easily detected. Further, he possesses the mysterious ability to mold his particular material until it expresses the ideas of his fantasy faithfully; and then he knows how to attach to this reflection of his fantasy-life so strong a stream of pleasure that, for a time at least, the repressions are outbalanced and dispelled by it. When he can do all this, he opens out to others the way back to the comfort and consolation of their own unconscious sources of pleasure, and so reaps their gratitude and admiration.

Note that Freud makes only one distinction between writers and readers. It's essential to understand that both have nothing more than "meagre daydreams." Some artists claim to be more sensitive or gifted than non-artists, but don't listen to them. There's only one difference, and it has to do with the work you put into the task. Remember the formula for writing a good poem is b + T = P, with that capital T standing for "time." We all have the same daydreams. The writer simply takes his or her time to make those daydreams more pleasurable.

The poet Donald Davie once said, "I will not trust dreams to do what only a composed fable can do," which is another way of saying the same thing. We all have dreams, and artists simply turn theirs into fables. When you or I read those fables, we are dreaming again, but this time in a sustained and exhilarating way.

That might sound like a tall order for the artist. But I'd be misleading you if I were to suggest that creative people have to put in twelve hours every day and collapse with exhaustion. Remember, the secret is time, not how many calories you burn.

Let me give you a homey example. Let's say you're going to lunch. You run into me, who has just had lunch and is ruminating on the delicious salad I have eaten. You ask me where to go, and I point you to the bistro on the corner, and naturally you want to know what to order. If I say, "Oh, I had this salad there, and it was really good," you're likely to nod your head but not feel much enthusiasm. But suppose I say this: "It was a salad of Boston lettuce that was very tender and a delicate shade of green. It had feta cheese on it and walnuts and some kind of dried fruit—dates, maybe? Anyway, the dressing was a simple one of olive oil and balsamic vinegar, with a sprinkling of salt and oregano. On the side were some wedges of what looked to be vine-ripened tomato. Oh, yeah, and the server brought out one of those pepper mills. You know, the kind that's the size of a medieval mace?" And here I hold my hands apart and make the size-of-a-medieval-mace gesture.

If you're not hungry now, it's probably because you don't like salad. I did my part. I like you, and I want you to eat well, and that's why I just told you where to go and what to order. Poetry works the same way. A poem isn't an expression of my sensitive feelings. A poem is a gift from me to you.

A poem is a gift, a meal is a gift, and a joke is a gift, too, right? There are a lot of poems and meals out there that aren't that great, and the same goes for a lot of jokes. But you remember the ones that had you gasping for breath and wiping your eyes, just as you try to forget the ones that left you wincing or tapping your watch and saying, "My goodness—look at the time!" In a marvelous essay that shows how one might link two things that most people would think of as entirely different, Howard Nemerov argues that a poem and a joke are pretty much the same thing. You either get the joke or you don't, says Nemerov. If you don't get the joke and everyone else does, you never say that the joke doesn't make sense, which is something that people say about a lot of poems; after all, it made sense to everyone else. If you are wise, you'll smile politely, and if you're not, you'll give a forced laugh that the others will recognize as fake. Should the person who told the joke have to explain it to you, the mystery might be cleared up, but it'll be too late. You may laugh weakly, but not with the spontaneity of the others. So a poem, too, is a way of getting something right in language, according to Nemerov, "save that the proper response will be not laughter but silence, or the acknowledgment that it is so, it is as it is, that the miracle has happened again."

When Robin Williams died, then secretary of state John Kerry said, "We will all miss Robin's uncanny impressions, zany observations, and cutting-edge quips that found the truth as well as the humor." As though the two are distinct. When a comic says something funny, isn't it only funny because it's true?

Robin Williams is the guy who said, "Cricket is basically baseball on valium." Now he could have said, "Cricket is slow." But everybody knows that.

If you ask TV critics who really stood out during the early years of the twenty-first century, many of them will point to *Parts Unknown*, the travel and cooking show hosted by the late Anthony Bourdain. Who's got the best show on television? Anthony Bourdain. Who's the funniest man on television? Anthony Bourdain. Who's the smartest man on television? Anthony Bourdain.

In one episode, a farmer in a Central American country said half-jokingly that he was going to beat his overly playful dog. Bourdain says, "Don't do that. We can't mistreat dogs on this show. We can eat them, but we can't mistreat them."

What does that tell you? Everything. Everything about kindness, about the different customs of different countries, about culinary diversity, and, mainly, everything about the play of the human mind, which is limitless.

Speaking of fine dining, Robin Williams also said, "Death is nature's way of saying, 'Your table's ready.'" I'm not even sure what this means, but I love it.

POETRY CAMP

Okay, ready for a poem that illustrates everything I've been talking about for the last ten pages? Then go online and read "The Lanyard" by former U.S. poet laureate Billy Collins, one of our best poets and teachers of poetry.[1]

Sad, huh? Not really. The boy was ungrateful, and you get the sense the mother is dead now and unable to hear her son's apology. But the rendering of the poem is not lugubrious or sloppy. It's thoughtful, sharp. So there's a sense of completeness, of having done the right thing. It's also funny in a head-shaking way: I've read this poem to audiences a hundred times, and the room always explodes in laughter when I read the lines "She gave me life and milk from her breasts, / and I gave her a lanyard." And then a look of ruefulness comes over the crowd's face, because we've all taken our mothers for granted.

As Collins says, poetry has sad content but happy form, and out of that tension comes the reader's pleasure.

The first six lines of "The Lanyard" show the poet summoning the vatic voice as he moves from one object to another until he chances on a dictionary and then the word that sets him on his journey. The craft item he made in camp ("with a little help from a counselor") is his starting place, but ultimately the subject is the one poets probably write about the most, namely, the complicated geography of love.

Speaking of geography, note the meandering nature of "The Lanyard." It wanders all over the place, doesn't it? Just as we do when we go out for a walk. I'm talking about a recreational walk, of course. You might walk down to the drugstore to get some razor blades and a pack of gum, but I'm talking about the walk where it's a nice day and you go out and you turn left or maybe right and you walk a mile or maybe two miles or just a hundred yards before you turn around and head home. You might see Jamal or Miz Williams or Lulu or that guy whose name you forgot and are too embarrassed to ask for again, or you might meet a stranger that you end up despising. Or loving. Or marrying! You might get rained on or bit by a dog—anything can happen on a walk.

But the one thing that all walks have in common is that you'll end up where you started. You'll feel better for having been outside for a while, and you'll see the world differently. Every walk contains

---

1 For full poem, visit link: https://bit.ly/thelanyard.

the potential for wonder. Barbara and I usually take a walk in the late afternoon, but we had too much going on the other day and didn't get out until dark. We've lived in our neighborhood for thirty years, but we found ourselves seeing things we'd never noticed before: that a neighbor had installed lighting in his entryway, for example, and how Archie, who lives two streets over and used to be an outdoor cat, has put on weight and likes to sit in the window now, looking out solemnly at us as we look back at him. And then we were home again, the better for having taken a brief and pointless and absolutely wonderful walk.

The main point I want to make here is that Billy Collins starts his poem with something small, even trivial: a lanyard. I once heard Collins give a talk about the appeal of what he called the elemental in poetry, and then he held his hands a foot apart and said, "A plate of lemons."

ONE TERRIFIC COOKIE

Can't you see the white plate with the lemons on it? If that doesn't do it for you, try reading this poem by Julie Danho without your mouth watering.

The Best Chocolate Chip Cookie in New York City

In case there's a line, I show up at seven
but the man at the counter says the cookies
won't be ready until eleven and by then
I'll be on the train, nearly halfway back
to Providence. He and the dozen people
behind me are waiting, so I quickly choose
a ham croissant and a blueberry muffin
glittering like a hotel lobby chandelier.
The shop's a dab of yellow on the block,
its only seats along the front window
where I sit and look at bleary people stopped
at the bodega across the street, touching

apples and mangos until they find the ones
most untouched. With my first bite,
the croissant comes undone, its shawl
falling to the floor. I break off the peak
of the muffin and hear the sugar overfill
the valleys of my back teeth. I'm trying not
to think about how it must taste, the best
chocolate chip cookie in New York City,
how big, how warm, how it would've
collapsed in my mouth, traveled my blood,
made wild pinwheels of my cells.
How much time have I lost
hunting perfection? Once, before cell phones,
before the days when cars couldn't linger
outside the airport doors, my plane was
delayed on the runway for four hours,
and my husband, before he was my husband,
waited for me in his cramped Plymouth
battered from years of lake effect snow.
He just waited, reading a book, turning on
the car every so often to listen to the radio.
When I finally arrived, he was surprised
that I thought he'd be gone. He said
no one asked why he was there so long
or what it was he was waiting for.

Of course, Danho's poem is no more about a cookie than Collins's is about a lanyard. Both are about elemental emotions: in his case, gratitude, in hers, patience. Yet you can't attack emotions like gratitude and patience directly in a poem. You have to start with something simple: a knickknack you made for your mom at camp, a bakery treat. But look at how eloquent those simple objects are.

Talking Points

What point in this chapter do you find most helpful? What's the point you agree with most strongly? What point or points do you disagree with and why?

How do you trigger the vatic voice? How do you summon poems—what works for you?

Think of a time when you started a poem with one subject and then abandoned it for a subject that worked better. Real-life examples are good, too: how about that time you went to buy a bike and got roller skates instead? And don't forget the night you were going to pick up your blind date but then saw her roommate.

Following the example of the salad I described above, think of a common noun: sandwich, song, movie, clothes, game, mom, dad, sweetheart, car. One by one, start applying descriptive phrases until you have a paragraph that turns the abstraction you started with into something very specific and desirable.

Like a poem, a joke has a center that needs to be filled in for you to get it. Example: "Why can't you trust an atom? Because they make up everything." This joke centers on the something that's implied but not stated, which is that to "make up everything" has two meanings, "to lie" and "to constitute all reality." Think of your favorite joke and fill in the missing center. (This will ruin the joke, but we're learning a lesson here, not auditioning for the Upright Citizens Brigade.)

Prompts

Read all these prompts before you settle on one. Don't be surprised if you find yourself mixing and matching and coming up with your own prompt. For example: I can see myself starting with "Perfect Setting" but then tripping over a movie or food or person or pop song that deserves "Faint Praise." The whole point of *The Knowledge* is to get where you want to go, and you don't always do that by following the rules.

PERFECT SETTING

Think about the places in which your favorite memories are set. It might be a family picnic by a lake, you with a sweetheart on a beach at sunset, you by yourself on a country road at night. Now write down the five senses—sight, smell, taste, touch, hearing—and cluster as many images as you can around each one. Don't be eager to rush this exercise to its conclusion; the more time you take, the more opportunity you'll give yourself to be surprised by what you really remember and how you really feel about it.

As your picture grows, don't overlook its negative aspects. Often it's the unsettling moments—those few minutes when nobody could find the baby, that barking dog who rushed at you and then stopped—that make the beautiful ones all the more delicious.

DRUNK ON WORDS

Open the dictionary, point your finger blindly, and come up with an unfamiliar word. Do this for as long as you feel like it; you'll end up with a list of words you can select from, put in a sequence that makes sense to you, and then write about.

You might come up with *cramoisie* (crimson cloth), *supranational* (an adjective meaning "transcending national boundaries"), *ortolan* (a European bunting), and *tampion* (a plug or cover for the muzzle of a gun), for example. Let there be a supranational Ortolan Festival, then, with people draping themselves in cramoisie and tossing tampions in the air.

FAINT PRAISE

While half of all writing seems to be telling us things we already know—love is sweet, beauty doesn't last, and so on—the other half tells us the opposite of what we might assume. For example, while most of us are doing our best to stay alive as long as possible, in the "Ode to a Nightingale," Keats speaks of being "half in love with easeful death." And the New Testament tells us to be tolerant of thieves and prostitutes.

In this exercise, praise something that, in the minds of most people, doesn't deserve it. Kimchi, for example, or head cheese. Or a TV program that everyone else thinks is silly. Or a pop star whom the critics can't stand. Or hangovers or mothers-in-law or nearsightedness.

This is another of those exercises in which you can tell yourself in the morning to look out for unusual objects or people to write about, then collect them as the day goes on. By supper time you'll have a good-sized list; you can choose your subject from it and discard the others or, better, save them in a notebook and give them a chance to grow into projects themselves.

1.2

Accidents Will Happen

The previous chapter amounted to an entire undergraduate curriculum. Look at all the subjects you studied: poetry, of course, but also math, philosophy, neurophysiology, and Freudian psychology, among others. There were even some fun electives: food tasting, stand-up comedy, camp craft.

Let's review quickly and then loosen up a bit and have a laugh or two. Jimi Hendrix said, "Learn everything, forget it, and play," and we'll be pausing from time to time to do just that in *The Knowledge*.

You remember the basic formula to use when you write a poem, which is $b + T = P$, with "b" standing for "beginning" (it's a small "b" because all beginnings are small); the capital "T" standing for "Time," which you're going to need a lot of; and the capital "P" equaling poem, which is going to be a dandy because of all the "T" you lavished on your "b."

So that's the basic formula. Here's the advanced formula: $b + T^2$

= P^2.

The lessons you figure out on your own are more valuable than the ones that are served up to you on a silver platter, so let me give you a minute to decipher this new formula.

Okay, time's up. Huh? You're right! The "T" is squared in the advanced formula because you're not just bringing "time" to the process but "lots of time." And the "P" is squared as well because this poem is not going to be just a good one but a "truly terrific poem" thanks to the extra time you poured into it.

The "b" doesn't change, though, because all beginnings are small.

You can also sum up the creative process this way: art is the deliberate transformed by the accidental.

That is, you start deliberately, in your studio or office with your paints or pens or whatever it is you use as well as a cup of tea or coffee to get you going. Then you put some colors on the canvas or some words on the page. You might work that way the whole morning in a calm and steady way, but sooner or later, something will happen—you'll hear a sound outside or get a phone call or remember something that you'd read the day before—and what you're doing will change.

If you're lucky, your painting or poem or short story will get better; it'll certainly be different. It might even get worse, but that's just part of the process. And that process is far from over, because you're going to go back and forth between all the deliberate things you need to do while you stay open to the accidents that always happen and that, in the end, are going to take what you're doing up to a whole other level.

Ciaran Carson says, "There's a whole language out there, and one's role as a writer is to stumble around in it."

By the way, if art is the deliberate transformed by the accidental, so is science. Think of Gutenberg looking at a wine press and then his signet ring and coming up with the printing press, or Eli Whitney inventing the cotton gin after he sees his cat pulling feathers through the bar of a bird cage. I know that these stories sound too good to be true, but this is poetry, not history, and factual or not, they illustrate how the creative mind works.

The same is true for gumbo: you run out of shrimp, so you use twice as many oysters, and your gumbo tastes better. Or romance: I've already alluded to the scenario where you go to pick up Betty at her apartment but Veronica answers the door, and the next thing you know, you and Veronica are married and have a kid and another on the way and are thinking about adopting a rescue dog.

But let's stick to poetry. It's complicated enough. If only readers would tell us what they want! Thing is, they don't know themselves. As Steve Jobs said, "It's not the customer's job to know what they want." Who could have described the iPhone ten years before it was invented? In artistic terms, think not of the texts or shows or songs you merely enjoyed but of the ones that made an indelible impression, the poems and stories and movies you describe to other people, the ones about which you say, "And you wouldn't believe it, but then this happens. . . ."

Maybe this will help illustrate how deliberateness and accidents work together. Some companies use a test to evaluate potential employees that sounds goofy but is said to work. It goes like this: subjects are given six rings and asked to place them in any way they choose over a peg in the middle of the testing room.

The most highly motivated subjects (that is, the ones the company will want to hire) are going to place themselves at an intermediate distance before they toss the rings. Sure, you could stand next to the peg, drop the rings on it, and achieve a 100 percent success rate. But that would be too easy, meaning it'd identify you as someone who is afraid to accept challenges. On the other hand, to get too far away would almost certainly guarantee a poor result; this person is willing to take chances but usually ones that don't pay off.

In other words, an ideal employee would be neither a slacker nor a self-defeater but someone who enjoys working with reasonable and satisfying challenges.

This is what the person who is reading your poem wants. You, the poet, supply the pegs and the ring, and the reader plays the game. The reader wants not to breeze through your poem or be baffled by it but to engage with it in a way that requires an effort yet satisfies.

It's kind of like taking a swim in the ocean. Yeah, you had to change out of your clothes, and the water's chilly, and that one big wave roughed you up a bit.

But now that you're back on the beach, didn't it feel good?

ALL THOSE HENRYS

Check out this poem by Carrie Fountain. It's made almost entirely of accidents.

Will You?

When, at the end, the children wanted
to add glitter to their valentines, I said no.

I said *nope, no, no glitter,* and then,
when they started to fuss, I found myself

saying something my brother's football coach
used to bark from the sidelines when one

of his players showed signs of being
human: *oh come on now, suck it up.*

That's what I said to my children.
Suck what up? my daughter asked,

and, because she is so young, I told her
I didn't know and never mind, and she took

that for an answer. My children are so young
when I turn off the radio as the news turns

to counting the dead or naming the act,
they aren't even suspicious. My children

are so young they cannot imagine a world

like the one they live in. Their God is still

a real God, a whole God, a God made wholly
of actions. And I think they think I work

for that God. And I know they will someday soon
see everything and they will know about

everything and they will no longer take
never mind for an answer. The valentines

would've been better with glitter, and my son
hurt himself on an envelope, and then, much

later, when we were eating dinner, my daughter
realized she'd forgotten one of the three

Henrys in her class. *How can there be three Henrys
in one class?* I said, and she said, *Because there are.*

And so, before bed we took everything out
again—paper and pens and stamps and scissors—

and she sat at the table with her freshly washed hair
parted smartly down the middle and wrote

WILL YOU BE MINE, HENRY T.? and she did it
so carefully, I could hardly stand to watch.

Any conversation involving children is going to have more accidents in it than a demolition derby; you never know what the rascals are going to say. Actually, adult life is pretty much all accidents, isn't it? At least compared to a child's view: children think God is in charge and that He only makes correct decisions, always. Boy, do they have a surprise coming. At least we grownups have poems, some of which are as beautiful as this one. Notice that this isn't a minute-by-minute diary of an entire evening but a selection and sequencing of a few key events, complete with a quick trip to the future ("I know they will someday soon / see everything").

The poem ends with a final accident. How *can* there be three Henrys in one class? In the last line and a half, the poet/mom states the lesson without stating it: no matter how young or old we are, all we have to do is be patient with and kind to each other and let the accidents take care of themselves.

Talking Points

Okay, you may have to rein yourself in if you tackle this one, because you'll probably be bombarded with examples. Look over your own life and discuss a moment where something unexpected happened that was better than or at least different from what you anticipated. I bet you have an endless supply of such stories. You could also give examples from the lives of others (how your mom met your dad) or the headlines (a bullet aimed at one person struck another) or history (how penicillin was discovered).

You were a kid once, right? Everybody has family stories about the goofy thing the kid said or did that didn't make sense but was just right. In my life, I think of the kid next door who was crazy about the musical based on that Victor Hugo novel *Lame as a Robin.* Anecdotes like these will furnish you with an endless supply of poetry.

Ever taken a psychology class? I bet you have designed or participated in or at least heard of an experiment where subjects were told to do one task while they were secretly being tested to see if they could do another. The famous example here is the Invisible Gorilla Test: as you watch a short video of a basketball game (you can find it on YouTube), you're supposed to count the number of times the players pass the ball. In the middle of the video, someone in a gorilla suit walks through. When subjects are asked how many times the ball was passed, most come up with fairly accurate answers, but only half the subjects remember seeing a gorilla. Point: there's a lot going on that we don't see. And when it's pointed out to us, even then we're not sure what we saw. The impulse to figure out what's really happening in this world has triggered many a great poem.

Prompts

As with the last set of prompts, read through all three of these first. You may end up combining two prompts. Or these three might generate a fourth that comes from your own experience.

THE INCIDENT

People sometimes say they "dine out" on one or more good stories, tales so mesmerizing that people never tire of hearing them. Example: a friend of mine told me recently that when he was a young man, he was in New York one day and saw the actress Ingrid Bergman about to step in front of a car. He grabbed her by the shoulders and said, "Watch out, Miss Bergman!" He saved the life of someone who had been in *Casablanca*, *Spellbound*, and *Notorious* and would go on to make many more films and be adored by fans who would never know that she had been saved from a terrible accident.

If nothing comes to mind immediately, you can give yourself the assignment of writing about an incident you or somebody else brings up in the next twenty-four hours. It's good to get in the habit of programming yourself to latch on to the poetic materials that are almost certainly headed your way.

STUPID STUFF

Nobody does something stupid on purpose. Write about stupid things you've done, like leaving the yeast out of a bread recipe because you didn't "have any."

A variation on this exercise and one that requires a lot more courage is to write about shameful things you've done, such as when you were part of a group of children who made fun of someone else in school who was different. Don't just wallow in remorse, though. Without letting yourself off the hook, figure out a way to get yourself and your reader out of this poem with insight rather than emotional overkill. (There will be more on how to do this in the upcoming chapter called "This Is the End, My Only Friend.")

Or if you were the person who was made fun of, here's your chance for revenge. The revenge should be comical, though; self-pity is no more attractive in writing than it is in life.

FUCHSIA MUSKETEER

There's nothing like banging a bunch of unrelated words together to create a bunch of happy accidents. On the left side of a page, write down a dozen adjectives: say, "fuchsia," "murderous," "sugary," "false," "electric," "Italian," and half a dozen more; use a dictionary, if you like. On the right side, write down the same number of nouns: "pie," "raccoons," "ukulele," "schoolboys," "cathedral," "musketeer," and so on. Now attach an adjective to each noun until you've used up all your words; swap parts of speech or create new ones until you're satisfied.

Begin writing about one of your combinations or several or all twelve. And let them be whatever they want to be: a Fuchsia Musketeer could be a person, but it could also be a pub, and it might be a fancy French dessert as well.

1.3

This Isn't Cryptology

Some years ago, I wrote a poem called "Broken Promises." I'm not quite sure what happened, but every spring, polite high-school juniors from Alabama and well-mannered Wyoming sophomores started calling or writing to tell me that they were getting to recite my poem, and they hoped I wished them well, which, of course, I did. But after a couple of springs, I began to wonder why these young women and men from Sacramento and Topeka were doing this, which is when I discovered that "Broken Promises" had been adopted by the Poetry Out Loud project for its annual competition. What that means is that high school students can recite it or one of several hundred other poems and maybe advance through regional and state competitions to the nationals, where some serious money is at stake. None of which ever filtered down to me, I might add, but then what would I do with money?

"Broken Promises" deals with just that: the promises we break and how they limp around and gaze at us reproachfully while enjoying an immortality denied to the promises we've kept. Here it is:

Broken Promises

I have met them in dark alleys, limping and one-armed;
I have seen them playing cards under a single light-bulb
and tried to join in, but they refused me rudely,
knowing I would only let them win.
I have seen them in the foyers of theaters,
coming back late from the interval

long after the others have taken their seats,
and in deserted shopping malls late at night,
peering at things they can never buy,
and I have found them wandering
in a wood where I too have wandered.

This morning I caught one;
small and stupid, too slow to get away,
it was only a promise I had made to myself once
and then forgot, but it screamed and kicked at me
and ran to join the others, who looked at me with reproach
in their long, sad faces.
When I drew near them, they scurried away,
even though they will sleep in my yard tonight.
I hate them for their ingratitude,
I who have kept countless promises,
as dead now as Shakespeare's children.
"You bastards," I scream,
"you have to love me—I gave you life!"

Recently I spoke with a group of high-school teachers who wanted to discuss my famous poem—rather, to tell me what it meant. "It's about your own poems!" said one teacher, and another shouted, "I think it's about your children!" They seemed a little crestfallen when I said, no, the poem's about the promises we break, as the title and, as far as that goes, the poem itself says.

The teachers thought my poem said one thing but meant another, and it's the reader's job to figure out what the poet is really saying. No wonder poetry doesn't have a bigger audience. All that code cracking! Who has the time?

True, no poem speaks to us as directly as a stop sign or a six-pointed star. But nobody listens to Kendrick Lamar rapping and says, "Hmm, I wonder what he meant by that?" A well-made poem works the same way. As Susan Sontag says (more about her in a second), we need "an erotics of art": poetry is for lovers, not cryptologists.

Both in the classroom and here in *The Knowledge*, I want to give poets "an empty prescription." That is, I want to show them how to write, not what to write. I certainly don't want them to try to limit what they write to one meaning. Or, really, to a meaning at all.

Here's another poem that is exactly what it is and doesn't call out to be interpreted. It's by Hera Lindsay Bird. (Note: Whereas the other poems in *The Knowledge* are single-spaced the way most poems are in books and journals, Ms. Bird chose to double-space her poem and not end it with a period.)

Jealously

Anytime someone I'm dating mentions someone they used to love
in a semi-nostalgic or non-cynical way
I immediately want to drive my car head-first into a swamp full
  of battery acid
ruining Christmas for everyone!!!
it's so unreasonable
to be afraid of so many sad and distant women
who have escaped into the future
only occasionally looking back through their naturally thick eyelashes
when I think about the possibility
the person I'm currently with has ever been remotely romantically
  interested

in another person ever
I felt a great self-antagonism
for being the kind of woman who came afterwards
like a bad sequel with a higher budget
O I feel sorry for the people I love and where it is I am taking them
because I don't think I'm good enough
I think it's okay to admit the people you love are better than you
I wouldn't date anyone who wasn't
imagine dating someone worse than yourself on purpose
that's the kind of fucked up thing only everyone I've ever loved would
do

See what I mean? Bird's poem is one you can reread with pleasure and pass around and talk about, but you're more likely to talk about your own experiences and human nature in general than you are to try to figure out what the word "car" means. For what it's worth, my guess is that it means "car."

The problem the English teachers had with my poem about broken promises is that they wanted to "get" it. When strangers ask what I do and I tell them I'm a poet, a typical reaction is, "Gee, I just don't get poetry." But do you get Rossini's String Quarter in C Major, I reply? Or if you're at a dance recital, do you stand up in the middle of row H and shout, "Stop! I don't get it!"? Just give poetry a chance, I say. Many poems don't work for me, either, but most are short, so I just keep reading until I find one that, as Emily Dickinson put it, takes the top off your head when you read it or gives you a chill no fire can warm.

That's the way a poem works. That is, if it works. Yes, there's a lot of bad poetry out there. As I said early when I quoted Adrian Mitchell, most people ignore poetry because most poetry ignores people.

So no wonder people don't get poetry. Or think they don't: in his essay "The Poet," Emerson writes, "some stars, lilies, leopards, a crescent, a lion, an eagle, or other figure which came into credit God knows how, on an old rag of bunting, blowing in the wind on a fort at the ends of the earth, shall make the blood tingle under the rudest or the most conventional exterior. The people fancy they hate poetry, and they are all poets and mystics!"

But notice what Emerson is talking about here. He's talking about images, not words. Words create images that resonate emotionally, but they're not images per se. After all, language tends to be serial and analytical by nature, whereas an emotion is an irreducible, all-at-once phenomenon.

LARVAL LIFE FORMS

Let me give you an example. Do you like maggots? Okay, come back. I know how you feel. There's actually a treatment called maggot therapy in which the squirmy little fellows are used to debride and disinfect wounds that don't respond to other types of treatment. But most of us non-medical types just get the creeps when we open the garbage can and find it crawling with the larvae of the common housefly.

Maybe this poem by Yusef Komunyakaa will make you think differently.

Ode to the Maggot

Brother of the blowfly
And godhead, you work magic
Over battlefields,
In slabs of bad pork

And flophouses. Yes, you
Go to the root of all things.
You are sound & mathematical.
Jesus Christ, you're merciless

With the truth. Ontological & lustrous,
You cast spells on beggars & kings
Behind the stone door of Caesar's tomb
Or split trench in a field of ragweed.

No decree or creed can outlaw you
As you take every living thing apart. Little
Master of earth, no one gets to heaven
Without going through you first.

In this poem the humble maggot expresses everything contained in an entire library of philosophy books. The maggot is the ultimate egalitarian. To it, everything is equal: beggars and kings, every decree and creed. Sooner or later, the maggot will take each and every one of us apart, rich as well as poor, ugly and beautiful alike. There's good news, though—we're going to heaven! But we have to go through the maggot first. Since the first humans crawled out of their caves, we have been dealing with the fact that each of us will die. Nobody deals with it more succinctly than Yusef Komunyakaa does here with his tidy if initially disquieting image.

Notice how you react to the images in this poem by Laurie Uttich. We've all known people who are going through hard times, and we probably know even more who say things like "I feel a little blue today" or "I'm so depressed." But watch how these feelings spring to life and become visceral when they are laid out in terms of images, starting with the poem's grab-you-by-the-collar title.

To My Student with the Dime-Sized Bruises on the Back of Her Arm
Who's Still on Her Cellphone

Oh honey, you can text him, you can like his meme, you can
follow him on Twitter and to Target, you can ride shotgun, hold
his anger on your lap, pet his pride, be his *ride or die*. You can
wear those jeans he likes. You can discover Victoria's
secret, buy a bra with a mind of its own. You can
recite *I'm sorry* like it's a Bible verse and Snapchat the shit out

of those purple roses he bought you at Publix. You can try
every one of Cosmo's *30 Ways to Give an Ultimate Blowjob.*
You can remember the name of his mother, his best friend

in 2nd grade, the lunchroom lady who gave him extra
chicken strips on Tuesdays. You can grow out your bangs, toss
your hometown over your shoulder, sleep facing North
with your cheek in his back.
          You can strip yourself for parts.   But, baby,

it still won't be enough. You can love him, but you can't pull
his story out of the dark and slide your arms into it. You can't
wash it and lay it flat in the sun to soften. You can't
hold his face in both of your palms and watch tomorrow
bloom from the sheer wanting and waiting of it. It doesn't
matter if his daddy talked with his hands   or his bloodline
is marinated in booze   or his mama loved his brother best.
          You can't fix what somebody else broke.

    So, girl, put down your phone and pick up
your pen. Take a piece of the dark and put it on a page.
Sylvia Plath waits to wash your feet. And look,
Virginia Woolf has built you another room and painted
it pink. There's a place for you at the table. Sit next to me;
I got here late.   Oh, baby, don't you feel it? You were knit
for wonder in your mother's womb.
          You were born for the driver's seat.

Of course, not every reader will react to Laurie Uttich's images in the same way: some will flinch and turn away, others will wish they could soothe the girl in the poem, and so on. It's hard to explain how any art form sparks the emotional reaction it does. Film scholar J. Clover says that "the processes by which a certain image (but not another) filmed in a certain way (but not another) causes one person's (but not another's) pulse to race finally remains a mystery—not only to critics and theorists but even, to judge from interviews and the trial-and-error (and baldly imitative) quality of the films themselves, to the people who make the product."

On the other hand, when art works, it really works. Many movies, like many poems, are lousy. But then there's always *Casablanca*, not to mention "Ode on a Grecian Urn."

But how exactly does poetry make the blood tingle? Again, that's something not easily explained. As Emerson says in "The Poet," quoting the Neoplatonic philosopher Iamblichus, "things more excellent than every image are expressed through images." So words create images, and images express . . . things?

That might be about as close as one can come to a formal statement on how poetry works. Or an informal one, because if it works, a poem is more likely to be half understood rather than fully comprehended. After all, unless Sigmund Freud and Carl Jung and Joseph Campbell are all wet, a poem tends to have one foot in the unconscious and one in the sunshine, one foot in the base camp and one foot already heading up the mountain.

Susan Sontag says we need "an erotics of art." The phrase occurs in her essay "Against Interpretation." Here's what the Wikipedia entry on the essay says:

> Sontag argues that in the New Critical approach to aesthetics the spiritual importance of art is being replaced by the emphasis on the intellect. Rather than recognizing great creative works as possible sources of energy, she argues, contemporary critics are all too often taking art's transcendental power for granted, and focusing instead on their own intellectually constructed abstractions like "form" and "content." In effect, she writes, interpretation has become "the intellect's revenge upon art." The essay famously finishes with the words, "in place of a hermeneutics we need an erotics of art."

In the next chapter, we'll take a closer look at the erotics of poetry. By the way, I'm using "erotics" as Sontag does. I'm not talking about the kind of thing they went over in eighth-grade biology class when they took the boys into one classroom and the girls into another and showed them a movie nobody understood anyway. When I say "eroticism," I mean "desire." How does poetry make you want something you don't have? Even better, how does poetry make you want something you've never had? Better still, how does it make you want something you never even knew existed?

Talking Points

Think of a specific artistic experience that gives you intense pleasure. It can be a book you reread every year or a favorite movie, but I suggest a song. The great thing about songs is that most of them don't make any sense, none at all. When I was in middle school, there was a song on the radio called "Sally Go 'Round the Roses." The lyrics said something about . . . well, something. There was the central image of the rose bush and then references to a secret of some kind as well as a straying boyfriend. Or girlfriend—you couldn't even tell the gender of the person who broke Sally's heart, if that is, in fact, what happened. Man, we talked about that song endlessly. The bubblegum songs came and went. Meanwhile, no Department of Philosophy at an Ivy League school devoted more time to one of the eternal problems that plagues mankind than we did to that song. So what's your "Sally Go 'Round the Roses"?

How about an experience that gives you indescribable pleasure that shouldn't? Once I was talking about the sense of taste with a friend of mine, and she said that when she was a kid and wanted to make herself feel terrible, she'd sneak into the kitchen and get her mom's tube of anchovy paste and squirt a big ribbon of it out on her tongue. What is or was your ribbon of anchovy paste? By the way, my friend grew up to get a PhD in epidemiology and is happily married and has two kids of her own and works for the

World Health Organization. So she wasn't a weirdo. She just knew that weirdness has charms about which normalcy knows absolutely nothing.

What did you once love that you now hate? What did you hate that you now adore? Once again, food rears its head: I used to loathe beets, and then one night a cook in Florence put down a plate of fusilli in front of me that was with dripping with the smoothest, creamiest, pinkest, most delicious pasta sauce I've ever tasted, and now I can't get enough of that root vegetable. As with the other talking points, don't look for rational explanations. As you writhe with pleasure or shudder with distaste, think details, not ideas.

Prompts

MYSTERIOUS PAINTING

Create a story or poem around the events depicted in a mysterious painting, such as Giorgione's *The Tempest*, the magnificent Renaissance representation of a woman nursing a child on a hillside while a soldier stands guard and a terrible storm threatens in the background.

Or you can use a painting from your local art gallery. There are lots of possibilities here: you could write a poem about the painting or based on it, just as you could write a story with a character who comes back to this particular painting again and again—why?

You can always use an art history textbook as a source for paintings to write about, but do try this exercise at least once in an actual gallery. For writers, they're terrific work sites, since they're not only filled with suggestive images but also, except during openings and visits by noisy school groups, usually very quiet.

YOUTHFUL CRUSHES

Recall your youthful crushes. What movie and TV actors and singers did you adore when you were a kid and how did you show your affection: by imitating their walk or clothes style, kissing fan-magazine or album covers, writing gushy letters?

This exercise could go off in any number of directions. Suppose your favorite actor did write you back, declaring undying love; suppose you did marry him or her; and so on.

KISSES

How many different kinds of kisses can you come up with? There is the Lover's Kiss, Aunt Gerty's Cheek Peck, the Guilty Kiss, the Kiss in Which the Kisser Is Keeping One Eye on Himself in the Mirror, and so on. Write down as many kinds of kisses as you can think of, then write a paragraph or a poem stanza on each. Keep going until the material takes on a life of its own and the idea for a larger work on kisses suggests itself to you. End with that Special Kiss you give that Special Someone who means more to you than life itself. Don't have a Special Someone? You will. In the meantime, dream one up.

BODICE RIPPER

At your local bookstore, study the covers of a dozen romance paperbacks. One will depict a hunk with a bad tan and a couple of babes hanging over his shoulders; another will show a frightened maiden looking up at a sinister caped figure on the parapet of a castle.

Make up a life for these people. What fears and insecurities trouble the sleep of that hunky chap, for example? And suppose that the scared-looking woman is really in charge, that her paleness doesn't stem from fear but from the fact that she's a vampire in dire need of fresh blood.

Let your imagination go here, and remember: be just as ironic as you like.

1.4

Images, Images, and More Images

In an exhibition-catalog entry in 1961, sculptor Claes Oldenburg uttered a famous manifesto:

> "I am for the art that a kid licks, after peeling away the wrapper. I am for an art that is smoked, like a cigarette, smells, like a pair of shoes. I am for an art that flaps like a flag, or helps blow noses, like a handkerchief. I am for an art that is put on and taken off, like pants, which develops holes, like socks, which is eaten, like a piece of pie."

I saw these words not long ago at a Museum of Modern Art show of Oldenburg's work that includes a huge nine-foot-long wedge of cake called *Floor Cake* sitting on the floor next to a seven-foot-wide hamburger called *Floor Burger*, a sandwich so big you have to walk around it. "I am for the art of underwear and the art of taxicabs," Oldenburg went on. "I am for the art of ice cream cones dropped on concrete." Lying near the gigantic hamburger is the eleven-foot-long *Floor Cone*. Then there's the burlap and plaster *Baked Potato*, with its pat of melting butter, and the *Banana Sundae*, with its accompanying spoon painted with drips of enamel ice cream.

An actor, Hamlet says, holds a mirror up to nature. Just so, Oldenburg's art reflects the lives we live. "I am for an art that takes its form from the lines of life, that twists and extends impossibly and accumulates and spits and drips, and is sweet and stupid as life itself."

The Palestinian poet Taha Muhammad Ali says writing poems is like playing billiards, that you aim over here to strike over there. (He also said, "The more mosques, the less poetry," but that's a topic for another day.) Everyone who has ever written a successful poem knows what Mr. Ali is talking about. Here's my own metaphor: in the time necessary to get from the start of a poem to its conclusion, the poet is operating like a pilot in the early days of aviation, relying less on external controls, even in the case of highly formal poetry, and more on his own experience and intuition to gauge the plane's position and performance as he tries to find his way and then bring the craft in for a nice soft landing.

Even with an accessible poem, though, it's important to remember that it is we who go after poetry, not the other way around. Poetry doesn't flirt with you the way ad copy does. As Mark Halliday says in his essay "The Arrogance of Poetry," you may upbraid the poem or give it the finger or simply let it slide to the floor, but the poem doesn't care: "while you're huffing or leaving the room," as Halliday points out, "poems keep stroking their own hair."

But as Adrienne Rich said in her National Book Award speech, "When poetry lays its hand on our shoulder, we can be to an almost physical degree touched and moved." And we can be affected this way at any time and by any poem. We come back to poetry again and again, because no other art form does a better job of capturing the emotions that matter most to us, the ones that we don't fully understand yet pierce our hearts like spears.

HOW POETRY CONSOLES

The week after the Trade Center towers fell, the *New Yorker* departed from its usual format and, instead of the cartoons and satires that usually appeared on its back page, published Adam Zagajewski's "Try to Praise the Mutilated World," a poem that ends: "Praise the mutilated world / and the grey feather a thrush lost, / and the gentle light that strays and vanishes / and returns." Here are words that make the blood tingle, as Emerson said; here are images that express things more excellent than themselves. Read the full poem and see if you don't agree.[2]

Now why does this poem work? Remember what Billy Collins says, that poetry succeeds because it has sad content (death, failed love) but happy form, so there's tension. Collins also says that television has happy content and happy form, so there's no tension there.

And Zagajewski's poem is deeply tragic, yet it's so well-turned that we feel that we are in the presence of something permanent, something real. Yes, the world is scarred. Some ships sail forever, and some sink. But we have our memories: those are permanent. A bird loses a feather, but there are other feathers and other birds. The light leaves, and it returns again.

MAKING A LIST AND CHECKING IT TWICE

Let's pause for a moment. I'll summarize what I've said so far by means of an image I haven't used yet.

I've taught or read to every age group, from toddlers to octogenarians, and what I've learned is that audiences like to use the familiar elements in a work as a base camp: you set up your tent, get a fire going, and then walk out through the ice and hope you don't (or do) run into the Abominable Snowman.

As you know, I see art as the deliberate transformed by the acci-

---

2 For full poem, visit link: https://bit.ly/trytopraise.

dental: story, image, and sentence are the deliberate aspects, and what happens after that is unpredictable. The known is always the same—same tent, same fire—but the unknown changes, because you never know what you'll find when you climb the peak.

And now let's talk about form for a minute. We'll come back to this topic from time to time, but for the moment, let me quote David Shields, who says in *Reality Hunger* that "every work needs to find its own form. But how many do?"

Every poem is a formal poem, in a way. Even a poem that looks wild and crazy has a form: it has a wild and crazy form. That said, the whole concept of form can be paralyzing to young poets because it seems to argue against natural and free expression, as though you're being asked to capture a leopard and put it in a cage too small to hold it. But one relatively simple type of poem that's sure to find its own form, as David Shields says, is the list poem.

The list poem is as old as poetry itself. It's also one of the most timely ways of writing at the present moment, but let's begin with some lines from back in the day. And I mean way back in the day. Together, "The Songs of Solomon" in the Judeo-Christian Bible amount to a timeless love poem. But except for a few "thys" and verb forms that end in "-eth," it reads as though it might have been written this morning. Consider these lines from the seventh song in which the bridegroom lists the beauties of his beloved:

> Thy navel is like a round goblet, which wanteth not liquor:
> thy belly is like an heap of wheat set about with lilies.
> Thy two breasts are like two young roes that are twins.
> Thy neck is as a tower of ivory. . . .
> And the roof of thy mouth like the best wine for my beloved, that goeth down sweetly.

And he's just getting started. The poem goes on and on as the biblical bridegroom enumerates his beloved's body parts, praising each with a startling image ("thy belly is like an heap of wheat") every time.

There's more to love poetry than the hey-baby-give-me-a-big-kiss poem, though. Christopher Smart's *Jubilate Agno* is a mid-eighteenth-century testament to the poet's adoration of God. But the reason why Smart is one of my Elvii (that's the plural of "Elvis," if that's not apparent already) is that he sneaks his cat Jeoffry into his poem. One of the best things about poetry is the wacko combinations you can come up with, and Christopher Smart is the master of that. Smack dab in the middle of his glorification of Our Creator, he clears his throat and says:

> For I will consider my Cat Jeoffry.
> For he is the servant of the Living God, duly and daily serving him.
> For at the first glance of the glory of God in the East he worships in
> his way.

Clever Jeoffry! He worships God in ten ways, in fact:

> For first he looks upon his forepaws to see if they are clean.
> For secondly he kicks up behind to clear away there.
> For thirdly he works it upon stretch with the forepaws extended.
> For fourthly he sharpens his paws by wood.
> For fifthly he washes himself.
> For sixthly he rolls upon wash.
> For seventhly he fleas himself, that he may not be interrupted
> For eighthly he rubs himself against a post.
> For ninthly he looks up for his instructions.
> For tenthly he goes in quest of food.

But Jeoffry's not all about grooming and snacks—hell, no. Look out, Satan!

> For when his day's work is done his business more properly begins.
> For he keeps the Lord's watch in the night against the adversary.
> For he counteracts the powers of darkness by his electrical skin
> and glaring eyes.
> For he counteracts the Devil, who is death, by brisking about the life.

For he camels his back to bear the first notion of business.

There's a chapter in *The Knowledge* about endings that's coming up soon, but for the moment, notice how easily and simply Christopher Smart ends his tribute to his kitty. He's like a pilot who has taken us on a beautiful flight and is now bringing us in for a nice soft landing.

For, though he cannot fly, he is an excellent clamberer.
For his motions upon the face of the earth are more than any other quadruped.
For he can tread to all the measures upon the music.
For he can swim for life.
For he can creep.

One of the swell things about poetry is that if you can do something in one poem, you can do something completely different in the next poem—in fact, you better if you want to keep your reader (not to mention yourself) happy. So if you've written a list poem about a person or a feline you adore, how about doing the same in a hate poem? Julie Sheehan did.

Hate Poem

I hate you truly. Truly I do.
Everything about me hates everything about you.
The flick of my wrist hates you.
The way I hold my pencil hates you.
The sound made by my tiniest bones were they trapped in the jaws of a moray eel hates you.
Each corpuscle singing in its capillary hates you.

Look out! Fore! I hate you.

The little blue-green speck of sock lint I'm trying to dig from under my third toenail, left foot, hates you.

The history of this keychain hates you.
My sigh in the background as you pick out the cashews hates you.
The goldfish of my genius hates you.
My aorta hates you. Also my ancestors.

A closed window is both a closed window and an obvious symbol
of how I hate you.

My voice curt as a hairshirt: hate.
My hesitation when you invite me for a drive: hate.
My pleasant "good morning": hate.
You know how when I'm sleepy I nuzzle my head under your arm? Hate.

The whites of my target-eyes articulate hate. My wit practices it.
My breasts relaxing in their holster from morning to night hate you.
Layers of hate, a parfait.
Hours after our latest row, brandishing the sharp glee of hate,
I dissect you cell by cell, so that I might hate each one individually
and at leisure.
My lungs, duplicitous twins, expand with the utter validity of my hate,
which can never have enough of you,
Breathlessly, like two idealists in a broken submarine.

Elizabeth Barrett Browning's best-known poem begins "How do I love thee? Let me count the ways." Julie Sheehan traffics in hate rather than love, but her list is so long and varied—a list, a pencil, an eel, some lint, a keychain—that you begin to wonder whether or not the speaker protesteth too much and is signaling that she really loves the object of her hate after all. In other words, this poem works: if you really want to know how you feel about someone or something, start making a list. There's no better way to get a clear picture of how you really feel.

Of all the great list-makers in poetry, Walt Whitman is without doubt the one who got the most out of this simple yet effective device. Whitman's readers sometimes refer to the lists that make up his 1855 poem "Song of Myself" as "catalogs." Those who feel Whitman gets a bit windy at times call them "laundry lists," but no matter what term you use, the point is that, since Whitman's subject is the entire cosmos, no single object in it can suffice as the organizing principle of his big poem.

Actually, the poet himself forms the spine of "Song of Myself," and each image that pops up is a kind of vertebra. As he did throughout his career, Whitman wanders through the universe, a passionate yet detached observer who strings together perception after perception until his poem is finished. Consider just a few lines from "Song":

> The little one sleeps in its cradle,
> I lift the gauze and look a long time, and silently brush away flies
> with my hand.
>
> The youngster and the red-faced girl turn aside up the bushy hill,
> I peeringly view them from the top.
>
> The suicide sprawls on the bloody floor of the bedroom,
> I witness the corpse with its dabbled hair, I note where the pistol
> has fallen.
>
> The blab of the pave, tires of carts, sluff of boot-soles, talk of the
> promenaders,
> The heavy omnibus, the driver with his interrogating thumb, the clank
> of the shod horses on the granite floor,
> The snow-sleighs, clinking, shouted jokes, pelts of snow-balls,
> The hurrahs for popular favorites, the fury of rous'd mobs,
> The flap of the curtain'd litter, a sick man inside borne to the hospital,
> The meeting of enemies, the sudden oath, the blows and fall,

The sleeping baby, the shy lovers, the dead man, the crowded street scene, the snowball fight, the protests, the sick person, the chance encounter that ends in a punch-up: what you've just read is less than 1 percent of the entire "Song of Myself." You don't have to do this. Few of us are Whitmans, thank goodness. One is plenty. For the rest of us, let it suffice to use the list technique as a way to capture something in our experience that affected us strongly. The next couple of pages will tell you how to go about that.

Talking Points

Go back as far as you can in memory and think of words or phrases to which you reacted intensely one way or another. They could be pleasurable words ("football" or "breakfast") or hateful ("claw" or "itch"). Include words that could be pleasurable to some people and hateful to others: "tobacco," say, or "rockabilly" or "video games." Recognize that a slight variation makes a difference: "summer" could suggest stifling heat to someone who might react completely differently to "summer afternoon." Now summon up images that tell you why these words mean what they do. Take "football": it might be that you or someone you know broke a leg in practice and walks with a limp to this day, just as that word might trigger a video of someone catching a kickoff on the one-yard line and running it all the way back for a touchdown.

With your friends or classmates, write the five sense verbs across the top of a page: see, hear, touch, smell, taste. Below each, make a column of experiences that correspond to each. You might put "skin" or "hot stove" under "touch," for example, "perfume" or "body odor" under "smell." Compare lists. What experiences are most common? Which ones are most surprising?

Go to an art gallery, either on campus or in town. Or visit a gallery online. I suggest you start with the contemporary wing, because more abstract or experimental art is liable to work better with this exercise, in which you look for pure images (like an action painting by Jackson Pollock or one of Mark Rothko's big monochromes) and ask yourself what ideas and emotions these art works trigger. But it's okay to look at the older work, too. Just look closely. A Renaissance portrait of Mary and Jesus makes a very clear statement about faith, but Mary is a mother like any other: what does her expression say to you? And how about the background of the painting: who are those people and those buildings, and how do they contribute to what you think or feel?

Prompts

ISLAND PARADISE

Think of everything you like best: strawberries, Tolstoy's *War and Peace*, the cop show you watch on TV every Wednesday night, that harmonica you're learning to play, your favorite shoe store, coffee. Now put all these things on an island that you will make into your earthly paradise.

Think of the form you want everything to take: do you want Tolstoy himself there or his characters or a building that looks like a huge copy of the novel? Pay attention to location and distance: make sure the right things are next to each other (and the wrong ones not) and see to it that your objects are neither too close together nor too far apart.

You could also create a neighboring island that contains everything you dislike.

MY LIFE: THE MOVIE

Quickly make a list of the big events of your life. Using your list as a rough script, begin to imagine your life as a movie, keeping most things the same but changing a few, say, or keeping just a couple of things the same and changing the others.

There are lots of possibilities with this exercise: your movie could begin to veer off in a totally unexpected direction, for example. On the other hand, the script as you've actually lived it thus far might turn out to be pretty darn satisfying—or to contain a hidden drama that you weren't aware of until you began to look at things this way.

THE NEW NOBELS

You know there are Nobel Prizes in Literature, Peace, Economics, and so on. How about a Nobel for Getting Your Homework in On Time? What about a Nobel Prize for Dogs? For Non-Competitiveness? Make a list, pick your prizes, and describe the ceremony.

A TOWN CALLED AMNESIA

Write a series of short poems or paragraphs about towns: the town of the chocolate lovers, for example (what kind of statues would they have?). Then the town of the Freudian psychoanalysts. The town of the escaped laboratory animals. A town inhabited only by men (or women or children). The ex-lovers' town. The amnesiacs' town—which one is that, now? The town where pets keep people.

Like several of the longer poems referred to earlier, this exercise will lead you to a bigger poem with many different parts rather than a short one that takes a close look at one thing.

If "towns" doesn't work for you, try "planets."

1.5

Okay, Control Yourself

So far I've shown you poems by Billy Collins, Carrie Fountain, Adam Zagajewski, Hera Lindsay Bird, the anonymous author of the biblical "Songs of Solomon," Christopher Smart, Laurie Uttich, Walt Whitman, and yours truly. At the risk of being caught sneaking in a compliment to myself by means of what appears to be an objective statement about other poets, I'd say they've all achieved their form.

But let's look at a fourth that is extremely formal, from Barbara Hamby's *All-Night Lingo Tango.*

Mambo Cadillac

Drive me to the edge in your Mambo Cadillac,
    turn left at the graveyard and gas that baby, the black
night ringing with its holy roller scream. I'll clock
    you on the highway at three a.m., amen, brother, smack

the road as hard as we can, because I'm gonna crack
    the world in two, make a hoodoo soup with chicken necks,
a gumbo with a plutonium roux, a little snack
    before the dirt and jalapeño stew that will shuck
the skin right off your slinky hips, Mr. I'm-not-stuck
    in-a-middle-class-prison-with-someone-I-hate sack
of blues. Put on your highwire shoes, Mr. Right, and stick
    with me, 'cause I'm going nowhere fast, the burlesque
queen of this dim scene, I want to feel the wind, the Glock
    in my mouth, going south, down-by-the-riverside shock
of the view. Take me to Shingles Fried Chicken Shack
    in your Mambo Cadillac. I was gone, but I'm back
for good this time. I've taken a shine to daylight. Crank
    up that radio, baby, put on some dance music
and shake your moneymaker, sweetheart, rev it up to mach
    two. I'm talking to you, Mr. Magoo. Sit up, check
out that blonde with the leopard print tattoo. O she'll lick
    the sugar right off your doughnut and bill you, too, speak
French while she do the do. Parlez-vous français? Okay, pick
    me up tonight at ten in your Mambo Cadillac
'cause we got a date with the devil, so fill the tank
    with high-octane rhythm and blues, sugar cane, and shark
bait, too. We got some miles to cover, me and you, think
    Chile, Argentina, Peru. Take some time off work,
'cause we're gonna be gone a lot longer than a week
    or two. Is this D-day or Waterloo? White or black—
it's up to you. We'll be in Mexico tonight. Pack
    a razor, pack some glue. Things fall apart off the track,
and that's where we'll be, baby, in your Mambo Cadillac,
    'cause you're looking for love, but I'm looking for a wreck.

Did you read "Mambo Cadillac" aloud? I hope you did. You should read every poem aloud. They all have their own built-in musicality, and reading a poem without hearing it is like doing the same with song lyrics. You'll understand the words, but you won't be dancing. So when you hear yourself read "Mambo Cadillac," of course you'll notice that "k" sound that ends every line. But look (and listen) again. Bouncing off all those crackly "k" sounds are all the "ohs" and "ooos" that occur in the middle of the lines.

So there are two tightly controlled features that make this a formal poem. But if those two complementary rhyme schemes aren't enough—the harsh sound of the "k" softened by the cooing of the "o"—notice one more thing: each line also contains exactly 13 syllables.

It's hard to imagine a poem more tightly wired than "Mambo Cadillac." And while the rest of us needn't use all the sounds and syllable counting that Barbara does, we're still obliged to write poems that are tight.

RESTRAINT, RESTRAINT, AND MORE RESTRAINT

For when an emotion is promised but never quite delivered, the audience will come back for more. We all know that an actor fighting tears is more moving than an actor who weeps; the same idea operates in poetry.

Indeed, the same idea operates in all the arts. There's nothing like emotions under pressure so great they enter the heart like bullets, like water that lies quietly in a pool but leaps from a hose with a force that knocks down doors. Macduff trying not to weep for his slaughtered family, a Bernini statue that seems to want to speak, Keats's odes about a silent urn or a bird whose song he can't understand: these flood me with joy.

In fact, let's look at that scene from Shakespeare. Here is an abbreviated version of the dialogue in Act IV, scene 3 of *Macbeth*, when Ross tells Macduff that his wife and children have been slain by Macbeth:

ROSS

Your castle is surprised; your wife and babes
Savagely slaughter'd.

MACDUFF

My children too?

ROSS
Wife, children, servants, all
That could be found.

MACDUFF
And I must be from thence!
My wife kill'd too?

ROSS
I have said.

MALCOLM
Be comforted.
Let's make us medicines of our great revenge,
To cure this deadly grief.

MACDUFF
He [Macbeth] has no children. All my pretty ones?
Did you say all? O hell-kite! All?
What, all my pretty chickens and their dam
At one fell swoop?

MALCOLM
Dispute it like a man.

MACDUFF
I shall do so;
But I must also feel it as a man:
I cannot but remember such things were,
That were most precious to me.

Thus does Macduff the warrior prepare himself to resume the battle while Macduff the husband and father reins in his emotions. Result?

The audience's heart breaks. Macduff could howl and roll around on the stage, and as we watch him, we might think, "Poor fellow. To lose your whole family! What a blow." But imagine Macduff as he starts to leave. There's a war on, and Macbeth must be stopped. But then Macduff turns to Ross once more and says, "Did you say all?" Macduff doesn't cry, but when I see this play, I sure do.

Here's a story about a composer named Doc Pomus. A 1972 Rock & Roll Hall of Fame inductee, Doc is responsible for dozens of hits by some of the greatest rock and soul groups ever.

Doc had a gift for making songs out of what happened before his eyes. Take, for example, "Save the Last Dance for Me," a song recorded by the Drifters that was #1 on the pop chart for three weeks in 1960. Pomus was heavyset and used crutches because of a childhood bout with polio; he could barely walk and eventually was confined to a wheelchair. Nonetheless, he married a gorgeous blonde actress, and the song comes from Doc's memory of his wedding day, as he sat with his crutches and watched his brother Raoul whirl the new bride around the floor.

Now imagine the recording session. Ahmet Ertegun is producing the song for the Drifters. The group has done several takes of "Save the Last Dance for Me," but lead singer Ben E. King can't nail the song, can't quite get it right. Then, just before King steps up to the mike for the final time, Ertegun tells him the story of the fat cripple watching another man dancing with his pretty new wife. King's eyes moisten, and he fights tears as he gives one of the most moving performances of his life.

Here is a short poem by Marilyn Nelson that gains great power because of emotions under pressure.

How I Discovered Poetry

It was like soul-kissing, the way the words
filled my mouth as Mrs. Purdy read from her desk.
All the other kids zoned an hour ahead to 3:15,
but Mrs. Purdy and I wandered lonely as clouds borne

by a breeze off Mount Parnassus. She must have seen
the darkest eyes in the room brim: The next day
she gave me a poem she'd chosen especially for me
to read to the all except for me white class.
She smiled when she told me to read it, smiled harder,
said oh yes I could. She smiled harder and harder
until I stood and opened my mouth to banjo playing
darkies, pickaninnies, disses and dats. When I finished
my classmates stared at the floor. We walked silent
to the buses, awed by the power of words.

There are so many missing parts to this poem that one hardly knows where to begin. The main one is that well-meaning Mrs. Purdy asks the black poet-as-child to read an embarrassing dialect poem to her white classmates, but there are others. Who has the darkest eyes? How does the poet react to being asked to read the poem, and how do we know? How do her classmates react immediately and then later?

In theoretical terms, the missing parts of Nelson's poem are what is variously called a "gap" or "blank."

The German critic Wolfgang Iser has described how gaps work in *The Act of Reading: A Theory of Aesthetic Response*. Iser argues that texts contain gaps or blanks that powerfully affect the reader, who must explain them, connect what they separate, and create in his or her mind aspects of a work that aren't in the text but are motivated by the text.

A more homey way to put it is to say that Nelson is offering the reader a very effective version of the ring-toss experiment that I talk about in Chapter 1.2. People seldom say everything they think or mean when they are interacting with others. Here we are given the basics—really, the least important elements of the interaction. The crucial elements are the ones we come up with ourselves.

Talking Points

Cue up some comedians or comedy sketches on YouTube and discuss how the most successful ones operate. A good stand-up comic comes across very casually, like someone who was walking through the room and just found themselves with a mike in their hands. They've spent hundreds of hours perfecting their routine, though. And you can see that prep work in the little things: the timing, the inferences rather than the big revelations, the sudden switches in direction. Not all poets are funny, but all comedians are poets: they use the same tricks we do.

Play a favorite song for friends or classmates and have them do the same, then look at those songs in terms of what's been discussed in this chapter. What's said, but, and more important, what's unsaid? Look at tempo. How do the beats affect your emotions? Is the song packaged in that typical verse-chorus-verse-chorus-bridge-verse-chorus format? Maybe so, but likely not: there are a hundred variations on that template. If you were the producer, would you change your song to make it tighter or looser? If so, how? As with the point about comedians, don't expect an easy correlation between poetry and the other art forms, but study other art forms anyway. There are lessons there that you'll absorb and use later in ways that may surprise you.

Switch on your phone or tablet and look up the Italian word *sprezzatura*, which means something like "studied carelessness." What are some examples? Here's one: a baseball player who catches a fly ball over his shoulder, smiles to the crowd, and flips the ball to a kid in the stands. Here's another: a poet reads aloud a poem that sounds like him or her talking but with just a slight difference, just a little more speed, say, just a few more rhetorical peaks and valleys.

Prompts

CONTROL FREAK

Someone, maybe even well-intentioned, wants to control you: a parent or older sibling or coach or lover. Sound familiar? If not, this exercise isn't for you. As a writing teacher, though, I can tell you I've read a lot of poems and stories arising out of this precise situation. A lot of poets and fiction writers have produced moving and insightful works about the dynamics of this kind of relationship, and some have even learned what they needed to know to make healthy changes in their own lives.

If you tackle this exercise, you'll need to be ready to look at yourself as well as the other person. A one-sided indictment isn't good writing; all things being equal, an evenhanded and sympathetic examination of both sides of a complex relationship usually is.

In the spirit of this chapter, expect to look unflinchingly at your subject. But expect as well to defer, conceal, displace, hint. A big emotional goo fest will turn your reader off, but a poem that withholds just the right amount of information will be a gem.

ANCESTOR WORSHIP

Write a poem to or about a grandparent. This exercise is based on my own encounters with such works—I can't tell you how many poems and stories my students have given me about a grandparent, male or female, who is either saintly and adorable or else stingy and mean.

You'd think the moms and dads of the world would be getting all the love or taking all the heat, but my experience suggests that it's *their* moms and dads who best grab a writer's attention. Doctor Freud would probably have to come back and explain why, but apparently it's that next generation that really gets under a writer's skin.

Maybe there's a greater freedom in the child-grandparent relationship; maybe it's just easier to say "I love you" or "I hate your guts." Either way, take a good look at your parents and then look past them at theirs; the older people might be the ones you'll want to focus on.

CONSTELLATIONS

You know the familiar ones: Orion, Cassiopeia, the Big Dipper, and so on. Constellations are compelling because they consist of a dozen or so stars, yet from these highly restricted patterns viewers have come up with a warrior in full battle gear or a queen on her throne. Come up with three or four new constellations: they might be representative people of our time or historical figures or personal favorites of yours or the person you love or the person you used to love but no longer do. Be sure the "stars" are surprising: they might be personal attributes, but they could be any number of other things as well. Within this tight pattern, work up a complete portrait.

1.6

Mind the Gap

We think of our artists as oracles, prophets, truth tellers. We think of them as two-legged talking machines who dig up the facts, uncover secrets, find out what the rest of us don't know, and, by singing or printing or painting it, make the world a less mysterious place. As we've seen, though, sometimes less is more. Sometimes the artist who holds something back gets our attention better than the one who shouts and thrusts pamphlets into our hands.

There's a Neil Young song called "After the Gold Rush" in which the singer says he's lying in a burned-out basement, thinking about what a friend had told him and hoping that what the friend had said was a lie. And that's it: we don't know who the friend is, and we don't know the content of his message, but we do know that it was unpleasant enough for the singer to hope it's untrue. You might play "After the Gold Rush" for one of your buddies or just show them the lyrics and ask them what they think the friend said. I've done this maybe a dozen times, and eleven times the person I quizzed said something along the lines of "that girl you've been dating put a move on me last night" or "That girl you've been dating? You said she was in the library last night, but I saw her out drinking with Ricky." (The twelfth person said, "I don't know.")

For a young person, what could be worse than finding out that your baby doll is two-timing you? And sure, there are plenty of other possibilities, but isn't the song more powerful if we're free to guess?

Voltaire said, "The secret of being a great bore is to say everything."

A poem has a gap at its center, something only the reader can provide; look at Marilyn Nelson's poem again in Chapter 1.5 if you need to remind yourself.

A poem is incomplete, in other words. Wolfgang Iser says every work of literature has a "fundamental asymmetry," and it is we readers who make it symmetrical.

Besides, too much perfection misses the point of poetry, which is to bring pleasure. Sometimes a little roughness is exactly what's called for.

Michelangelo is the most sublime of artists, though he was more than a little rough around the edges. Here is what Mary McCarthy says about him in *The Stones of Florence*:

> The boundless conceit and ambition of the Florentines was based on a feeling of "natural" superiority, which required no outer polish, and Michelangelo, who liked to leave some roughness on a finished statue, to show the mark of the sharp tools he had used on it, in the same way left some roughness on his speech and manners, to show the mark of Nature, which had formed him in a certain mould.

Not long ago, I was talking with Alan Walden, who managed Lynyrd Skynyrd. I asked Alan what projects he was working on at the moment, and he told me that recently he declined to manage a band that was going to fire a guitarist who smoked pot all the time, wouldn't rehearse, and wouldn't write songs with the others. Alan told the band this guy was the one who gave them their distinctive sound, that without him they'd sound like any other Southern rock band. But the other band members said no, they were going to fire this guy, so Alan turned them down.

Sometimes you have to let the rough stuff in, whether it's a slip of your carving tool or a pot-smoking screw-up who plays like an angel.

Later in *The Knowledge* we'll be looking at a variety of very tightly constructed formal poems, but while we're in the Department of Rough Stuff, take a look at this loosely wrapped poem by Maggie Estep:

The Stupid Jerk I'm Obsessed With

The stupid jerk I'm obsessed with
stands so close to me
I can feel his breath
on my neck
and smell
the way he would smell
if we slept together
because he is the stupid jerk I'm obsessed with
and that is his primary function in life
to be a stupid jerk I can obsess over
and to talk to that dingy bimbette blonde
as if he really wanted to hear about her
manicures and
pedicures and
New Age ritualistic enema cures and
truth be known, he probably does wanna hear about it
because he is the stupid jerk I'm obsessed with
and he's obsessed with doing anything he can
to lend fuel to my fire
he makes a point of standing
looking over my shoulder
when I'm talking to the guy who adores me

and would bark like a dog
and wave to strangers
if I asked him to bark like a dog
and wave to strangers
but I can't ask him to bark like a dog
or impersonate any kind of animal at all
cause I'm too busy
looking at the way the stupid jerk I'm obsessed with
has pants on that perfectly define his well-shaped ass
to the point where I'm thoroughly frantic
I'm just gonna go home
and stick my head in the oven
overdose on nutmeg and aspirin
and sit in the bathtub reading The Executioner's Song
and being completely confounded by the fact
that I can see
the stupid jerk I'm obsessed with's face
defining itself in the peeling plaster of the wall
grinning and winking
and I start to yell,
Get the hell out of there
You're just a figment of my imagination
Just get a life and get out of my plaster
and pass me the next painful situation please
but he just keeps on
grinning and winking
he's the stupid jerk I'm obsessed with
and he's mine
in my plaster
And frankly, I couldn't be happier.

Did I say loosely wrapped? Hell, this poem is hardly wrapped at all: it's repetitive, the line lengths are all over the place, and except for a comma and a period, there's no punctuation at all. But haven't you felt this way about somebody? I sure have, and I relate a lot more to this tossed salad of a poem than I would had Maggie Estep handed me a scholarly article on the nature of romantic obsession.

Jack White of the White Stripes didn't want drummer Meg White to practice because the more primitive the drumming, the better the music sounded.

Critics sometimes accused jazz pianist Paul Smith of emphasizing flash over substance, and some were put off by playfulness. "They don't seem to realize we ain't doin' 'Hamlet' up here," Smith said in 1991. "So when I toss in a shot of 'Santa Claus Is Comin' to Town' in the middle of 'Take the A Train' or a few bars of 'School Days' in 'Jumping at the Woodside,' that's my way of saying, 'Stay loose.'"

YOU WANT IT ROUGH

English philosopher Edmund Burke says while the beautiful is well-formed and aesthetically pleasing, the sublime arouses feelings of awe in the observer. In his 1757 treatise on the subject, Burke says "sublime objects are vast in their dimensions, beautiful ones comparatively small: beauty should be smooth and polished; the great, rugged and negligent." There is an element of darkness in the sublime: "beauty should not be obscure; the great ought to be dark and gloomy." Finally, the sublime exists on a much larger scale: "beauty should be light and delicate; the great ought to be solid, and even massive." The sublime needn't scare or threaten us, but it should have the ability to do so.

Compare a cute kitten to a tiger, for example. Or consider that while a well-proportioned athlete is beautiful, only a god (or a demon) is sublime.

The pioneering special effects artist Ray Harryhausen, best known for the Fighting Skeletons sequence in *Jason and the Argonauts*, used a stop-motion technique in which he shot a frame, moved his figures slightly, and shot again. Computer-generated effects, says Harryhausen, make movies appear "too realistic" and lacking in an essential "dream quality."

The Italians have a saying: the perfect is the enemy of the good.

In a *Rolling Stone* interview over a breakfast of waffles, Eagles guitarist Joe Walsh says that at one point "a really bad thing happened to the Eagles: somebody went and invented Pro Tools [an audio workstation platform for Mac OS and Microsoft Windows]. Digital editing. So now we can REPLACE EVERY NOTE! And so WE DO! We can replace the space between notes where there's NO MUSIC! And so WE DO! We can replace the commas BETWEEN THE WORDS! And so WE DO! Why? Because WE CAN!" The outburst concludes with Walsh dropping his forehead into his waffles.

The latest version of Pro Tools, according to Wikipedia, "supports sample rates of up to 192 kHz and bit depths of 16 and 24 bit, opens WAV, AIFF, mp3 and SDII audio files and QuickTime video files, and features Time Code, tempo maps, automation and surround sound capabilities."

When I listen to a pop song layered over with too many synthetic instrument tracks and too much echo, sometimes I think, "Gee, I wonder what that would sound like without all the bells and whistles?"

Wait, wait: I've got one more for you. This one's from the Bible. "Where no oxen are, the crib is clean," says Proverbs 14:4, "but much increase is by the strength of the ox." Want the job done, whatever it is? Better get an ox. Sure, you're going to have to shovel out his stall from time to time, but if you want that cart pulled or those logs dragged from here to there, you're going to need more than a hamster.

The good news is that you don't have to be Neil Young or Michelangelo to do the kind of work I'm talking about here. And while it might seem as though I'm saying you need to create something magnificent and then rough it up in some way, the most effective way to write a poem with a gap in it is to simply put two unrelated subjects next to each other and leave space for them to interact. Let them work it out! This will take some trial and error, but what have you ever done that you're proud of that didn't involve trial and error? Once you get the right two subjects, they'll figure out how to talk to each other. All you need to do is listen and write down their conversation.

Here's a poem called "The Crybaby in the Library" by Carolyn Knox.

The Crybaby in the Library

There was a crybaby at the library.
Tears were pouring heavily down his face.
He had omitted to do his math
and thought of the anger of his teacher
as the tears fell on his knitted
mittens between the fingers and thumb.

It is raining all over inside the library.
Parts of the brick walls are curling up
and plaster is falling on the heads and beards of students.
It is very dangerous for the books.
The rain comes down from every beam
and the professors do not know whether they should wrap
their articles in themselves or themselves in their articles.
The beautiful new botany professor who is only twenty-six and has
  marvelous dark eyes
has makeup running down her face as she runs out the door.

A precious incunabulum inside a glass case
is swimming gently as if in a dishpan.
Tiny letters and pieces of gold that were put there in 1426
are lifting off and turning into scum.
The assistant librarians are afraid to use the telephones
because yellow sparks are coming out of them.
Several young men go up to the attic, saying that the trouble may be
  from up there.
The electricity goes off and people are standing
between the floors in dangerously wet elevators.
The librarians' Kleenex and aspirin are wet and are melting into each
  other in the desk drawers.
The Shakespeare professors come out of the Shakespeare Room
and look around and go back in again; they must stay with the ship.
Fog is rising like rugs between the bookstacks.

People are laughing in a brittle way to disguise their well-grounded
panic.

The botany professor is a redemptive figure.
She goes to the Maintenance Department and reports what is
happening in the library.
Eventually the Maintenance Department goes over and fixes things.
The crybaby is definitely *not* a redemptive figure—he sits
still self-absorbed and shivery, and crying and crying,
and not at all trying to catch up on his math, nor even trying to fake it,
and all the time waves of water dash over his Bean boots
and up onto his lap, splashing his notebooks.
For the impending disgust of his teacher is foremost in his mind
as tears are foremost on his cheeks, where he sits crying and crying in
the library.

Silly crybaby! Don't you kind of hate him? I do, yet I feel sorry for him as well. Let's face it: we all have an inner crybaby. We all feel sorry for ourselves from time to time. We know we shouldn't, so we get annoyed with ourselves, and that just makes us tearier. Maybe for that reason it just seems natural for the little sniveler to slump among the books, destroying valuable manuscripts and threatening everyone with drowning, and after a while the poem becomes so horrific and goofy that we wouldn't want him to be anywhere else.

This next poem is one of Emily Dickinson's shorter poems, and it brings together two things that appear to be even more unrelated than a crybaby and a library. Dickinson didn't have to title her poems. You do. Or if you don't plan to title your poems, at least make sure you're as great a poet as she is.

A Route of Evanescence,
With a revolving Wheel—
A Resonance of Emerald
A Rush of Cochineal—
And every Blossom on the Bush

Adjusts its tumbled Head—
The Mail from Tunis—probably,
An easy Morning's Ride—

Dickinson has a great little trick that she uses in poem after poem, and she uses it here. She forces us to be literary detectives, yet the questions she poses aren't that hard to answer. What's red and green, or "emerald and cochineal," to use the poet's ten-dollar synonyms for those primary colors? The ruby-throated hummingbird, of course. What else is the bird like? Okay, there's that revolving wheel. . . . Ooo! I know—a locomotive! But not just any choo-choo. Now the hummingbird is a high-speed train as well, its wings spinning like wheels as it delivers the mail it picked up in Tunis just that morning. Not that a hummingbird isn't exotic enough on its own, but Dickinson gives the extraordinary little creature a further upgrade and, in so doing, reminds us what a miracle this world is, that it's always sending us messages.

Talking Points

Actually, if you haven't worked your way through all the talking points in the last chapter, go ahead and look at any you didn't use then—the two chapters are that closely related. Or consider this: conventional wisdom says that we find others beautiful if they have symmetrical features. Really? Think of the celebrities you're attracted to as well as people of your own acquaintance. The French have a wonderful expression (actually two) for people who are good-looking but in a slightly weird way: *beau-laid* or "handsome but homely" for the *messieurs* and *belle-laide* or "beautiful but unattractive" for all the *mesdames* and *mademoiselles.* A beautiful person can appear vacant and boring, but often the people we find charismatic and engaging are just a little bit off. Now why is that?

Think of some things that you like that don't make sense to anyone else. Recently a student wrote a poem in which she said her father caught her cutting a bagel "the wrong way," and he showed her how to do it so the bagel would end up in two equal halves. The student had to explain to her dad that she didn't like her bagels that way and she preferred a bigger half and a smaller one. The poem goes on to discuss bigger topics, but it begins with the incontrovertible fact that one person's idea of perfection can differ sharply from someone else's.

Telling Points

Prompts

WAFFLE HOUSE

Go to a Waffle House or your favorite diner and order coffee and then populate the booths and the counter seats with people: the ones you see, yes, but also the ones you invent. Go from one to another; when you get tired of sketching in someone's background, just go on to someone else until you have a roomful of interesting characters. Then watch them while they interact—I bet you'll be surprised.

You could also try this same exercise at the barber shop the next time you're waiting to get a haircut or in a doctor's or dentist's office.

THIS WAY TO BOZEMAN

Look at the map of the United States in an atlas or click on a U.S. road map; close your eyes and point. Now write about your life in the town your finger lands on, though if you have even the slightest information about the town you've picked, choose another one. In other words, if you live in Atlanta and your finger lands on Macon, Georgia, don't write about your life in Macon, because it'll be too similar to what you already know.

But say your finger lands on towns in states you've never been to and don't know anything about: Akron, Ohio, say, or Bozeman, Montana. Now your imagination can take off. What sort of shirt would you wear if you lived in Akron? What music would you listen to, and what instrument would you yourself play? And say it's breakfast time in

Bozeman; what would a Bozeman breakfast consist of? And where did those boats come from that you see on the canals of Bozeman? What language do the boatmen speak, and what do they say to you?

JOB SEARCH

Start taking notes describing the inner life of someone in a job very different from yours: an executioner, say, or a prostitute or a terrorist. For that matter, you might get interested in what a chimney sweep thinks, or a stuntman.

If no contemporary profession appeals to you, search back through history. For example, I wonder what it would have been like to be the taster for a nobleman, the person who tries the wine or the soup to make sure it hasn't been poisoned. Or a galley slave. Or a eunuch in some sultan's harem.

FUNNY MARRIAGE

Marry something you can't. A room, say: "When my room and I got engaged, my mother said, 'You can't marry your room!' and my room overheard her and ran crying from the house."

Or a piano: "Every night we strolled slowly to the café to hear the Brazilian guitarist who always asked my piano if he wanted to request something, and my piano always said, play the Brahms, man, play the Brahms. . . ."

How about a novel? "*Crime and Punishment* asked, 'Will you marry me?' and I said, 'I don't know, it's not very nice to kill an old lady with an ax,' and he said, 'That wasn't *my* idea!'"

This will be a highly visual piece, so pick something easily seen. A garbage truck will work better than a computer, for example: "My first husband was a garbage truck . . ." and so on. (Okay, you take it from there.)

Poetic marriages are a delight to perform because anything goes. Come one, come all. Say you're driving along, and you're thinking of your days at summer camp, and you pass a field of cows. Camp. Cows.

How about a camp for cows? After a lifetime of boredom in some stupid pasture, the cows would probably love to play softball or head for the archery range, and can't you just see them around the campfire at night, telling bovine ghost stories?

Or somebody says something about Homer Simpson, but you think of Homer the poet, and then you think of Ulysses, only not Ulysses in Greece. Homer the poet beat you to that scenario a couple of thousand years ago. Why not have the epic hero walking around the streets of San Francisco or, even better, some one-stoplight town in Mississippi? Man might have adventures in those cities that make the events of *The Odyssey* seem tame in comparison.

1.7

Cruelty, or Readers Like Pleasure but They Adore Pain

What do you remember of certain movies or television shows? In the BBC series *Downton Abbey*, the family that owns the vast estate of the title can only retain it if the aging husband and wife have a male child. At last she's pregnant! But a servant who harbors a grudge against her ladyship deliberately leaves a bar of wet soap by the bathtub. The servant has second thoughts, though, and starts back to pick up the soap, but too late—there's a scream from the bathroom. The next scene shows the master of Downton in tears. His wife has miscarried as a result of her fall. It was a boy baby; that was the family's last chance, and now they must leave.

In the movie *Sunshine*, a Hungarian Jewish family is detained in a camp during World War II. While waiting in line with his son on a bitterly cold day, the father somehow offends a militia man who ties him to a post and sprays him with water, which freezes in the wintry air as his little boy wails. As the scene goes on, you think, surely this is going to stop. Surely the people who made this film are not going to make us watch a man die this way. But it doesn't, and they are.

The death of the baby is the main thing I remember about *Downton Abbey*, which I saw fairly recently. I saw *Sunshine* some years ago, and the horrible freezing death of the father in that movie is all I remember of it.

It's hard to admit, but there's something in us that is drawn to cruelty. Now none of us has lost an estate thanks to a treacherous servant or seen a parent tortured to death by a fascist militia man. But cruelty can arrive at any minute. It's built into life. We aspire to joy, and there's no better expression of joy than a poem. But hard times, from snubs and bullying to crime and car crashes, are wired in.

Sooner or later, physical ills will weigh in. Some of us are born with problems or acquire them along the way. All of us grow old (if we're lucky) and all of us die. In the meantime, we have life.

HURTS SO GOOD

Let me tell you about my own experience with pain. One of my poetry collections is called *Get Up, Please*, and on the Amazon site, it says the poems in it are "cheerful and boyish." Actually, it says it twice: for some reason, that information shows up a second time on that page. So maybe the poems are doubly cheerful and boyish. Anyway, I hope Amazon doesn't fix this. What guy wouldn't want to be described as cheerful and boyish?

To be frank, though, I believe my poems are called cheerful and boyish because (a) some of them are but (b) in general, most poems by other poets aren't. Like me, you probably belong to one or more poem subscription services, such as Poetry Daily or Poem-a-Day. Think about it: when is the last time you opened your email and saw a cheerful, boyish poem?

In the great tradition, art pretty much equals the blues. Actually, the best art does. Art showcases pain, perfidy, the breakdown of the body: art does all that for you so you don't have to do it yourself.

Take a Puccini opera. You don't have to die spitting blood into a handkerchief—let Mimi cough her lungs up instead. Or a country song. You don't have to go to jail. Johnny Cash went to jail for you, for us all. Dante went to hell for us, and if that doesn't make you feel better, nothing will.

As you know by now, I'm a music journalist as well as a poet, and I not only write mainly about but also steal frequently from roots music, from the early country and rhythm and blues tunes that gave us today's music. And my greatest theft from roots music is the theft of pain. The best songs hurt—they hurt a lot. I'm thinking of Otis Redding's "I've Got Dreams to Remember," which is Otis's saddest song.

And that's saying a lot, because he had a lot of them—even his happy songs are sad. In this song, though, Otis gets something out of himself that you can't hear anywhere else in his music, something so painful that it seems to come from the underworld.

You'll have to hear the whole song to experience it; it can't really be excerpted. Here, though, suffice it to say that the singer says he dreamed they were walking down the street together, him and his girl, and a stranger comes up and grabs her, and she just turns and walks away with him. That stranger's got your baby now and you're, like, dead. I mean, you can see what's going on around you and hear people talking and laughing and having fun, only you're not having any of it.

That's what I want in my harder-hitting poems, not the cheerful and boyish ones. It's what I try for in a poem called "I Had a Girl" in *Get Up, Please*. That's a poem about two early rockers, Buddy Holly and Ritchie Valens, but the poem is really about the two girls they left behind, Peggy Sue and Donna. The poem begins with a fatal crash, not of the plane that killed the musicians but a car wreck I witnessed when I was sixteen. There's so much death in this poem; so much love dies. So at the end, I want to take you to not the end of love but love's beginning. Because if you're an artist, it's good to hurt people, but you also have to heal them.

"I Had a Girl" is a long poem, though, so let me give you a short example of what I mean. Look how Molly Fisk uses poetry to make the best of a medical diagnosis no one wants to hear.

Cancer, again

this time a slow-
growing rarity
tracing delicate
tendrils through
kidney and liver,
the lung's sturdy
wall, artery
somewhere I
can't remember,
though twice
I've been told.
How the mind
aches to abandon
the salient data
and amble back
to the meadow
we lingered in
only last week,
the one with
a stream, some
late-summer
columbine
nodding their
colorful heads
in a whisper

One diagnosis of cancer is cruel enough. The fact that the cancer has returned can be a death sentence. What to do? Wail and wring one's hands, of course. But after that, if you're a poet, your job is to make something that will provide consolation and insight to yourself and others, because a diagnosis like this will befall all of us sooner or later.

Notice what Molly Fisk does here: she lays out the worrisome medical issue succinctly and then segues to a scene so beautiful that you almost forget what came before: instead of being lost by herself in that paralyzing isolation, she places herself and her beloved together in a sylvan setting where the stream and the breeze and the flowers create a kind of Eden for them. I always urge my students to end their poems with what I call an aesthetic uptick: not a Pollyanna-ish zip-a-dee-doo-dah note that masks the truth but a place from which the reader can comfortably survey what has happened and think it through. In this case, the key to getting to that kind of ending occurs in the middle of the poem, where the speaker wishes her mind could amble to a happier place and time. This doesn't deny the gravity of the cancer diagnosis. Indeed, it makes it all the more poignant.

THE BLUES IS MY BUSINESS

One of my favorite things to do in a poem is set up a problem that's driving me nuts and then solve it. But that doesn't always happen in my poems, and it probably doesn't happen in the majority of the poems out there. When it comes to pain and suffering, sometimes the poem just lays everything out on the page. And somehow, often that's all that the poem needs to do. Consider this one by Terry Ann Thaxton.

Getaway Girl

Inside the house, red
as a bruised peach, someone
kicked me saying *this*
is love, but
I found my broken
perfume bottles at the edge
of the stone steps, my
clothes hanging
off branches,
and my only escape
was over homemade ball fields
where I found myself

chased by headlights
of the drunken car
he drove that made the baby
inside die. To remind me
of the baby,
he buried—under a pile
of old garbage bags—
the dog he shot. I put my hands
through the front
window to make him
stop, but every night, in my dreams,
I looked for the baby I lost, tearing dress
after dress out of the branches.
My black coat hid the face
I kept trying to lose. And when he left
to buy apologies
at the card shop
I hoped he would
not return. There were other
times I waited
for him, committed crimes
for him, like the time I kept
the motor running
in a truck at the edge
of a deserted road while he
rolled heavy electric spools
from construction sites,
carried stacks of lumber,
and then scattered
nails, hammers, and paint
into the truck bed. I was his
getaway girl. I remember
him urinating on me
as if I were a stone
statue by Picasso.

I wanted someone to take him
to Africa and lay him under
the heads of elephants.
I wanted to see him dead
in a lake of grass. Instead, he kept
pinning me against the wall,
tying me to the floor,
and I smelled the heat of Florida
coming up through
the tiles in the bathroom.
I begged my grandmother
to lift her arms from her grave,
grab his fists, his ankles
and tie him to the damp,
unforgiving earth.

Were you waiting for a resolution of the speaker's problems with this guy? Did you expect the law to step in or a father or brother? Did you think a chivalrous new boyfriend would appear in a burst of laser lights and stage fog and give the villainous old boyfriend the thrashing he deserves? Well, it didn't happen. But when I read Thaxton's poem, I feel better about things the way I do when I listen to one of those blues songs I mentioned earlier. Somehow you know that things turned out the way they should. You get the impression that all the bad stuff took place years ago. And you can tell by the tone of the poem that, though the speaker was furious at one point in her life, she has a sense of perspective now, and if she hasn't found happiness, at least she has found peace. Bonus image: no stone-shouldered hero steps in to set things right, but you're left with the indelible visual of a skinny-armed grandma storming out of the earth like an avenging angel and giving this bastard what for. Hooray for Granny!

When you hear the word "blues," of course you think first of a musical tradition that traffics in dejection, depression, despair, despondency, moodiness, melancholy, misery, and mourning. And that's just for starters. But there's also a sassy side to the blues. You hear it in songs like "The Blues Is My Business" by Etta James: "I'm open for business in your neighborhood, / The blues is my business, and business is good."

And you hear a lot of sass and jive and back talk in this bluesy poem by Yeney Echevarria as well.

The Learning Channel, or, Why I Take the Long Way

Sometimes I think about being knocked
in the back of the head with a dumb brick
then crammed inside the trunk of a green Supra.
This is it, this is how I'll go. In a sports bra,
clutching a bag of Funyuns that's mostly hot air.

In school, they had this whole presentation
on Stranger Danger, with the video of a little
brown dog and a man in an oversized peacoat
making small talk by the swing set, saying things
like *oh, yeah, orange is my favorite color too.*

Which is bullshit, because who the fuck even likes
orange. Everyone in Ms. Wallace's class got a bag
with a fat whistle and a pamphlet with the faces
of the milk carton and corkboard kids, plus three
round stickers of white police officers showing teeth.

The first time a guy corners me in the prop room
of a community theatre, I'm wearing eyeliner
and my nails are the right kind of pink, and when
he cups my head he doesn't even need a brick.
Barely happened, but I learned the shape of almost.

In school, they put me in advanced math and science
and I tore a patch of dead skin cells with clear tape
just to look at a bunch of empty squares, magnified 20X

and that's the way it should be when they pull me
out of the water, body geometrically sound and vacant.

At that juncture, it's pointless to have all four limbs,
but hey, a trophy is a trophy. Though it doesn't feel
much like winning when I'm not worth the trouble
of a lateral slice or being done *allumette* or, shit, rolled
into a tarp after a quick try with the kitchen shears.

In school, we never used the burners during home ec
and the only thing they had us do with eggs was carry
them around in shoeboxes stuffed with cotton like they
meant something, and we gave them names and painted
their shells, and learned three cracks still got you a B minus.

Don't put me in a shoebox. Don't put me in a box,
period. Maybe it'll be a glass bottle and not a brick.
I keep thinking why that guy didn't do more. Who
raised him half right? Wouldn't my face look good
on a lamp post? I promise I look better quiet.

This is a flirty poem, by which I mean that the speaker doesn't flirt with dangerous strangers but with danger itself. Why not? There's tons of it out there. Fortunately, most danger just bumps our shoulder instead of flattening us like a steamroller. Or cups our head in the prop room but then lets us go. Most of us aren't bad, but a lot of us try bad things and then realize they aren't for us. Somebody raised the would-be assailant "half right," and the speaker lives to tell her tale in a voice that's jokey, yes, but in a dark way, a way that recognizes that people do end up in the trunks of cars or in lakes, with or without all four limbs.

The world is beautiful and terrible, too. Poetry celebrates the one quality and reconciles us to the other. When we are troubled, poetry always helps. I got that from a friend whose adult daughter was grieving the death of a beloved pet, and the friend said her daughter replied, "Poetry always helps." I think that's true. I hope it is, and I can guess why. Think about the last time you wrestled with a swimsuit or a pair of pajama bottoms or some other article of clothing that has a drawstring and you had to grapple with a knot, teasing it out with your nails until the hard center dissolved and you could separate it into two strands. No poem by someone else speaks directly to your moment, but when your mind's in a knot, a well-turned piece of writing can untangle that knot, and then you can retie the strings in a new way or just let them dangle, if you like. The materials that made the knot haven't changed, but you can deal with them now. It helps if the poem is about whatever is troubling you—a poem about the loss of a pet if you've just lost one, say—but that's not essential. Any good poem will have the same effect. Try a Keats ode, for example, or anything by Emily Dickinson or your favorite contemporary poet. Poetry always helps.

Welcome to the end of Section One. I've laid a lot on you, so let's review before we move on. We've learned that poetry works through images, which means it works half-consciously, and the way you organize that complex mass of materials—or complex mess of materials, either one—is to arrange for some kind of cooperation between content and form that will surprise and delight the reader. Your poem is itself. It doesn't contain some hidden message. It's like a favorite person that way. It delights you, and you trust it. And it always leaves you just where you need to be.

Talking Points and Prompt at One and the Same Time

Let's keep this brief. Anyone who has been in this world for a couple of decades has enough woe to write about. What's interesting is how some woeful incidents lend themselves to the poetic treatment while others don't. I've cried harder over the deaths of certain favorite musicians than I have for uncles and aunts. You might nearly die in a car wreck and find you don't need to write about it, whereas you might pass someone else's wreck on the highway and find yourself reaching for pen and paper when you get home. You're not going to have to search for a topic here. Just let yourself realize which dark events haunt you and which don't. Start taking notes and then writing, and when you get to the end, remember to get your readers out of the traffic and leave them in a safe place the way Molly Fisk does. You might even use her trick. Don't like the present day? Go back to one that was happier.

Be careful, though. One pitfall in poems of this sort is what I call unearned emotion. In class once, a student read a poem about a neighbor who ran over his own daughter while backing out of the driveway. The class was horrified, though they managed to make their way through the poem and give the poet some useful tips.

Just before we moved on to somebody else's poem, though, he said, "None of that happened, by the way—I made it up." To this day, I can't believe the other students let him get out of that classroom alive.

TWO: HOW TO [illegible] A REALLY GOOD POEM

2.1

Three-Dimensional Poems

Okay, Section One ended on a bit of a down note, but I hope I showed you that there's a way to handle life's darker moments and leave the reader, as Henry James said in the days following his mother's death, "almost happy." I'm sure James and his siblings weren't glad to see their mom go, but certainly they were glad to have found a place where they could put their grief as their world came back together. Because the one rule in poetry is the same rule that dominates the rest of our lives: pleasure first.

Sure, we want our food to nourish us, but it's more important for it to taste good. And we want our sweethearts to make our time on earth easier. But really, didn't we make them our sweethearts in the first place because we love to look at them and caress them and nuzzle their necks?

So pleasure first, and after that? In *A Few Good Voices in My Head*, Ted Solotaroff says that a piece of writing is often a writer's "only way to organize and to some extent comprehend life's fullness and perplexity." Surely that's equally true for readers.

And not just readers, either: anyone who takes the time to look at a painting or listen to music or watch a TV show is organizing their experience and, to use Solotaroff's modest phrase, "to some extent" comprehending it.

To understand "to some extent" is plenty, is it not? What monsters we would be if we understood everything!

In this poem by Alejandro Escudé, a man is going through that prolonged and painful disengagement that takes place when a couple breaks up. This is a terrible thing to happen, which means it's a perfect example of the kind of experience Solotaroff is talking about, one we have to organize in our minds and try to understand if we want to go on with our lives.

Bed Sheets (Moving Out After Separation)

I wanted my soul out of the house, too.
So, I took all my diaries—twenty or so,
from the past twenty years. And I slipped them
into the recycling bin. I took all my photos,
baby, childhood, adolescence, college years,
and trashed those, too. I took my blood pressure reader,
and I took the white carnival mask I bought in Venice.
I wasn't going to leave myself at the house.
She offered me sheets for my bed. I took them
to the new place then dumped them in the trash bin.
She offered me the dog's bed, and I accepted,
but it never even made it close to his food bowl.
I took my bicycle, the one that folds up to fit inside a car.
I was proud to buy it for myself. She didn't understand
the purchase. She looked at me, I remember this,
as if I'd acquired a reptile who we'd now have to feed
live mice and crickets. A bicycle so I could get in shape.
A fucking bicycle! Do you understand what I'm driving at?

She wanted my father to help her move out, too.
Her brother-in-law would be there, but they needed
my father's truck. My father loved her like a daughter.
In many ways, he was just as hurt as me.
I lied and said my father couldn't help. If she wanted
the patio furniture then she'd have to figure out a way
to haul it. The moon that night was a harvest moon.
Yellow. Smudged by leftover rain clouds or wind.
What the hell do I know about weather?

For a short poem, the level of detail here is staggering, from diaries and photos to the dog's bed and that bicycle that sounds like the straw that broke the camel's back but was probably just the indicator of a much deeper divide between the two people. There's a beginning and a middle and something approaching an end to this poem, meaning the speaker has organized his experience as best he can. But what has he understood about it? Where's that comprehension or partial comprehension Solotaroff says a poem provides? Maybe it's not in the action of separating at all but in that slightly offbeat yet strangely soothing reference to the weather in the poem's last few lines. Maybe there's nothing more to say about the couple's parting except that it happened and it's over, that the speaker and the woman and the dog and the brother-in-law and the father are still here, just as much a part of the world as the moon and the clouds and the wind. The world changes, but it endures, and the same is true for the people in it. For the moment, maybe that's all we know, which means it's all we need to know.

But if understanding life is difficult and maybe even impossible, there's nothing that says we can't try. In the words of Sir Thomas Browne, "What song the Syrenes sang, or what name Achilles assumed when he hid himself among women, although puzzling questions, are not beyond *all* conjecture."

Indeed, isn't that what every work of art is on one level or another: an attempt to know what we can't? And isn't the pleasure we take in the work the pleasure of the attempt?

ART RENEWS PEOPLE

Across the lintel of the Teatro Massimo, the opera house in Palermo, are carved these words: L'ARTE RINNOVA I POPOLI E NE RIVELA LA VITA. That means "Art renews people and reveals life to them."

Is this not a Sicilian way of saying that art allows us to organize and understand?

Tolstoy is supposed to have said that a work of art should make people love life more. That's not exactly it. What he really said was, "The aim of an artist is not to solve a problem irrefutably, but to make people love life in all its countless, inexhaustible manifestations."

But close enough. Do we not love life more because art renews and reveals?

Which brings us to the subject of this chapter. The reader will have the best chance of doing all this (organizing life, comprehending it) the more fully dimensional the poem is.

You can open any magazine and find a wise poem (in the Frost tradition, say). Or an intellectually challenging one (Rilke). Or a comic poem, like one by Dorothy Parker or Ogden Nash. But an Emily Dickinson poem has all three of these elements.

Now rather than get into the question of whether Dickinson is a better poet than Frost or Rilke, let me illustrate what full dimensionality is by stepping away from poetry for a moment.

Think instead of pop music: why did Sinatra have the impact that other singers didn't, and why did the Beatles spur Beatlemania—why is there no Gerry and the Pacemakers-mania? It's because the Beatles' work was fully dimensional. Those songs contain every emotion we've ever felt, and they hint at mysteries we can't articulate; in other words, you get the whole roller-coaster ride.

Or think of love. If you've found the person you want to spend your life with, it's because you spent years trying out relationships with other people who didn't quite give you everything you needed. And if you haven't found that person yet, you're still selecting, dating, rejecting, being rejected, and so on, all in an attempt to find that best person: not the best person in the world but the one who's best for you.

We love the music we love and the people we love because they bring out the best in us. That's why music is generational: Sinatra was right for my parents, the Beatles for my contemporaries, and the young people I pass on the sidewalk with earbuds in are listening to the music that makes them feel most like their best selves.

I had a student who had only one tattoo, which was of a Red Hot Chili Peppers album cover. That band gave him such power that he devoted a significant amount of his very limited skin surface to their cover art.

Same thing with love. You may have been in a relationship with someone who held you down. Aren't you happier with the person who makes you feel as though you can do anything?

SERIOUSLY FUNNY

Now back to poetry. Let's read the poems that bring out the best in ourselves, and let's write the poems that bring out the best in our readers and make them want to read more—let's make our poetry addictive to them, like a song they listen to again and again or a sweetheart's kisses.

I'm going to go over a poem like this with you. Recently I had an undergraduate class choose and write on their favorite poems in that anthology edited by Barbara Hamby and me, the one called *Seriously Funny: Poems about Love, Death, Religion, Art, Politics, Sex, and Everything Else.*

It's a big book, and the students could have chosen from among hundreds of poems. Again and again, though, they came back to Adrian Matejka's "Understanding Al Green." Now obviously Al Green had his moment before these students were born, so what in this poem draws them to it? Let's find out.

Understanding Al Green

When I was twelve, a wiser sixteen-
year-old told me: *If you really want*

to get that, homeboy, you best be bringing
Al Green's Greatest Hits. And if you ain't
in the mix by song five, either she's
dyking it or you need to re-evaluate your
sexual orientation. Know what I'm saying?

With those words, I was off—borrowed Al
Green in the clutch in search of that thing.
Socks pulled up to my neck. Jeri curl. Real
tight Hoyas jersey was nothing but regulation
and I knew I was smooth and I knew
I was going to be in the mix by song five.
The whole walk from the ball court,

the wise man's words echoed like somebody's
mama banging on the door: *the panties*
just be slippin' off when the women hear
Al's voice. Slippin'. Slippin' because Al
hits notes mellow, like the silk that silk
wears. His voice is all hardworking night time
things. Not fake breasts, but you

and your woman, squeezed onto the couch,
taking a nap while the aquarium stutters
beside you. Nodding off on drizzly days
when you should be at work. The first smoke
after a glass of fine wine you know
you can't afford. Nobody, not woman
or man, knows how to handle Al Green.

That Girl from Ipanema would have
dug Al. Her panties, flip-flopping right
there by the sea. That sexy passing
the Pharcyde by would have stopped to say
What up? if they were Al. But they weren't.

And neither were you, last night when
that woman at the club shut you down:

I got a man . . . blah, blah, blah. Hate to tell you,
player, but she's at Al's place right now asking
for an autograph and maybe a little sumpin-
sumpin. What is sumpin-sumpin? I don't know.
But Al knows. And I'm sure you've heard that old
jive about Al getting scalding grits thrown on him.
You have to recognize those lies because

he would have started singing and those grits
would have been in the mix, too. For real.
I never believed the pimp-to-preacher story
anyway. The point is, Al's voice is like g-strings
and afro wigs and trying to be quiet when
the parents are home. The point is Al Green
hums better than most people dream.

Let's begin by looking at the unavoidable fact that romance, if you want to call it that, is rather narrowly defined here. The Al Green fan in this poem is a straight male in his mid-teens talking about females, and not always in the most respectful terms. The class that read this poem was roughly half young men and women, and they represented every possible type of sexual orientation there is: gay, lesbian, straight, transgender. The fact that the guy dishing out advice is not an authority figure but just a schoolyard loudmouth like any other made it easy for them to overlook his boorishness and get to the heart of the matter: how do we make others love us? This class's ability to cut to the heart of the matter made me think of the feminist music critic Ellen Willis, who said that whenever she heard the Rolling Stones' "Under My Thumb," which is a very danceable misogynistic manifesto, she got out on the floor and boogied for 3 minutes and 41 seconds and then went back to her feminism.

Most of the students in this class had had several other poetry workshops, meaning that they knew by the time they got to me that often a poem has to overstate its case if it's going to have an impact. They knew that poems are like people—poems are written by people, after all—in that the most energetic and engaging ones are likely to break something from time to time, and in that way does an ambitious poem distinguish itself from the bland little poem that sits in the corner and talks about the weather. The students who declared this the best poem in the *Seriously Funny* anthology recognized that here Adrian Matejka is addressing the perilous teen years that they've just left behind and that there's no easy way to do that.

Mainly, though, they appreciated the fact that he addresses his topic with everything at his disposal, including sex, romance, music, friendship, humor, violence (having scalding grits thrown on you can't be fun), maturity or its lack, and mainly hope, because, more than anything else, the speaker expresses every kid's hope that he'll grow up cool and that, with the right music and a little luck, he'll talk somebody into loving him.

That's three-dimensionality. You can't just say, "Be hopeful, twelve-year-old person!" You've got to give that middle schooler a lot of options, including some stupid ones. That's the only way he'll have the confidence to proceed. Notice, too, how the speaker here conveys a sense of his own supple mind at work. He's listening to the politically incorrect advice of the older boy (who is probably more bark than bite) but he isn't putting anything objectionable into practice, and I doubt that he will. He's thinking things through. He is also—did you notice?—winking at us. He's letting the older boy lampoon himself.

Talking Points

Using an anthology you had for another class or an online anthology, find a one-dimensional poem on any subject of your choosing and then a three-dimensional one. Compare and contrast.

Ted Solotaroff's statement that a piece of writing is often a writer's "only way to organize and to some extent comprehend life's fullness and perplexity" is too good not to revisit. Discuss this proposition, especially that "to some extent" part, from the standpoint of your own experiences. Is partial comprehension better than full understanding or is it simply the best we can do?

Almost every song or movie or novel we read that's truly memorable has objectionable elements. Slogans are easy: love your mom, floss twice a day, don't roll through stop signs. But art is a lot gnarlier. It needs complication, argument, internal disorder. Why is that?

Prompts

CITY BENEATH THE EARTH

It's sad to think of the dead being gone forever, so give them a new life underground. Would their life be like ours or more formal (or more primitive)? What sort of transportation would the dead have? What would they talk about? What do the dead eat, if they eat at all? Take your time. Make their world memorable. Make it three-dimensional, in other words.

THEN/NOW/SUPPOSE

Take yourself or someone you know or a group of people (your roommates, your family, everyone in the United States). Without a great deal of forethought, simply start writing sentences that begin with the word "then": "Then I gathered turnips for a living," "then they were only one foot tall," and so on. Go on for as long as you can, taking a break if you need to. What you want to do is make a long list and eliminate the items that don't work that well and put the rest in a sequence, paying special attention to the way you begin and end.

After you do that for a while, try beginning a sentence with the word "now": "Now I'm speaking French, though it sounds like English to everyone I know." And then "suppose": "Suppose the people slept outside and let animals stay in their houses." This exercise could result in at least one piece of writing but more likely three and maybe more.

REINCARNATION

Imagine you return, not as someone else but as an object: a mailbox, a square of sidewalk, a refrigerator. You might also try being an object that will itself have several lives: a sheaf of wheat that becomes bread, a tree that is turned into furniture, recycled paper (it might be the pages of a racy novel in one lifetime, scripture in another). Keep evolving! Think you're hot stuff in your human form? Hey, you're just getting started.

2.2

Overdetermination (It's Not as Boring as It Sounds)

Another way to define three-dimensionality is to think of it as a state of being fully alive: not just present but fully alert with everything switched on and ready to go. Music makes us feel that way. A great dinner with someone we love does, too, especially if the right music is playing. And dreams can have the same effect. We forget most of our dreams, but we remember the ones we do because they're electrifying. Often we wake from our dreams laughing or screaming because a dream can seem more real than life itself.

What music, love, poems, and dreams have in common is that they're all made of more than one part: the lyrics and melody and percussion of the song, for example, or the food and drink and guests at an ideal meal. Likewise with dreams.

Freud says that dreams aren't determined but overdetermined, that is, that they don't have a single cause but many.

That's why a typical dream will incorporate a childhood memory, an occurrence that took place the day before, the sudden appearance of someone you haven't heard from in years, a loud sound from just outside your bedroom, and so on. Say you're on an iron roof, fleeing a lion, but you're dressed like a ballerina except that you're wearing magnetic shoes. Now there are iron roofs in the world and lions and ballerinas and shoes and magnets, and you yourself are in the world as well. But these six ingredients have never come together anywhere except in your dream, and it's this overdetermination that makes your dream something that frightens and delights you and that you tell others about the next day.

So how do you overdetermine rather than merely determine a poem? You keep a bits journal. A bits journal is just that: it's a collection of random images, childhood memories, dreams, snatches of overheard conversations, quotes from books you've read or lectures you've heard, bathroom graffiti, mistranslations, thoughts that come out of left field, notes to yourself ("Start using longer lines"), and so on.

You can't write poems every day, but you can write in your bits journals every day. This really takes the pressure off: you don't have to write memorably in your bits journal, you just have to write.

For that reason, you should never censor yourself. If you're trying to write a poem, you might say, "Oh, that's not appropriate" or "No one could ever make a decent poem of that." Kim Stafford says, "I call myself an eavesdropper on the world. Constantly taking note of the things that are coming in. Things that come from my mind. Things that come from the street. People around me. Reading. There's a constant river into the spirit and the mind." That's how a bits journal works.

But when you're writing bits, you throw in everything. Will a particular bit start moving toward poemhood? If so, fine. And if not, that's fine, too. A bit might not be useful to you for a couple of years. Or it might never be useful, but that's okay as well. It's not as though you wasted any time on it. It's not a poem, after all—it's a bit.

If you don't keep a bits journal, start today, and if you do, go back and have a look and see what you can use and what you might add. How you handle your bits journals is up to you, but I know I get antsy if my bits journal grows beyond twenty pages or so.

When that happens, it's harvest time: I'll look for bits that speak to each other, maybe three or four that might coalesce into a poem. I've heard that Walt Whitman had a box of a certain size that he filled with scraps of paper on which he'd written, and when the box filled, he'd pull out the scraps and look to see which ones would become a sequence and which he might use in another poem or return to the box.

If this method is good enough for Whitman, it's good enough for us, right? The only difference is that, instead of a box, you'll be using the bits file on your computer. I used to let students keep old-fashioned paper bits journals, but now I insist that they make them Word documents. That way, when one bit wants to cozy up to another, you just cut and paste. Too, often I go to record a bit that might consist of three words, and when I look up, twenty minutes have passed, and I've written a stanza.

NO SUCH THING

Occasionally, someone will say they have writer's block, but that's a fictitious disease. The phrase "writer's block" suggests that there's this immense warehouse of riches that you can't get into, a huge barn full of gold and frankincense and myrrh and canned hams and I don't know what all. But the fact is that people who say they have writer's block have an empty warehouse. The bits journal is your warehouse, and it's easy to fill. If you add just three or four bits a week, in a month your journal will be five or six pages long, which is more than enough material to make several poems of.

Like some examples? Here are some bits students have shown me.

A tense memory

A student visits Costa Rica and ends up sharing a room with his group's bus driver, who only speaks Spanish. Each takes a bed; they turn on the TV and start to watch a Spanish-language version of a movie the student has seen before, one that features a scene in which one man rapes another. As the rape scene approaches, the student pretends to fall asleep.

A factoid

In the first Olympics, they played Wiffle Ball.

[Note: Can that be true? Doesn't matter—it's a great start for a poem.]

Overheard conversation 1

"You make a better door than you do a window."

[Note: This bit works by itself or as a pattern along the lines of "you make a better ______ than you do a ______."]

Overheard conversation 2

Little girl can't get the lid off a pill bottle. When the mommy says it's child-proof and only an adult can open it, the wide-eyed child says, "How does it know it's me?"

Poignancy/Bittersweetness

Lady Jane Grey sees her husband before they are both executed.

Quotes from books

From a biography of eccentric chess master Bobby Fischer: after Fischer visited a brothel in Curaçao, he said, "Chess is better."

Montaigne scholar Sarah Bakewell writes that, as he thought he was dying after a terrible riding accident, "Montaigne and life, it seemed, were about to part company with neither regret nor formal farewells, like two drunken guests leaving a feast too dazed to say goodbye."

Note that a bit doesn't have to lead to its immediate topic. Many bits, perhaps most, and certainly the best bits lead to ideas beyond themselves, just as poems do. Take the little girl and the pill bottle one as an example. I can't see myself making a poem about childhood or parenting or pharmaceutical packaging out of that story. But I can see myself writing about self-knowledge and identity. Who are we, and how do we know who we are?

One of the games I like to play with poems is to imagine how they began. Take a look at this poem by Franny Choi in which the speaker wrestles with her childhood, with the sounds and sights and textures of a time out of which her adult self grew.

Bedtime Story

Outside, cicadas threw their jagged whines into the dark.
        Inside, three children, tucked in our mattresses
flat as rice cakes against the floor. Pink quilts,
        Mickey Mouse cotton—
why is it that all my childhood comforts
        turn out to be imperialism's drippings?
I was suckled on sugar cane, plague songs.
        My mother swaddled our soft bodies
in all the warmth a long day's work in America could spare.
        New world love, wrung from her heart-rag,
heating her hands from the bones, heating our bodies,
        teaching them how to be loved.
Outside, crickets gnawed all the way through their tongues.
        A perfect memory. It was night, and my mother loved us
and most of my clothes were stitched by slaves.
        At school, I sang the names of génocidaires.
Years later, my father thought himself conquistador.
        Searched for new soil, and found it. Years later,
my mother decided for the last time
        not to leave.

What triggered "Bedtime Story"? You could say it was the sound of the cicadas at night, since that's the poem's first image. Or it could be the parents' aspirations for themselves and their children. Wait, I know—it's those Mickey Mouse quilts! In fact, the poem has numerous references to fabric—"cotton," "swaddled," "rag," "clothes," "stitched"—so obviously cloth is very important to the poet. In the end, though, that doesn't mean a thing. Choi could have started with "rice cakes" or "sugar cane" or "crickets." Be patient with your bits. Let one bit lead to another, and once they're all there on the page, let them tell you what they want to say.

Remember, the main thing is not to discount anything. If you start to write a bit down and tell yourself it'll never be a poem, you're cutting yourself off from your supply chain. Try to be as literal-minded as possible. Once I was in Chicago and saw police officers shoving a guy into their squad car as a woman screamed, "Liar! You're a liar!" It's a situation that would be easy to explain if I wanted to: probably the guy had grabbed the woman's purse or something like that and then pled innocence when she had him arrested. Instead, I said to myself "Wait—it's a crime to tell lies in Chicago? What do you get for talking back to your teacher or tearing off a mattress tag?" Before I knew it, I was well into a poem that never would have been written if I'd used my rational mind.

A writer named Joseph Mitchell wrote fascinating essays about people on the fringe: alcoholics, the homeless, and so on. Many of these are included in a book called *Up in the Old Hotel.* Mitchell said that he was a good interviewer because, over time, he lost the ability to detect insanity. He listened to everyone, even those who were crazy, as if they were sane. Joe Mitchell, you, too, are one of my Elvii.

FROM BITS TO KITS

Here's how I use my bits journal to write poems—indeed, here's how I operate when I'm composing in any fashion, whether I'm working on a poem, an essay, a book review, a letter to the editor, a grant proposal, or a pitch to my wife to make a change to our house or yard or plan a trip.

First I identify six or eight like-minded bits and move them to a separate file so I can sequence them. I always know the one I want to use first and I'm fairly sure I know the one I want to end with, which leaves four or five bits floating around in the middle. But that's what they should be doing; experience has taught me that if you start right and end right, the middle will take care of itself.

Then I get going. I start making what I call a poem kit. And as I go, the middle bits begin to fall into order. Or not: usually at least one turns out to be unusable, just as, sooner or later, a bit comes to me out of the blue that I hadn't thought of before. And often, as I head toward the bit that will end my poem or whatever it is that I'm writing, sometimes I realize it needs to be the second-to-last bit. Or maybe that bit, too, should be discarded and something else put in its place.

In other words, I start with all due deliberation, but some happy accidents need to occur if the poem/newspaper article/book proposal is to end well.

Think of anything in your life that you're pleased with and you'll get an idea of how the bits journal works. It's all a series of workable combinations, isn't it? A series in which the whole is so much more than a sum of its parts. Your house isn't one room but several, each with a different function and some with more than a single function. Your sweetheart has not a single excellent attribute but many. You're happy with your education because it was varied, often contradictory; you took a class where one viewpoint was offered and then another in which it was contradicted, and out of that came your own ideas. You like your soup or the song you're listening to because of its different flavors and textures.

Here's Emerson on Napoleon's observations about one of his favorite commanders, André Masséna:

> Napoleon said of Masséna that he was not himself until the battle began to go against him; then, when the dead began to fall in ranks around him, awoke his powers of combination, and he put on terror and victory as a robe. So it is in rugged crises, in unweariable endur-

ance, and in aims which put sympathy out of question, that the angel is shown.

That's from Emerson's address to the Divinity School at Harvard in 1838. Now usually we don't look to generals for artistic guidance. But Emerson's message to the future ministers and theologians of young America still works today for artists and, for that matter, anyone who wants to have a full life:

- Collect stuff.

- Amass more than you can use.

- Pick the bits you want for the task at hand and assemble your kit.

- Start somewhere—anywhere—and keep moving bits around until your kit starts to take shape.

- Revise, revise, revise. Then ignore your work for a while, return to it, and revise some more.

New York Times writer David Brooks says, "Creativity rarely flows out of an act of complete originality. It is rarely a virgin birth. It is usually the clash of two value systems or traditions, which, in collision, create a transcendent third thing." His example is "Help" by Lennon and McCartney, originally written by John, who was in the throes of depression, with a "slow, moaning sound" till Paul added the manic countermelody that makes it a pop masterpiece.

"Sometimes creativity happens in pairs," continues Brooks, "duos like Lennon and McCartney who bring clashing worldviews but similar tastes. But sometimes it happens in one person, in someone who contains contradictions and who works furiously to resolve the tensions within." That's you.

And don't worry if what you're working on doesn't seem promising. Barry Mann and Cynthia Weil wrote hits like "We Gotta Get out of This Place" for the Animals as well as "You've Lost That Loving Feeling" for the Righteous Brothers, a song identified during their induction into the Rock & Roll Hall of Fame as the most frequently broadcast song of the twentieth century and one that's still going strong today. Yet Mann and Weil would go through periods of writing what they called "slump songs" just so they were writing something.

Some of those slump songs became hits.

John Singer Sargent's portrait of Mrs. Edward Darley Boit hangs in the Boston Museum of Fine Arts. The text accompanying the painting says that the artist "demanded thirty sittings to complete this seemingly spontaneous likeness."

ACTION-PACKED POEMS

Now that you have some background, let's look at some poems that are just chock-full of yummy bits. By the way, I wasn't there when these poets wrote these poems. I have no idea how they wrote them or whether or not they gathered lots of bits and sequenced them or if they wrote first drafts based on three or four bits and then put others in as they occurred or used some other method. The point is that, no matter how these poems were written, they ended up full of bits—ended up three-dimensional, in other words.

Let's begin with a joy-filled poem by Nick Holt that's organized around food and the end of the world, two topics that have a lot in common, or at least they will by the time Nick finishes with them.

Half of a Pizza in the Nuclear Apocalypse

I begin the way I always do, after
a six o'clock drive during daylight
savings time, slamming gas station
sodas in the backyard bunker, twisting
the knobs on the radio until I find
a station that sounds like linen being

crumpled in the large hands of a mountain
man. It sounds like the music that dust
mites listen to, a lullaby for the cans
of beans and apricots twiddling their fruit
thumbs on the steel shelves.

I have decided that when I hear the bombs
whistle I will save no one, except for
one very lucky pizza delivery person,
who will not be tipped in the traditional sense,
but with a forty-inch-thick bubble of steel
and half of a pizza in the nuclear apocalypse.
I wish I were joking, but there's only one cot—
so twist that dial o' angel of better ingredients,
kick off your no-slip sneakers and dance
to the music of the new world, our world,
and tell me how the old one was doomed
from the moment the Three Wise Guys brought
leftovers to Jesus' rage-in-the-cage-and-danger-
in-the-manger-and-welcome-to-the-common-era-
I-hope-you-dressed-sexy-for-it-birthday-
Christmas-pizza-party.

Like a lot of poems that are busy on the surface, this one is pretty simple in its way. The idea is as old as the ancient Greek and Roman poets who encouraged us to have fun while we can and especially when things are going south. The world is ending. Oh, dear—what shall we do?! The only answer is that of course we'll do the things we like to do best when everything was ducky. We'll scarf a pie, and we'll dance. If the universe is going to implode anyway, there's no point in wringing our hands and pounding our heads against the wall. Let's go out in style.

Okay, let's look at another poem by the same poet. "Half of a Pizza in the Nuclear Apocalypse" is a nice piece of work built around two big bits, the pizza and the fallout shelter. Now consider "My Cows," which is composed of even more bits, although less attention is paid to each. And then we'll talk about the differences between the two poems.

My Cows

My whole life I've given credit to the wrong people—
thank you for this balloon, I said to the man at the zoo
selling twisted intestine animal balloons,
when I should have stuck my face in the dirt

and thanked the cave we stole the helium from.
My great-great-grandpa thanked the bootleggers—
the ones who wore cow hooves on their feet
when running their shine from distillery to table

so as not to catch the fifth grade theatre production
spotlight eye of the law, when he should have thanked
the cows, whose worst crime was burping so much
methane that the polar ice caps melt and unleash a long-

frozen virus that shakes the Earth like an Etch-
a-Sketch, and even that part's our fault. On road trips,
my friends and I have this game called My Cows
where every time you see a field of cows you shout

My Cows! and those are your cows, and we worry
about the numbers but never about how much sleep
they're getting. When I sleep I tend to dream,
and sometimes I'm in a pasture with the cows from

the planes before Chicago, a pasture near Tacoma, my
runs when I lived in Georgia, and I jog from cow-
to-cow giving each a kiss on the nose, like a very
polite bovine Halloween, and some nights, I look up

and in front of me is a man, and he says *Thank you,*
and I say *For what?* and a crescent-moon scythe
slips out of his sleeve and he says *For the cows,*
and whenever I'm afraid of being cut to ribbons,

I calm myself down by re-reading the first
law of thermodynamics: teaching myself
that I don't own my body, it's just something
I'm renting for a while.

It's easy to see that the poet's voice here is the same as the one in the earlier poem. It's smart, funny, and fast-moving. But this poem incorporates so many more bits. Whereas "Half of a Pizza" was built around eating and dancing, this one features someone who makes balloon animals, bootleggers who wore fake cow hooves when transporting alcohol, and the First Law of Thermodynamics, not to mention friends, a car trip, the speaker's great-great-grandfather, polar ice caps, an Etch-a-Sketch, more cows, a fifth-grade play, and so on.

Whew! What's it all amount to? As with Nick's earlier poem, in the end this one isn't all that complicated. The First Law of Thermodynamics states that since matter can't be created or destroyed, the matter that makes up your body isn't really yours, so you may think you own your body, but in reality it's just a rental. Let us be humble, then, but grateful, too, for the bounty that is ours. Mainly (and this is how you know it's a Nick Holt poem), let's have fun.

I love both these poems, but I love the second one more.

I bet by now you have guessed that Nick is my student. For that reason, there's an insight into this poem that you wouldn't know about if Nick hadn't told me and which I am about to tell you. Here it is.

In addition to the dozen or so bits that make up "My Cows," Nick told me about a bit that he began with but then discarded. Apparently the tip on the end of the angler of a football fish glows because it is covered in luminous microorganisms, which they can spit on other fish to dazzle them. This is a bit "I riffed on to open the poem," Nick told me, "but took out later because it was no longer needed. It was, however, crucial in helping me write my way into things." Sometimes you have to kill your darlings.

When I quoted examples from students' bits journals earlier, I mentioned that a lot of great bits come from the books we read. Long before e-readers had a highlighting function that allows you to save your favorite quotations, readers from the Renaissance forward were copying theirs into what are called commonplace books or handwritten compilations in which educated folk recorded recipes, poems, proverbs, prayers, and so on.

It's said that behind every piece of writing there stands an entire library, and certainly that's the case with this poem by Danusha Laméris.

Fictional Characters

Do they ever want to escape?
Climb out of the white pages
and enter our world?

Holden Caulfield slipping in the movie theater
to catch the two o'clock
Anna Karenina sitting in a diner,
reading the paper as the waitress
serves up a cheeseburger.

Even Hector, on break from *The Iliad*,
takes a stroll through the park,
admires the tulips.

Maybe they grew tired
of the author's mind,
all its twists and turns.

Or were finally weary
of stumbling around Pamplona,

a bottle in each fist,
eating lotuses on the banks of the Nile.

For others, it was just too hot
in the small California town
where they'd been written into
a lifetime of plowing fields.

Whatever the reason,
here they are, roaming the city streets
rain falling on their phantasmal shoulders.

Wouldn't you, if you could?
Step out of your own story,
to lean against a doorway
of the Five & Dime, sipping your coffee,

your life, somewhere far behind you,
all its heat and toil nothing but a tale
resting in the hands of a stranger,
the sidewalk ahead wet and glistening.

This poem might be a little intimidating at first, especially if you haven't read all the works the poet mentions. As with those two Nick Holt poems, though, take a step back and look at what's really going on. This isn't a poem about scholarship or literary criticism. Each character mentioned in each of the bits is someone just like you, someone who wants to not get caught up in the oppression of the daily grind. We want to be our own bosses—who wants his or her story to rest "in the hands of a stranger"? So, yes, the bits here are all literary, but despite that (better yet, because of that), the poem as a whole is deeply relatable.

Now let's look at an example of a poem that consists of even more bits than the three previous poems do. The poet here is Claire Wahmanholm, and her voice is unlike any you've heard yet.

O

> Once there was an opening, an operation: out of which oared the ocean, then oyster and oystercatcher, opal and opal-crowned tanager. From ornateness came the ornate flycatcher and ornate fruit dove. From oil, the oilbird. O is for opus, the Orphean warbler's octaves, the oratorio of orioles. O for the osprey's ostentation, the owl and its collection of ossicles. In October's ochre, the orchard is overgrown with orange and olive, oleander and oxlip. Ovals of dew on the oatgrass. O for obsidian, onyx, ore, for boreholes like inverted obelisks. O for the onion's concentric O's, observable only when cut, for the opium oozing from the poppy's globe only when scored. O for our organs, for the os of the cervix, the double O's of the ovaries plotted on the body's plane to mark the origin. O is the orbit that cradles the eye. The oculus opens an O to the sky, where the starry outlines of men float like air bubbles between us and oblivion. Once there were oarfish, opaleyes, olive flounders. Once the oxbows were not overrun with nitrogen. O for the mussels opening in the ocean's oven. O for the rising ozone, the dropping oxygen, for algae overblooming like an omen or an oracle. O Earth, out-gunned and out-manned. O who holds the void inside itself. O who has made orphans of our hands.

Isn't this a beauty? Read it aloud. It's a song of sorts, isn't it? A celebration of sound. It's a poem that takes one of the most common letters in our language and uses it as a tool to crack open the whole wide world. It's a poem that looks way back in time, to the moments when our earth pulled itself together and its species began to appear in all their splendor and variety. But then a turn occurs. A little whitecap of fear flickers across the face of "O" as the speaker reminds us that all of this is in peril, that we'd better take care as earthly life evolves and changes if we don't want to lose the original world to technology and overpopulation.

I found "O" on the Poets.org website, which encourages poets to comment on their poems. Here's what Claire Wahmanholm says about hers.

> Since becoming a parent, more and more of my time has been spent with children's books. Their reliance on sonic play—rhyme, meter, alliteration, assonance—make many of them a delight to read. They were a way of re-entering the lushness of language in those early months when I was away from my own writing. When I did get back to the page, I kept thinking about alphabet books, especially those featuring animals. They say to children: look, the world is a vast kaleidoscope; look, its creatures are miraculous. But what if we were honest? If we said that koalas will vanish, and zebras, and orangutans, and that we—the authors of these books—are ensuring their vanishing? O is the sound of both praise and dismay. It's the sound my mouth is always making.

So far in this chapter you've seen four very different poems, all of which have in common the fact that they consist not of a single big idea or statement but of a lot of chewy, crunchy bits. Now in every case there's an idea or statement that underlies all that glitter, but it's the bits that draw us in. All great works are simple, in their way. But they attract us because they sparkle and shock and pulse just as life does.

Here's a poem by Rita Mookerjee that illustrates how bits can accumulate in such a way that they start to create a complex portrait. Rarely, a poem springs from its creator's consciousness fully formed, but more often, the poet starts with just one tiny thing and then adds another and another till a picture emerges. That's what happens here.

Umbrella Girl, Diamond Street

Lightest of the cousins, her family smiles at New Year's: red
envelope, white hand, with a crow's foot and dark circles from reading
and sunchapped lips, but no brown on her cheeks
the umbrella kept her clean
because brown would be great-grandparents knee-
deep in field muck, brown would be butchering chickens

on wood slabs, brown would be the relocation
of continents: cha and chai both mean tea.

Brown reminds you, be a white Asian,
be a twinkie, a coconut, a rice
ball, a zebra cake, banana pudding,
IT-Apple-queen-savvy-engineer-
Asian-it-girl-big-apple-tristate-but-
don't-you-try-her-father-spelling-bee-
Princeton-bound-review-dermatologist-
do-better-with-headshots smirking down
ancestral family shrine, aren't you
so proud of me, incense poised, a pen
at the reception desk: write your English
name, not your family name, excusing yourself

from mixing with jungle Asians,
sand Asians, mud Asians, sweet and sour
sauce Asians, sesame Asians, Sesame Street
all of us who can't umbrella-duck our
way out of the side-comments
model minority takes the long
way home to buy rosewater and lemon
skips the fish market, the smell will linger.

It's never easy to have a foot in two cultures, each with its own foods, social customs, dominant skin tones, even ways of naming oneself. It's the sort of conundrum that seems to call for a statement of some kind, but poems, especially good poems, seldom begin with a statement. Instead, they begin with a bit. I'd like to know which bit Rita Mookerjee started with here. Was it the cousin? The umbrella? The coconut? The rosewater? We'll never know, and it doesn't matter. What does matter is that bit after bit accrues here until a problem is not solved but expressed in all of its complexity.

By the way, not every poem has to be born out of a bits journal.

But other things being equal, the best poems tend to be bitsy. Take a look at this one by Michael Steffen.

Which of These Is Not Like the Others?

206 bones in my body, and I use each one
to love you. I know that *El Etowasni*
in Lakota means *Pay no attention*, my darling,
but I wish I could focus on one topic
for more than a moment; I never know when
or where my brain will wander. I guess
no one's entitled to the one life they want
when God spins his rolodex of ailments—
we're all accidents of birth—but latitudes
girdle the earth, butterflies pamphlet the air
on sorrow's wings, the wind speed-reads
a magazine lying in the street, dogwoods
offer a promise you and I will keep
in waking or sleep. I know dreams
are our most tangible possessions,
that it's impossible to hum
while holding your nose, and the area code
for Antarctica is 672. One percent
of women can achieve orgasm
just by stimulating their breasts,
and when I press my ears to yours, my love,
your quickened pulse thunders.
France still executed people by guillotine
when the first Star Wars movie came out.
I'd follow you, love, into hell, or worse,
into heaven. You appeal to my better angels.
A more appropriate title for *The Odyssey*
would have been *Troy Story 2.*
Almost is the longest word in English
with letters in alphabetical order.

My scarred heart beats roughly
100,000 times a day, but I will love you
until the sun becomes another red giant
in a dying cosmos, and I will pay attention
to the one thing that matters most
to all people, whether they know it or not.

Like a lot of poems that look pretty fancy when you first bump into them, this one is simple at its core. I will love you till the sun dies, it says. There are a bunch of things banging around out there in this busy world, but only one matters, and that's my love for you, baby. Okay, I'm putting words in Mr. Steffen's mouth, but he sounds like a happy smart guy, so I doubt if he'd mind. He certainly sounds like the rest of us when he says "I never know when / or where my brain will wander." Isn't that the point? Our brains are all over the place, and that's fine as long as they come back to "the one thing that matters most."

While we're at it, notice something else about this poem. By my count, there are nearly twenty images or other references in this poem, yet Steffen doesn't explain any of them. Not one. One thing I've noticed about beginning poets is that they'll say something and then explain it. Have faith in your readers, beginning poets! They'll figure it out. They'll probably figure out something you didn't intend, maybe something better. In Chapter 1.1 I mentioned Robert Bly and his love of swift allusion. "Which of These Is Not Like the Others?" is a perfect illustration of that.

Lest you get the idea that I want you to go absolutely bits-crazy and start slinging words and images like a kid in a snowball fight, let me say that one of the most satisfying uses you can put your bits journal to is to identify two or more bits that *seem to say something to each other* and then braid them together until they do.

Here is just such a braid by Chessy Normile. The poem begins with a bird in an airport terminal, which may or may not be an augury or sign that something is about to happen, and braids that image with the story of the Trojan War and the speaker's own story, which involves a guy named Thom.

And Send a Bird

I ignore omens all the time.

A bird in each airport terminal,
pale fruit split open in the grass,
a man bearing his low
center of gravity
just outside my house
talking loudly on the phone about seeds . . .

Someone even says "Augury" on the bus
as I ride to meet you. Nobody says augury.

But I don't quit my job
when the lights go out
the same moment as you say "tomorrow"
and I wake from dreams
of fire overtaking the town, but still
I light the stove for coffee.

In Greece, everyone said "augury"
and everyone watched as a snake,
the precise color of blood
pouring out of a bag at night,
swallowed nine baby sparrows
and then their mother.

And what I'm saying is everybody really reacted!
They set sail for Troy! And then stayed there! For ten years!

They left their wives, their favorite and least favorite
children, their soft and fallow fields, their vineyards
ripe with fat purple grapes, their beds and custom
fire pits, all because a snake

killed ten birds nine years ago.

I watch a small, brown bird
trying each window at the airport.
She is trapped and I am afraid
will die here. But I get on my plane anyway.

The layover is in Phoenix.

As if that weren't enough,
in this terminal again
appears a small, brown bird
charging towards the windows.

How is it
that I can ignore all this
and board a second plane?

In the ninth year, actually, the Achaeans forgot why
they'd agreed to spend so much time away from home
and asked to leave. But an auger everybody trusted
was there to remind them. Is that right?

I guess it doesn't really matter.

This poem is more-so about how
an identification with snake behavior/bird murder
cost a lot of people their lives.

Driving me home from the gym
Thom notices the moon.

"Hey," he says "that big upside-down moon
is the same as the one on my arm,"
and holds it up to show me.

"An omen," I say with authority from the passenger seat.

He asks what type.
The music on the radio
is from twelve months ago.

"It's a good omen, I think,
to drive towards something
you have on your body."
I shift around in the dark
as Thom changes the station.

"Years ago," he says,
"around the time when I began to lose it,
I saw omens everywhere
and followed all of them."

A train makes the customary sounds
and I wonder if I have been insensitive
by bringing omens up so casually.

I really love Thom
and want him to know
that in Ancient Greece nobody
would've thought he was crazy.

"And Send a Bird" is not a short poem and it skips all over the place, but it's pretty simple, in a way. It consists of just three bits—a bird, a war, and a boyfriend—and in the end, each of these bits says something that's perfectly consistent with anybody's hopes and fears about the relationship they're in. When we love someone, how do we know they love us back? We're always looking for auguries. But what works in poetry is what works in love as well: you listen, you pay attention, you give everything you can, and with a little luck, everything turns out just ducky.

By the way, you might like this quote from an interview with poet Jay Wright, who was asked about the braids (though he doesn't use that word) in his poems: "A young man, hearing me read some of my poems, said that I seemed to be trying to weave together a lot of different things. My answer was that they are already woven; I was just trying to uncover the weave."

The only way you can get in trouble when you're braiding is to talk too much. Notice that Chessy Normile just lays her images out in this poem. That's it. She doesn't explain. She trusts us. Barbara and I went to this James Taylor concert one time, and James sang one of the songs that put him on the map, "Sweet Baby James." In the first verse of "Sweet Baby James," we're out on the range with a young cowboy, and then there's a chorus, and in the second verse, we found ourselves on a snowbound turnpike between Stockbridge and Boston. As we walked to the subway, I said, "Hey, Barbara. How did James Taylor get us from way out west to Massachusetts? I don't get the connection." She looked at me as though I'm not too bright and said, "Easy. He just went there." Assemble your best bits, then, and just go there.

POETRY AND JAZZ

I'll end this chapter with one of the most thoughtful, unsettling, and beautiful poems I've read recently.

Each of the last two poems was a blitz, a barrage of bits bouncing off of us like bullets. That's a wonderful strategy, one that dazzles and delights the reader with its energy. Not so with this next poem. You've had a lot to absorb in this chapter, so I invite you to pour yourself a glass of cherry cola, put your feet up, and surrender to the smooth rhythms of Mr. John Murillo.

Upon Reading That Eric Dolphy Transcribed Even the Calls of Certain Species of Birds

I think first of two sparrows I met when walking home,

late night years ago, in another city, not unlike this—the one

bird frantic, attacking I thought, the way she swooped
down, circled my head, and flailed her wings in my face;

how she seemed to scream each time I swung; how she
dashed back and forth between me and a blood-red Corolla

parked near the opposite curb; how, finally, I understood:
I spied another bird, also calling, his foot inexplicably

caught in the car's closed door, beating his whole bird
body against it. Trying, it appeared, to bang himself free.

And who knows how long he'd been there, flailing. Who
knows—he and the other I mistook, at first, for a bat.

They called to me—something between squawk and chirp,
something between song and prayer—to do something,

anything. And, like any good god, I disappeared. Not
indifferent, exactly. But with things to do. And, most likely,

on my way home from another heartbreak. Call it 1997,
and say I'm several thousand miles from home. By which

I mean those were the days I made of everyone a love song.
By which I mean I was lonely and unrequited. But that's

not quite it either. Truth is, I did manage to find a few
to love me, but couldn't always love them back. The Rasta

law professor. The firefighter's wife. The burlesque dancer
whose daughter blackened drawings with *m*s to mean

the sky was full of birds the day her daddy died. I think
his widow said he drowned one morning on a fishing trip.

Anyway, I'm digressing. But if you asked that night—
did I mention it was night?—why I didn't even try

to jimmy the lock to spring the sparrow, I couldn't say,
truthfully, that it had anything to do with envy, with wanting

a woman to plead as deeply for me as these sparrows did,
one for the other. No. I'd have said something, instead,

about the neighborhood itself, the car thief shot a block
and a half east the week before. Or about the men

I came across nights prior, sweat-slicked and shirtless,
grappling in the middle of the street, the larger one's chest

pressed to the back of the smaller, bruised and bleeding
both. I know you thought this was about birds,

but stay with me. I left them both in the street—
the same street where I'd leave the sparrows—the men

embracing and, for all one knows (especially one not
from around there), they could have been lovers—

the one whispering an old, old, tune into the ear
of the other—*Baby, baby, don't leave me this way.* I left

the men where I'd leave the sparrows and their song.
And as I walked away, I heard one of the men call to me,

please or *help* or *brother* or some such. And I didn't break
stride, not one bit. It's how I've learned to save myself.

Let me try this another way. Call it 1977. And say
I'm back west, south central Los Angeles. My mother

and father at it again. But this time in the street,
broad daylight, and all the neighbors watching. One,

I think his name was Sonny, runs out from his duplex
to pull my father off. You see where I'm going with this.

My mother crying out, fragile as a sparrow. Sonny
fighting my father, fragile as a sparrow. And me,

years later, trying to get it all down. As much for you—
I'm saying—as for me. Sonny catches a left, lies flat

on his back, blood starting to pool and his own
wife wailing. My mother wailing, and traffic backed,

now, half a block. Horns, whistles, and soon sirens.
1977. Summer. And all the trees full of birds. Hundreds,

I swear. And since I'm the one writing it, I'll tell you
they were crying. Which brings me back to Dolphy

and his transcribing. The jazzman, I think, wanted only
to get it down pure. To get it down exact—the animal

wracking itself against a car's steel door, the animals
in the trees reporting, the animals we make of ourselves

and one another. Flailing, failing. Stay with me now.
Days after the dustup, my parents took me to the park.

And in this park was a pond, and in this pond were birds.

Not sparrows, but swans. And my father spread a blanket

and brought from a basket some apples and a paring knife.
Summertime. My mother wore sunglasses. And long sleeves.

My father, now sober, cursed himself for leaving the radio.
But my mother forgave him, and said, as she caressed

the back of his hand, that we could just listen to the swans.
And we listened. And I watched. Two birds coupling,

one beating its wings as it mounted the other. Summer,
1977. I listened. And watched. When my parents made love

late into that night, I covered my ears in the next room,
scanning the encyclopedia for swans. It meant nothing to me—

then, at least—but did you know the collective noun
for swans is a *lamentation*? And is a lamentation not

its own species of song? What a woman wails, punch drunk
in the street? Or what a widow might sing, learning her man

was drowned by swans? A lamentation of them? Imagine
the capsized boat, the panicked man, struck about the eyes,

nose, and mouth each time he comes up for air. Imagine
the birds coasting away and the waters suddenly calm.

Either trumpet swans or mutes. The dead man's wife
running for help, crying to any who'd listen. A lamentation.

And a city busy saving itself. I'm digressing, sure. But
did you know that to digress means to stray from the flock?

When I left my parents' house, I never looked back. By which
I mean I made like a god and disappeared. As when I left

the sparrows. And the copulating swans. As when someday
I'll leave this city. Its every flailing, its every animal song.

You may not have recognized the name Eric Dolphy when you saw it in the title, but in the middle of the poem, it's revealed that he was a jazz musician who composed music as well. In fact, while primarily a saxophonist, Dolphy was a multi-instrumentalist known for his wildly improvisational style that tried to incorporate sounds from the natural world.

But you don't have to know that to appreciate what a magnificent assemblage of bits John Murillo's poem is, how one bit becomes a series of bits that opens a door to another series in a way that you probably wouldn't notice were it not for the poet's use of such phrases as "I'm digressing" (twice) and "let me try this another way" and "stay with me now" and "which brings me back to Dolphy / and his transcribing."

This is poetry as jazz, isn't it? It's soulful, thoughtful, improvisational, and self-referential, coming back to its beginning again and again until a wistful portrait emerges, that of an outsider artist, an observer and creator who keeps his distance from people and things in order to see them better. He's one who pays a price for his vision, but it's worth it. And the whole story is told bit by bit by bit.

Talking Points

According to Oscar Wilde, the most frightening sentence in the English language is "I had a very interesting dream last night." But this is poetry class, not psychology, so go ahead and take a look at the last really satisfying dream you had, one with lots of different elements. See if you can figure out where they came from. See if you can figure out what, as a whole, they mean—you'll probably be wrong, but what the hell, we're just playing here. And actually, the most frightening sentence in the English language is "my wife had a very interesting dream last night."

Do the same thing with a sandwich. A restaurant sandwich, that is: at home you're likely to throw together a simple PB&J or throw some tuna on a couple of slices of bread, but no self-respecting restaurant is going to offer anything less than a Roast Turkey and Bacon with Caramelized Onions on Fresh Pumpernickel with Provolone and Our Signature Honey Mustard Sauce or Our Sky-High Italian Combo with Lettuce and Red Onion Rings Doused with Balsamic Vinaigrette and Stuffed into a Tomato-Kale Ciabatta. Why was that sandwich so good? Or was it so good—was it too much of a muchness instead? What should the sandwich maker have added? What should she have taken out, and what should she have put in in its place?

Do the same with a short but sophisticated piece of music—not a pop jingle, in other words, but a tune that changes keys or tempo or uses a non-traditional instrument like an electric sitar or has some sort of surprise in the beginning or middle or end, such as a startling horn section or just a simple pause. What are the parts? How do they make a whole? What effect does it have on you?

The previous three Talking Points are designed to sensitize you to the granularity of the world at large, how objects in it are less monolithic and more composed of tens or hundreds of bits, little pieces that amount to more than their sum and that make our best experiences varied, self-renewing, and continually delightful. Now let's apply those lessons to poetry. Working with at least one other person, read this poem by Amy Woolard a couple of times and count the bits in it. When you compare your count to that of the other reader or readers, you should expect the numbers to be different, but that difference will lead to a spirited discussion of how bits work in a poem, singly and together.

Things Go South

Always trust a red door
On a black Camaro, thighs

Sticking to the vinyl in the June
Sun, pinking up the place.

Here, the apple don't fall
From the tree. Here, whatever you

Find lying on the ground is yours.
A scratch-off waiting to strike. The shade

From a sidelong glance. You're looking at
What happens when a body fights back

Three years after the fact. Three years
After the fact: the sweet morning

Stench of you sweating out last night's liquor
Just by pushing my tongue against the porcelain

Crown glued in my mouth, like hitting a switch.
Every town I leave, I leave on scholarship.

Nothing looks better to me than seeing
Nothing for miles. I can fit everything

I love into this trunk, into my own two arms,
Into my backhanded smile. And this gas station

Bathroom is more than just an American
Notion of the dirtiest place on Earth. It's where

I'll put on my face. I know how to wipe
A scene clean. And then I'm gone, love, like

I was never there. And even if it could hear
You at these speeds, the backseat don't

Care a lick what you have to say. Sweetheart,
I sympathize with the assassin in every story.

Prompts

ANOTHER YOU

If you get up around seven every day and have a cup of coffee and a bagel, have another you get up at six forty-five and make tea and toast.

Then follow that person around as he or she lives a life like yours, only different. Continue writing until your other self does something dramatically different, something that comes as a surprise to you.

MAURICE AND JOYCE

Write "My name is —" and fill in the blank with the first name you pick at random from a book or website. You pick Maurice, say, or Joyce. How does a Maurice dress? Immediately I see a man in a tuxedo but with the jacket draped over a chair; what little hair he has is long and wispy. He has a rather full mustache, and he's nervous about something.

When I see the name "Joyce," I hear the sound of chuckling before I get a visual image. Joyce is good-natured, a little younger than me, an attractive woman in a slightly horsey way. Mainly, Joyce is one of those people who can laugh at anything, no matter how terrible. In fact, her nonstop good humor is starting to get a little annoying. . . .

Start every stanza of a poem with the sentence "my name is —." You'll want to take most or all of these sentences out later, but for now use this basic sentence to generate a lot of material.

DRACULA CHILLING

Think of a big figure in our popular culture—Tarzan, Dracula, Sherlock Holmes, Superwoman, King Kong—and then imagine them on their day off. What would they do? Dracula might walk down to the village and have a cup of coffee in a diner. The townspeople would be terrified at first, but then what? Superwoman might go for a massage or a pedicure. Saving the world can be so stressful!

Sherlock Holmes, on the other hand, might try to stir up a little trouble. He's a guy who needs to stay busy, so he might steal a precious jewel from someone's safe or forge a letter blackmailing a cabinet minister.

CROSSTALK

Create a dialogue between two distinguished people in the same field who are greatly separated by time: Leonardo da Vinci and Einstein, for example, or Rembrandt and Jackson Pollock, Alexander Pope and Allen Ginsberg, Amelia Earhart and a contemporary astronaut.

It would be easy to make the more modern speaker the one who is "right," so be sure you give both equal time—if the older figure was right back then, they're probably still right today, though maybe in a way unforeseen by them.

MINOR CHARACTERS

Write about or from the viewpoint of a minor character on the margin of history: the driver of Archduke Ferdinand's car, for example, or Shakespeare's gardener. One of the workers who built the pyramids, now retired ("Man, these stones were heavy!"). A shopkeeper or schoolchild in Hiroshima the day the bomb fell. Napoleon's cook. Henry VIII's headsman—surely he can't have enjoyed his work?

In most cases, the viewpoints of the little people are going to be more interesting (or at least less self-serving and therefore more honest) than those of the big shots. After all, the person who wins the New York Marathon doesn't have to do anything except smile and go off to the victory banquet. The person who comes in second will probably have a lot to say, though, and the one who comes in last even more.

CRIMINAL LOVER

It's easy to imagine being the lover of a beautiful model or charismatic leader, so give your imagination a workout and imagine yourself as a criminal's lover. You dated Hitler when he was in high school, but then you broke up—why?

Or take somebody out of today's headlines. Many criminals are out-and-out psychos, whereas others are normal and neighborly, at least on the surface, and often it turns out that the terrorist or serial killer has a loving if bewildered partner much the way a banker or a store clerk might. What would it be like to be such a person—what kinds of tensions would shape his or her life? And what kinds of satisfactions would there be? Nothing human is alien to a writer, even (or maybe especially) the bizarre.

2.3

Hooks and Gimmicks

Well, I overdetermined that last chapter, didn't I? Wait, though: there's more to come. In this chapter, I'm going to talk about ways to develop the middle of that absolutely fabulous three-dimensional poem you're working on. And then there'll be a short chapter on how to end that poem effectively. And that'll be it for this section of the book—well, except for one more short chapter where I sum up everything so far.

In the meantime, you want your three-dimensional poem to be memorable, right? There's only one thing better than hearing your reader say, "Wow, this is a great poem," and that's for a month to pass and then hear her say, "That poem you showed me in July was really terrific. You know the one I'm talking about? The one with the cinnamon toast? Love that poem."

How? One way is by using hooks.

In musical terms, a hook is a short riff, passage, or phrase in pop, rock, hip-hop, and dance music designed to catch the ear of the listener and, beyond that, to "brand" the song. It's got to stand out, to be easily remembered. It can be repetitive—that helps—but it can be attention-grabbing in a single use, if it's powerful enough. Way back before Little Richard and the Beatles, classical musicians wrote great hooks. Think of the beginning of Beethoven's Fifth Symphony or Mozart's "A Little Night Music," and cue those babies up on your Echo Dot or YouTube if you don't know or would like to be reminded of them. In poetry, what you'll discover is that as the hook appears and vanishes and comes around again, your poem will assign different meanings to it and become richer and more fully dimensional.

At the Andy Warhol Museum in Pittsburgh, I saw a contemporary rabbi's justification of Warhol's technique of repetition in which the same image would appear again and again. The particular instance was Warhol's portrayal of Elvis as a gunfighter, which appears as a series of identical images side by side on a scroll that covers an entire wall. In his commentary, Rabbi Jonathan Kligler quoted his first-century predecessor, a rabbi with the marvelously alliterative name of Ben Bag Bag, who said this of the Torah: "Turn it and turn it, for everything is in it." That is, look at the work again and again, for it will never get old, and it will yield new meaning every time.

If that's true in art, think how much truer it is in music. You've got your own examples of hooks from your music, but here are a few from my mental jukebox. I bet you'll recognize a lot of them, but if not, these songs are just a couple of keystrokes away. (Side note: You can never listen to too much music. Not only is it enjoyable in itself, but music is an easy way for a poet to absorb half-consciously the rhythms and other musical effects that make our poems more sonorous than they might be otherwise.)

- Most elementally, Little Richard's "Tutti Frutti" with its recurrent "a-wop-bop-a-loo-bop, a-lop-bam-boom!" For that matter, all the very hooky songs that came out of Cosimo Matassa's studio on the corner of Dauphine and Rampart Streets in New Orleans are, for the most part, what Matassa calls "celebration songs." Matassa says that while songs like "Tutti Frutti" as well as Huey "Piano" Smith & The Clowns' "Don't You Just Know It," Jessie Hill's "Ooh Poo Pah Doo," and Sugar Boy Crawford's "Jock-A-Mo" feature phonetic vocalizations some might call nonsense lyrics, in each case the artist is using his own language to express the simple pleasures of living. "You can imagine children or adults dancing and skipping, finger-popping," says Matassa. "All of 'em move—that's the central thing with all of those songs. Some of 'em are totally childlike, but they were expressions of joy. These were expressions of emotion; you can't reject those. They get too analytical about the records. And most stuff isn't that cerebral—it's visceral."

- The Beatles' "She Loves You (Yeah, Yeah, Yeah)."

- Instrumentally, the theremin in "Good Vibrations" or the saxophone hook in Gerry Rafferty's "Baker Street."

- Lots of rap songs are hooky, of course. Take "How I Could Just Kill a Man" by Cypress Hill, who repeat that title over and over. It's a horrible hook! And it won't leave your mind.

- An example from a poem you might know and can easily locate on the Internet is Carolyn Forché's "The Colonel" with its unforgettable image of the severed ears.

And while it's not exactly the Torah, check out the hooks in this poem by Jennifer L. Knox.

Hot Ass Poem

Hey check out the ass on that guy he's got a really hot ass I'd like to
see his ass naked with his hot naked ass Hey check out her hot ass
that chick's got a hot ass she's a red hot ass chick I want to touch
it Hey check out the ass on that old man that's one hot old man
ass look at his ass his ass his old man ass Hey check out that dog's

> ass wow that dog's ass is hot that dog's got a hot dog ass I want to squeeze that dog's hot dog ass like a ball but a hot ball a hot ass ball Hey check out the ass on that bird how's a bird get a hot ass like that that's one hot ass bird ass I want to put that bird's hot ass in my mouth and swish it around and around and around Hey check out the ass on that bike damn that bike's ass is h-o-t you ever see a bike with an ass that hot I want to put my hot ass on that bike's hot ass and make a double hot ass bike Hey check out that building it's got a really really really hot ass and the doorman and the ladies in the information booth and the guy in the elevator got themselves a butt load of hot ass I want to wrap my arms around the whole hot ass building and squeeze myself right through its hot ass and out the other side I want to get me a hot ass piece of all 86 floors of hot hot hot hot ass!

What a beautiful act of subversion, huh? At first you think "oh, jeez" as she starts up in a manner that seems totally sexist and degrading, and then she does one of the things poets do best, which is to relieve the phrase that dominates her poem of its power and make it silly and fun instead. If you're prone to earworms, my apologies. I bet you'll be muttering this poem's hook for the rest of the day.

Back to music for a minute. In the music business, "gimmick" is a term closely related to "hook."

HANGING WITH NEWT COLLIER

One night in Macon, Georgia, I got a compressed history of rock 'n' roll gimmickry when I was out making the rounds with Newt Collier, who for ten years was the trombone player for Sam and Dave. He toured the world with them, once doing 280 shows a year, and these days you can catch him on YouTube performing "I Thank You" with the soul music duo on an archived episode of *The Ed Sullivan Show*.

Newt and I were at a club called 550 Blues, and a decent band was working hard onstage, though the audience was holding back. Suddenly a young woman walks up to the front of the stage, hooks her thumbs in the top of her dress, and pulls it down. I say, "What!" But Newt says, "That's just a gimmick." And I say, "Huh?"

"I'm guessing she's with the band," says Newt, which turns out to be the case, because after the show I see her chatting with the musicians and then scooting behind the merch table to hawk their T-shirts, CDs, and posters, all the while perching on a folding chair and making change out of a cigar box like the enterprising businesswoman she turned out to be.

Newt tells me that Sam and Dave had a gimmick called "getting the Holy Spirit," which means they'd be working up a sweat and "rocking back and forth the way church people do" when suddenly Dave would fall out and the roadies would rush over to revive him, and just when it looks as though the show will have to be called off and everybody given their money back, Dave leaps to his feet and rushes back to his mike—I'm a soul man, bah-bah-bah-bah-bah-bah-bah-bah-bah!

By the way, Newt says Otis Redding told manager Phil Walden he *never* wanted to be on the bill with Sam and Dave again, because Otis couldn't dance, and he couldn't stand it when Sam and Dave would "pull out that goddamned Holy Spirit gimmick every goddamned show!"

But a gimmick doesn't necessitate elaborate choreography and rehearsal time. Some of the simplest ones still work. Newt told me that sometimes when they had a soul revue at the historic Douglass Theatre, where all the great Macon musicians got their start, a guy would run up to the MC and whisper and point to the balcony, and the MC would shade his eyes with his hand and look up there, and a big grin would break out on his face, and he'd take the microphone and say, "Ladies and gentlemen, we have a very special guest this evening: Mister . . . James . . . Brown!" And the house would go dark, and there'd be a drum roll, and a pencil spot would shine down, and a guy crouching just under the balcony ledge would slowly raise a tongue depressor that had a picture of James Brown stapled to it.

"It was a gimmick," Newt said, "but a good one, because it worked."

So a gimmick is anything startling or unexpected that threatens to derail the poem but instead furthers it. Often, it's just a simple reversal of what's already underway, as in this poem by Mark Doty. Charlie Howard was a real person who drowned when he was thrown from a bridge by some other young men because he was gay. But now notice what happens in the fourth-to-last stanza.

Charlie Howard's Descent

Between the bridge and the river
he falls through
a huge portion of night;
it is not as if falling

is something new. Over and over
he slipped into the gulf
between what he knew and how
he was known. What others wanted

opened like an abyss: the laughing
stock-clerks at the grocery, women
at the luncheonette amused by his gestures.
What could he do, live

with one hand tied
behind his back? So he began to fall
into the star-faced section
of night between the trestle

and the water because he could not meet
a little town's demands,
and his earrings shone and his wrists
were as limp as they were.

I imagine he took the insults in
and made of them a place to live;
we learn to use the names

because they are there,

familiar furniture: *faggot*
was the bed he slept in, hard
and white, but simple somehow,
queer something sharp

but finally useful, a tool,
all the jokes a chair,
stiff-backed to keep the spine straight,
a table, a lamp. And because

he's fallen for twenty-three years,
despite whatever awkwardness
his flailing arms and legs assume
he is beautiful

and like any good diver
has only an edge of fear
he transforms into grace.
Or else he is not afraid,

and in this way climbs back
up the ladder of his fall,
out of the river into the arms
of the three teenage boys

who hurled him from the edge—
really boys now, afraid,
their fathers' cars shivering behind them,
headlights on—and tells them

it's all right, that he knows
they didn't believe him
when he said he couldn't swim,

and blesses his killers

in the way that only the dead
can afford to forgive.

Amazing, yes? Mark Doty could have written a perfectly straightforward elegy for Charlie Howard that would have done him justice and made the rest of us feel absolutely awful. Instead, he performs the kind of miracle that's only possible in a poem: he has the dead boy come to life again and climb the trestle and embrace his killers, who are not vicious men at all, just stupid frightened boys. The last two lines tell us that we can't forgive the killers, but Charlie does, and that makes him more memorable than he would have been in a more straightforward poem.

ALL GIMMICK, ALL THE TIME

So Mark Doty tells his narrative in a straightforward way but then introduces a startling surprise when he's almost finished. But a gimmick can be, in effect, the whole poem. Consider this one by Terrance Hayes.

I Want to Be Fat

I want to be fat,
I want a belly big enough to hold
A refrigerator stuffed with trout,
Big enough to house a husband with a beer gut,
A wife with a baby in her belly.

I want to be fat like a Volkswagen bug,
Candy-apple red, or cabbage green
With a burping engine and curving hood
Which opens to reveal my penis tucked
Safely between the crowbar and spare.

When I am fat,
Ladies sipping diet colas will whisper:
Look at him. My God how'd he get so big?
And beneath those questions they'll think,
I wonder if he still makes love?
I wonder what he looks like naked?

Love me skinny girls,
as you love jenny craig and vegetables,
Love me fat girls,
As you love insecurity and everything filling.
I'll let you kiss my triple chins,
I'll let you swim in the warmth of my embrace.

When I am fat
I'll scramble a dozen eggs each morning,
Brush my teeth after every meal
—this, of course, in the years
Before I am eight-hundred pounds,
Before I marry my mattress,
And lay all day swallowing
The light of tabloid TV.

I'll cry elephant tears
When *Cooking with Betty Crocker* is cancelled,
I'll curse flexing biker-shorts and ESPN,
And I'll never forget you, Fat Albert,
Your ass like heaving pistons of flesh,
Your stomach like a massive tit
Beneath your tight red shirt.

"You motherfuckers will have to give me
My own seat on the bus!"

I want to be the champion of excess,

The great American mouth with perfect snapping teeth,
I want fat children to send me letters
Of self-love and gratitude,
I want to swell thick with love and gratitude.

I want to be buried in an ocean of dirt,
This ocean of flesh, this heart
Like a fish flopping at the center of it;
This heart like a skinny man gasping
at the center of it;
This heart. This heart. This heart.

Almost nothing in American culture tells us to get bigger. Every explicit weight-loss ad, every photo of a model or starlet implicitly tells us to put down that fork, drop that doughnut, get skinny. Not Terrance Hayes, though. He's the one exception among the millions of spokespersons out there telling us that there's something wrong with us if we are not seriously underweight. He says it's okay to be a big guy, only that's not what he's saying. No, Hayes is telling us to be big in spirit—as the last line says (not once but three times), big in heart. Anybody can embrace a cliché. Turn the cliché on its head, though, and you're looking at a profound truth.

A few years ago, I was at a performance of *A Midsummer Night's Dream* in a downtown park. What a lovely setting: families had spread blankets and put out picnic dishes, and a couple of dogs wrestled over to the side as we all settled in and waited for the production to start. The show was well underway when suddenly a couple of jerks jumped up and played Lynyrd Skynyrd's "Sweet Home Alabama" on a boom box as they sang along and bumped their hips together. The audience went nuts, shouting, "Sit down, you idiots!" and doing all they could to stop the mayhem. But then the two miscreants jumped onstage. That's right: they weren't a couple of boorish drunkos at all but actors playing the parts of Peter Quince and Nick Bottom, two of Shakespeare's "rude mechanicals." The audience went from fury to revelry in an instant.

Good gimmick!

Talking Points

Think of your favorite songs. Why do you love them? It's because they have hooks, which are the parts that stick in your mind, the ones you sing to yourself as you're making dinner or jogging or riding your bike. You can't remember the rest of the lyrics, but there are parts to every popular song that enter listeners' minds indelibly. A few years ago, Barbara and I were sitting in a café in Santiago, Chile, when Toto's "Africa," which is one of the hookiest songs ever, came over the sound system. Two or three people began to sing along and then four or five. No one has ever figured out the third line of that song's chorus, however, so some people sang "I'll bash my brains out in Africa" while others sang "I'll catch some cranes down in Africa," and a third group warbled "I crashed my plane down in Africa." Everybody hit the last word really hard, though—"Aaaaaafrica!" So it turned out okay.

Every practical joke is a gimmick: a situation is set up, and then it's turned on its head. What's your favorite practical joke? Think of one that's kind, not mean; you don't want to make a kid cry or give Grandma a heart attack. I've never tried this joke, but it sounds great: you contact twenty friends of the birthday girl or boy and get each of them to invite one of *their* friends to your house on the special day, so when the birthday person comes in from school or work, there are twenty total strangers raising glasses in the air and shouting, "Happy birthday, Bob!" or Jill or whatever. Total bewilderment reigns for a few minutes, and then the twenty real friends emerge from where they've been hiding in the back of the house, and the real party begins.

Prompts

STUPID STUFF

Write about stupid things you've done, like leaving the yeast out of a bread recipe not because you forgot it but because you didn't "have any."

A variation on this exercise and one that requires more courage is to write about shameful things you've done, such as when you were part of a group of children who made fun of someone else in school who was different.

Or if you were the person who was made fun of, here's your chance for revenge. The revenge should be comical, though; self-pity is no more attractive in writing than it is in life.

FUNNY FOOD

Show someone eating, but not food. A woman is eating her own jewelry—why? Or the pages of books. Which authors taste best to her, which are most nutritious, which hardest to swallow?

Or someone munches on an abstraction, such as time. A man eats a handful of seconds, tossing them in the air like peanuts and catching them in his mouth, and then minutes, hours, days, weeks, months, years. He starts on the centuries—help! Soon he'll have eaten all of human history! Of course, that might not be such a bad thing, since it'll give us a chance to start over.

This is one of those exercises I like to set ticking in my mind early in the day. As I'm finishing breakfast (which is usually nothing more exciting than cereal and fruit), I tell myself to be on the lookout for surprising and exotic repasts for my imaginary characters.

"Food" and its many synonyms are just as beautiful as "kiss," so keep going as long as you please. Your reader will thank you.

This prompt triggers both hooks and gimmicks, since you're going to be repeating yourself but also reversing yourself. Women don't eat their jewelry any more than Terrance Hayes really wants to be fat. But if they chow down on their earrings and bracelets in your poem, you're going to be making a statement. You don't know what it is because you haven't written the poem yet, but you're on the trail of something fabulous, believe me.

A MASTERPIECE A DAY

This prompt might result in one good poem or a whole book. Using a one-volume encyclopedia such as *The Columbia Encyclopedia*, begin on page one, pick a topic, and write about it. For example, on Day One, you might come across "Aaron," Moses' brother. Try a dramatic monologue in his voice; do you think he'd be proud or resentful of his famous sibling?

On Day 153, you might be up to "British Thermal Unit." What would be a French Thermal Unit be like? What would it measure?

A hundred days later, you'd run into "Comoros" (island-state in the Indian Ocean between Mozambique and Madagascar) and "compound eye" (the kind flies have) and "Comstock Lode" (vein of gold and silver discovered in Nevada in the 1850s), any one of which is a marvelous metaphor.

Even after a year, you'd only be up to "Ezekiel" and "eye bank" and, best of all, "extraterrestrial intelligence."

2.4

This Is the End, My Only Friend

I've already talked about how to end a poem effectively earlier when I showed you Molly Fisk's "Cancer, again" in Chapter 1.7. You always want to end a poem right, but when you're dealing with something that's heavy (like cancer), you really want to take care. You want to end with an uptick so the reader is neither devastated nor consoled falsely but left in a place where he or she can comfortably contemplate.

Having your work turned down by a magazine is not exactly one of life's catastrophes, but it's an irritation every published author has to deal with. Look how Sean Thomas Dougherty handles the issue in this short prose poem of his.

> Dear Editor Who Apologized for Taking Six Months to Reject My Poems and Said They Came Close
>
> I was wondering how close? Close as a basketball rimming in and out

at the end of the Celtics game last night for the win, or close like how the moon is close to the earth, compared say to the nearest galaxy? Or was it close the way my wife lies next to me at night, almost no space between our bodies, so I can't tell whether sometimes it is she or I that is breathing.

Prose poems are notoriously hard to pull off, because they relinquish the control that only line and stanza can provide. So if you're going to write a prose poem, it better land. This one does. Note that the trick here is the same one that Molly Fisk uses. It's easy: you introduce the negative content, then you step away from it. Dougherty can whine or attack the editor (people do, believe me), but instead he shrugs it off. This is a poem that endorses perspective: yeah, my poem got turned down, but I still have basketball and the moon and someone who loves me.

Here are two more examples that show how endings work. The first poem deals with death, and it's by Peg Bresnahan. The second is a poem about heartbreak, and it's one of mine.

At the Sunny Ridge Retirement Center

During Harriet's memorial service,
Frances leaned, put her head
on my shoulder and died—quietly

as if she didn't want to interrupt
Harriet's program.
The minister didn't see us,

no one knew except me. At the piano,
Mary played the introduction
to *Going Home*. Everyone thumbed

their hymnals for page two hundred forty-three.
I didn't know what to do, since Frances

still looked like Frances, only not quite

and she was ninety-five. I put my arm
around her so she wouldn't fall
and waited for someone to notice.

Through the French doors
finches squabbled at the bird feeder.
The squirrel we call Rocky

contemplated his next move.
A laundry truck rolled by.
I looked down at Frances' navy blue crocs,

the ones she claimed felt so much
like bedroom slippers
she could wear them anywhere.

Thinking About What You Wanted Her to Say

You think about the times
you had to say to someone
I don't love you anymore
and even as you said it
you wanted to say
I take it back
it's not true
not because it wasn't
but because it caused
such pain that you thought
one or both of you would die

or the time that old song,
the good one,
came on the kitchen radio

as you were making supper
and you vowed
to learn the words this time
but when it was over
you were no closer
to knowing them
than you were
when you were seventeen,
in your car,
down by the lake,

saying please,
I don't deserve this,
take it back,
and you could tell
that she wanted to
but you both knew
that if she had
the words would have killed her
and by then
you were a dead man anyway
and so handsome.

See? In each case, the poem steps away from its subject and then concludes in a way that rounds the poem off. The first poem says, "Frances is dead, but when she was alive, she really got around, didn't she?" In the second, yeah, you got jilted, brother—hard. But you're a good-looking guy. You'll be okay.

CLICK!

Every part of a poem is as important as every other part, but getting the end right is one of the more exacting aspects of the process and one poets grind their teeth over more than any other. After all, it's the last thing the reader will see. Think of a guest leaving your house. You want to neither look and up and discover they've gone without saying anything nor hear a crash and see that they've leapt through your window and taken your cash and jewelry with them. You want a smile and a handshake before you close the door, a reminder that this meeting has been fun and can happen again.

Maxine Kumin wrote a perfect little essay on poetic endings, fittingly called "Closing the Door." At the end of every poem, says Kumin, there should be,

> if not the slam of the door . . . then at least the click of the bolt in the jamb. My *bête noire* is the poem that simply falls off the page in an accident of imbalance, so that the reader, poor fish, doesn't actually know how the poem has ended. He turns the page in expectation of further enlightenment, only to be caught red-fingered with the title of the next poem coldly sizing him up.

Instead of the clumsy non-ending, then, Kumin proposes four kinds of closure and quotes the endings of four canonical poems as examples.

First is the poem that comes full circle. This one's a no-brainer: you just repeat the poem's first line or title. Robert Frost's "Provide, Provide" ends this way:

> Better to go down dignified
> With boughten friendship at your side
> Than none at all. Provide, provide!

Then there's the poem that ends in an understatement that startles or arouses, such as Randall Jarrell's "The Death of the Ball Turret Gunner." Here a World War II aviator recounts his experiences in battle and closes with these words: "When I died they washed me out of the turret with a hose." The speaker's tone is flat and unsensational, which just heightens the reader's horror when he realizes the speaker is dead, is no longer a human being with soul and spirit but a sanitation problem.

A third type of poem concludes with a prophetic or apocalyptic statement, as is the case with "The Second Coming" by William Butler Yeats. Here the speaker foresees the passing of our world and wonders pessimistically what will take its place:

> And what rough beast, its hour come round at last,
> Slouches toward Bethlehem to be born?

Finally, Maxine Kumin points us to the poem that concludes with an aggressive shift that totally reverses the poem's meaning. Do you know Edwin Arlington Robinson's "Richard Cory"? Cory is handsome, wealthy, and therefore supremely confident, so naturally his townspeople are bitter and envious and wish they were him (they're the speakers here). Robinson's grip on the reader is so strong that no one, on reading the poem for the first time, can fail to be startled by its last lines.

> So on we worked, and waited for the light,
> And went without the meat, and cursed the bread;
> And Richard Cory, one calm summer night,
> Went home and put a bullet through his head.

Want some contemporary illustrations of how poems can be ended effectively? I got these from two poet friends of mine, Ada Limón (the first four are hers) and Landis Grenville (who came up with the last three). Ada uses a poem of mine for two of her examples. Sorry about that! Maybe she's right, though. You decide.

Flash of Light—a poignant image.

> "She burns like a burning bush / driven by a godawful wind."
> —"You and I Are Disappearing" by Yusef Komunyakaa

Flying out the Window—going in a new direction that chang-

es the poem but still fits tonally.

"The kind of grief that says the world / is so beautiful, that it will give you no peace."

—"More Than This" by David Kirby

Go out Singing—repetition of phrase or sound that feels as though it caps off the poem or a line that completes the rhythm.

"The haiku and the honey. The orange and orangutan slow dance."

—"Slow Dance" by Matthew Dickman

Slam the Door—strong "saying" moment.

"I lean back, as the evening darkens and comes on. / A chicken hawk floats over, looking for home. / I have wasted my life."

—"Lying in a Hammock at William Duffy's Farm in Pine Island, Minnesota" by James Wright

"The kind of grief that says the world / is so beautiful, that it will give you no peace."

—"More Than This" by David Kirby

Get off the Train—the poem feels as though it might keep going, stretching on.

"Your voice released into the night / like a song & the mice / grew wilder."

—"Bag of Mice" by Nick Flynn

Command—the poem ends on an action or a call for action.

"An ordinary woman who could rise / in flame, all he would have to do / is come close and touch me."

—"Fast Gas" by Dorianne Laux

Unanswered—the poem opens up or leaves itself hanging, an implicit or explicit unanswered question.

"She wants to get lost in that sad glowing square of blue. Don't you?"
—"The Backyard Mermaid" by Matthea Harvey

It's only fitting at this point to see how these two poets end their own poems. Let's have a look at a poem each by Ada Limón and Landis Grenville.

Crush

Maybe my limbs are made
mostly for decoration,
like the way I feel about
persimmons. You can't
really eat them. Or you
wouldn't want to. If you grab
the soft skin with your fist
it somehow feels funny,
like you've been here
before and uncomfortable,
too, like you'd rather
squish it between your teeth
impatiently, before spitting
the soft parts back up
to linger on the tongue like
burnt sugar or guilt.
For starters, it was all
an accident, you cut
the right branch
and a sort of light

woke up underneath,
and the inedible fruit
grew dark and needy.
Think crucial hanging.
Think crayon orange.
There is one low, leaning
heart-shaped globe left
and dearest, can you
tell, I am trying
to love you less.

Naturally you think the speaker is going to get in there and participate in all this gooey, syrupy love, but nope. Ada Limón's poem ends with a complete 180-degree reversal.

And here's Landis Grenville's poem.

Ode to the Swamp Monster from the '50s

You're the *Creature from the Black Lagoon*,
Gill-Man, *the Swamp Thing*, prehistoric
or the sad product of pollution
and night swimming. Still it's possible
(even though it's decades before climate
change) that you started as an eco-freak
diving for trash on the weekends, until
you forgot to go home to your wife,
forgot to put on a tie, just stayed, eating
algae and sleeping in the reeds. You stayed
so long that the swamp gobbled you back
and when you finally did remember
that you used to have a real bed and came
lumbering in through your old screen door
your wife didn't know you. She just
screamed and screamed and so you took
your toothbrush and went back to the water

and became the legend that boys pass on
to girls when they want to pull them close.
The girl always shivers at the thought
of you while the boy hooks his arm
around her waist, and they're both happy
to say it's fear stirring in them and nothing
a little sweeter. But when you come stumbling
out of the dark and water, woken by the flash
of headlights or the smell of metal, when you
walk towards their parked car, arms raised
and hung with swamp leaves and grasses,
you look like a father waving away a kid's
first date, your muscles softened and slackening
from age and the atrophy that comes when
there's nothing to hold. So if those teenagers
sliding around each other in the awkward oil
of first touches didn't scream their heads off
and hit the gas, if they stayed to see you loping
towards them, they might catch the resemblance,
might think you are just groaning because
it's past curfew, because you don't want them
to go too fast, because you know—and they don't—
that waiting for them in the tangled hedges
down that road, there are worse things than you.

This poem is so funny and so sweet. As you read it, where did you think it was going? Nobody would blame you if you thought the monster was going to devour those teenagers the way monsters do in most movies these days. But the monster was and still is a family man himself, and the surprise here is how kind he is at the last. The movies are one thing, but life? Now there's something that'll scare the pants off of you. By the way, don't forget the toothbrush in line seventeen. A lot of the best poems contain an element just like that. You're not sure quite how it works, but it's like the secret ingredient in your grandma's berry cobbler: no one knows what it is, but the recipe just wouldn't work without it.

While we're in gothic mode, check out this poem by Sarah Morrison. As with the two that precede it, be prepared for an ending that you're not prepared for.

Motel 666

The maid just found your latest victim's three-day corpse
        bled out and rotting on the purple paisley carpet,
ice bucket overturned and minibar wiped clean but
        you're bored; this is not your best work.
Motels are scum magnets, which makes it easy
        to do your job; you're practically on vacation when
you possess someone who is already doing bad.
        All you have to do is walk down the hall and
bam! there's the homeless ex-con you'll inhabit
        to kill the girl at the front desk, then tomorrow, bam!
there's a cheating husband who snuck out for the night.
        He did want that prostitute, but who knows? He
might have already wanted to kidnap her, too! You thrive
        in this universal symbol of desire, because there's nothing
more tempting than the ability to move in and out then in
        and out and in again without ever having to change the sheets.
This joint isn't always full of baddies, though. You often get
        the saddies, too, those families down on their luck, those
pregnant, runaway brides and abused wives, all of whom
        provide excellent opportunities for more creative haunts—
You become the room that goes black around the edges
        and creeps in on desperate mothers trying to sleep.
You are the warm milk in the bottle of the man who demands
        to be spanked when he makes an oopsie on the floor.
You are the scum in the toilets and the poison in the pills
        on the bedside tables but really, after all these years,
nothing puckers your pants more than subtlety.
        On a good day, you are the breath of a woman who leans

down chest first over her man, sprawled on the stiff must
of the bed, only to brush her lips against his ear.

See what I mean? As horror piles upon horror and you feel as though you're about to drown in a room that's filling slowly with body fluids the way it would in a particularly demented Poe story, suddenly there's a touch of tenderness that reminds you that doors do open, life does go on, and there may be something precious among the shadows, even love.

Talking Points

There are a dozen or so poems here that I just excerpted. I didn't include them in their entirety for space reasons. But most of them are online, so search them out and work your way through from start to finish. That's the best way to see how their endings work.

Without thinking about how they end, locate a handful of your favorite poems and see how they conclude. I'd be surprised if your affection for them didn't have a lot to do with how they wrap up.

Or close your eyes and just reach out and grab any old poem and analyze its end. I hope you find a couple of stinkers: sometimes the best way to learn how something is done well is to study how it's done badly.

Prompts

AFTERMATH

We've all undergone catastrophes—fires, deaths, tornadoes, break-ins. One good thing about being a writer is that you can always write about something that another person would have to undergo in frustrated silence.

So think back about that terrible thing that happened to you. It's quiet now, and you can take stock. What are the little things you notice? Taking your time, work up a list of all the details you remember, then gradually make them into a larger piece.

If you're one of the lucky ones who have enjoyed nothing but good fortune, make up your own terrible times. Say you shoot somebody, for example—you shoot somebody in the front yard, and while you're waiting for the neighbors to phone the police, you go in the house and sit on the bed for a moment and look at the shoes in the corner, the photos on the mantel, the books by the bed, that water spot on the ceiling from the big storm two years back, and you take a good long look at all this stuff you'll never see again, and about that time you hear the sirens.

A moment like this could be the end of a piece of writing, but it could be the beginning as well.

THE SECRET LIFE OF A KNIFE

Imagine and then write about the interior life of an object: a carrot, a screwdriver, a coffee cup, a catcher's mitt. Try an object that's had several owners, such as a watch that's been passed down from father to son or a mirror that's been moved from one house to another. You should expect your reader to be leaning into this poem and listening carefully to what your handsaw or fedora or football helmet is saying, so pay special attention to its final utterance.

The master of this kind of poem is Charles Simic, who can make a spoon seem downright evil or a rock as thoughtful as any philosopher. As with every poet who's had a career as long and distinguished as his, there are many, many Simic poems online, so go to town.

2.5

Accidents Will Happen 2.0

There is a lot in the first part of *The Knowledge* about the value of accidents, but that's because accidents often shape our lives more than our deliberate actions do. What we learn about accidents in music can teach us much about poetry.

Ray Davies of the Kinks once said he was liberated as a songwriter when he listened to a live recording of John Lee Hooker's "Tupelo, Mississippi" and heard a car horn in the background. Here's Mr. Hooker cranking away on his song as the studio technicians try to get it down on tape, and some fool out in the parking lot blows his horn at a dog or another driver. Ray Davies realized then that songs had imperfections in them because they were made by imperfect people—like himself, say.

As I write this chapter, a group named Haim is getting a lot of very favorable press. The band consists of three sisters (Haim is their last name) who released their debut album in 2013 and a second four years later. These two albums were well-received, but there was a certain studio slickness to them. Their third album is getting a lot of play right now and a lot more praise, in part because of what listeners describe as more of a day-to-day quality: the sounds of a saxophone and chattering voices drift in, and instead of being studio-perfect, a drum sounds more like someone walloping a trash can.

Reggae music has many sources—ska, rock steady, mento, calypso—and has itself evolved into other styles, such as dub and dancehall. As with all art forms, its origins are murky. At the heart of reggae is something called the one-drop rhythm, where the bass drum disappears on the first beat of a measure and returns (along with the snare drum) on the third; meanwhile, the keyboards and guitars play on the second and fourth beats.

Some scholars and even musicians from the early days of reggae point to what they believe to be the source of that syncopated beat. In the late 1950s and early 1960s, young music lovers in Jamaica became impatient with the pop music being played on official stations. Atmospheric conditions permitting, then, they tuned into rhythm and blues stations in Miami and New Orleans. Some say that the oscillating signals from these faraway stations were to blame for the fact that listeners didn't hear all the beats in a song, just the ones that were emphasized, while others say it was the tinny quality of the cheap radios of the day.

Okay, it's a little hard to think that one of the world's most infectious and influential musical genres was determined in large part by crappy technology. But wouldn't it be wonderful if it were?

And that takes care of Section Two. Let me sum up this discussion of the three-dimensional poem by listing some characteristics your three-dimensional poem might have. Every poem needn't have all of these qualities, and I can think of some dandy poems that don't have any. But most of the great poems have at least some of them, and a fistful of the poems that people will be reading a thousand years from now have them all.

- A poem features the voice of a speaker but other voices as well, at least by implication: the speech of an actor standing alone in a pencil spotlight is made richer by the eloquence of the players who are only temporarily silent.

- A poem will focus on the present moment but also convey an awareness of a larger world of time and space: a moment is most resonant when it appears to have a past and a future as well as dimensions on every side.

- A poem that deals in comedy will acknowledge tragedy. And the other way around: the funniest poem will have a dark heart, just as a good sad poem will seem to have been written by a poet capable of laughter.

- A poem that works onstage will work on the page as well: the best poems are a delight to hear aloud but will also grow richer during a silent rereading.

It's no accident that these characteristics of three-dimensional poetry are expressed as paired opposites, for the three-dimensional poem is willing to include or at least consider everything.

THREE: IMMORTALITY IS WITHIN YOUR GRASP

3.1

We're Hard-Wired to Tell Stories

We tend to think that works of fiction tell stories while poems traffic in images and impressions, but just as there is poetic fiction (see anything by Melville or Virginia Woolf or Jorge Luis Borges), so there is narrative poetry (Homer, Dante, Milton). Indeed, many of the first poems were stories: it wasn't until the rise of the novel in the nineteenth century that fiction began to reserve for itself the storytelling function.

And yet the purpose of many a great poem is to do no more than tell a rattling good tale. Here are the first six lines of Robert Browning's "How They Brought the Good News from Ghent to Aix," probably written sometime in 1844.

> I sprang to the stirrup, and Joris, and he;
> I gallop'd, Dirck gallop'd, we gallop'd all three;
> "Good speed!" cried the watch, as the gate-bolts undrew;

"Speed!" echoed the wall to us galloping through;
Behind shut the postern, the lights sank to rest,
And into the midnight we gallop'd abreast.

Talk about speed. The poem's speaker is in such a rush that he fails to introduce the third rider. Our soldier/messenger is in such a rush to deliver the good news that it isn't until the second line that he remembers to name his other companion. The poem seems to be set within one of those endless wars that crisscrossed Europe in earlier centuries, but Browning himself said "there is no historical incident whatever commemorated in the poem." Even better, we never find out what the good news is. Who cares? Now the poem's appeal lies purely in its story value. This isn't history, folks. It's showbiz.

Why have there always been stories? Also, who are they for? Maybe the phrase "bedtime stories" makes us think that they're for kids, but Emory psychologist Drew Weston says we all need them, all the time. Specifically, he's saying that it's the job of our political leaders to tell us stories that guide and inspire us, and that's because stories are hard-wired into our basic needs as much as the desire for food and shelter are.

> The stories our leaders tell us matter, probably almost as much as the stories our parents tell us as children, because they orient us to what is, what could be, and what should be; to the worldviews they hold and to the values they hold sacred. Our brains evolved to "expect" stories with a particular structure, with protagonists and villains, a hill to be climbed or a battle to be fought. Our species existed for more than 100,000 years before the earliest signs of literacy, and another 5,000 years would pass before the majority of humans would know how to read and write.
>
> Stories were the primary way our ancestors transmitted knowledge and values. Today we seek movies, novels and "news stories" that put the events of the day in a form that our brains evolved to find compelling and memorable. Children crave bedtime stories; the holy books of the three great monotheistic religions are written in para-

> bles; and as research in cognitive science has shown, lawyers whose closing arguments tell a story win jury trials against their legal adversaries who just lay out "the facts of the case."

Later in his article, Weston refers to "the repetition and evocative imagery that our brains require to make an idea, particularly a paradoxical one, 'stick.'" We, of course, call that "the hook" (see Chapter 2.3).

We have such a grasping, primitive need for stories that when we're not given them, we make them up anyway. We narratize, as the experts say. How else are we going to explain the world to ourselves?

THE ONLY EMPEROR

If you want to test that proposition, hand around this Wallace Stevens poem to a group of friends and ask them to describe what's going on, as though they're writing a plot outline for a movie.

> The Emperor of Ice-Cream
>
> Call the roller of big cigars,
> The muscular one, and bid him whip
> In kitchen cups concupiscent curds.
> Let the wenches dawdle in such dress
> As they are used to wear, and let the boys
> Bring flowers in last month's newspapers.
> Let be be finale of seem.
> The only emperor is the emperor of ice-cream.
>
> Take from the dresser of deal,
> Lacking the three glass knobs, that sheet
> On which she embroidered fantails once
> And spread it so as to cover her face.
> If her horny feet protrude, they come
> To show how cold she is, and dumb.
> Let the lamp affix its beam.

The only emperor is the emperor of ice-cream.

Your friends might start by noting there's a big fellow here. He looks to me like an old-fashioned circus strongman; he's got muscles, and he smokes cigars. It looks as though he's making something in the kitchen. Is he a caterer? Nah, probably just a dad, one of those guys who contributes one little dish to the feast and then expects to be praised for it all day long. What's the feast, though? Women arrive, and so do delivery boys with flowers. Somebody's face is being covered, and she's "cold" and "dumb," that is, not stupid but silent. Clearly this is a wake. Yes, folks, life is temporary. One minute it's there, and the next thing you know, it has melted away like a frozen dessert. There's no permanence in this world. The only emperor is the emperor of ice cream.

Recently I chaired a session on narrative at a scholarly conference. The papers were on every subject imaginable: World War I propaganda, Croatian immigrants in Pittsburgh, African American female preachers, circuit riders on the American frontier. I wasn't presenting a paper myself, so my job was to listen and respond. My focus was on the topics themselves, all of which had to do with storytelling.

But as I listened to the papers, I found myself jotting down a series of related words. Here they are: "consternation," "anxiety," "care, toil, and perplexity," "deep wounds and fears," "unjust laws," "suffering and oppression," "war," "disillusionment," "disenchantment." In other words, the scholars were talking about stories but without really underlining what their studies had in common (that was my job). They were pointing out that stories arise out of times of anguish and turmoil. When you're confused and upset and your mind is scattered, you need something to help you organize and at least partially comprehend your thoughts and feelings, as Ted Solotaroff says (in Chapter 2.1).

WHAT STORIES DO

That's what stories do. Every Sunday, there's a feature in the *New York Times* called "Metropolitan Diary" that consists of stories submitted by readers. The subjects vary; the stories are about overheard conversations, random acts of kindness, killer putdowns, quirky behavior. One consistent factor is that so many of the stories begin "I came to New York in the '60s" or "When I moved into my building twelve years ago" or "My parents used to take me to Central Park when I was little." In other words, these are stories that the tellers have been carrying with them for years, decades, a lifetime. They're telling their stories to the world now, but they tell them to themselves every day.

Who told the first story, and to whom? It was probably Adam to Eve or the other way around, and I bet it took place not long after they got kicked out of that garden. If you're in Paradise, you don't need stories. Once you enter the fallen world, though, you're going to need lots of stories to explain where you were, where you are, and how you got there.

Isak Dinesen observed that "all sorrows can be borne if you put them into a story or tell a story about them."

But in addition to quieting our anguished minds, stories have the capacity to accomplish great good on their own. As La Rochefoucauld says, "People would never fall in love if they hadn't heard love talked about." Of course, falling in love can lead to anguish as well as joy, but that just calls for more stories.

And G. K. Chesterton says that "fairy tales are more than true: not because they tell us that dragons exist, but because they tell us that dragons can be beaten."

I saw what looked to be a photo of a handwritten note on Facebook once. Here is what it said: "Every person you meet, every single one of them, is looking for their story. There are no exceptions. You become part of it by how you treat them."

Think how important it is to tell stories to others, then. Stories can entertain us, but they can yank the chain to that lightbulb over our heads as well. The best stories do both.

And they don't have to be *The Canterbury Tales* or *The Iliad*, either. "Blood History" is a poem by Reginald Dwayne Betts that takes up less than half a page.[3]

The key word here is "longed" (which becomes "longing" when it appears again). If someone asks a fatherless man if he ever "wanted" a dad, that's one thing. But if he "longed" for one, that's something else entirely. That one little ordinary word pierces the speaker's heart like a spear. Too, it prompts the whole second half of the poem, which is an extended reverie on fatherhood and what life is like for those without a male parent. No solution is offered, no quick fix. But you know already that poems don't necessarily solve problems. They untie knots, let you organize your thoughts and partly understand them.

IT DOESN'T HAVE TO MAKE SENSE

"Blood History" tells a quick story about one incident. Some stories unroll slowly, though, and don't even start to become stories until they approach their end. Here's a poem by Peter E. Murphy that does just that.

Doing Time

Each week my supervisor rejected
my lesson plans because my goals
and objectives were the same.
When I asked him to explain the difference,
he changed the subject. When I asked why
the syllabus makes no sense, he said,
You're not being paid to think, you're
being paid to deliver a curriculum.
When I asked how to teach teenagers
who can't read to read, he put a hand
on my shoulder, and with the other
pointed toward the horizon, which happened

3 For full poem, visit link: https://bit.ly/RDBbloodhistory.

to be the men's room at the end of the corridor,
and said, Take them where they are.
When I turned to ask what that meant,
he was gone. I figured he was off to help
another teacher or meet a parent, but when
I saw him first in line at the lunch counter,
I knew I was wrong again.
I also knew I wasn't meant to teach
anything important to the dark-skinned
students that sat in front of me.
Like them, I was meant to fail.
And because I was teaching *stupid kids*,
I figured I must be stupid too.
Even if I wanted to, I'd never be promoted
to supervisor like him. So, I thought,
Screw it, and I read my kids a poem
about nature, and they said, Man,
that's dumb. So I read them a poem
about love, and they said, Man,
that's stupid. So I read them a poem
about sports, and they said, Man,
that's nice. So I read them a poem
about death, and they said, Man,
that's deep. Then I read them a poem
that said something about their lives
they didn't know they knew, and they
said, Let me hold that, pulling it
from my hands, reading it over and over,
until they said, Why ain't nobody
ever told us this shit before?
And I said, You've got to be careful.
If they know how much you really know,
instead of more schools, they'll build
more prisons to teach you a lesson.

As with "Blood History," there's a beating heart to this poem. Only this case, it's not a single word like "longed." Here the revelation comes in five short pulses. A teacher is in over his head. He's teaching dead-end kids. He's not getting anywhere, and no one will help him. So he might as well try poetry. The poems probably won't work, but nothing else does either, so why not? His students think a nature poem dumb and a love poem stupid. A sports poem is nice, and one about death is deep. Then he reads "a poem / that said something about their lives / they didn't know they knew," and the kids can't get enough of it. It's a breakthrough moment for students and teacher alike. Different poems work different ways on different people. There's no one-size-fits-all in poetry. Peter E. Murphy doesn't say what the poem is that changed everybody's life because he knows it probably wouldn't work that way for you and me. He just tells us that there's a least one life-changing poem for each of us. It's out there, waiting.

By the way, while some poems end tidily, a great poem will be what I call *endable*. You don't want to leave the reader mystified, but think about that ring-toss experiment that I talk about in Chapter 1.2, where you want your poem to give the reader just the right kind of materials to play with so they can come up with an answer on their own.

In one scene in Karl Marlantes's Vietnam novel *Matterhorn*, two soldiers are talking about the lessons that can be learned from religion, and one tells the other that Jesus spoke in parables because when you speak in parables, it's the listener who comes up with the right answer, not the speaker.

Yes, stories can make sense. But aren't the best ones or the ones we like most (and what's the difference) the ones we treasure precisely because they don't always make sense? One of the people who can teach us the most about narrative is the English critic Frank Kermode, who says stories do two things at once: they proceed in a way that allows us to make sense of the world while, at the same time, they charm us with details that are indifferent, even hostile, to story. In his best-known book, *The Sense of an Ending*, Kermode says we want stories to have a clear beginning, middle, and end that make the whole fly like an arrow toward the target.

But stories, like life, need to include details that defy interpretation. Your reader is going to linger over your story that much longer if there's something in it that roughs up the flow of the narrative like a rock in the middle of the stream. In *The Genesis of Secrecy*, Kermode offers an example of just such a detail. It's the young man who runs away naked when Jesus is arrested at Gethsemane in the Gospel according to Mark.

I didn't believe it either. Go ahead. Look it up—I did. It's there.

Talking Points

Open a poetry anthology or find a website with lots of poems on it and stab your finger at a poem like "The Emperor of Ice-Cream," that is, a poem that clearly is not a story. As I did with Stevens's poem, make a story of it.

You have an arsenal of half a dozen stories you tell other people, right? Imagine you're sitting down with your friend's friends or family members. These are people you're comfortable with; thanks to the presence of your friend, you're already connected to them in a casual but real way. Think back to similar situations that you found yourself in over the last couple of years. What stories did you tell them? Which ones did they tell you?

The kinds of stories you swap when you're meeting your friend's friends for the first time tend to be short. You don't want to dominate and come across as a blabbermouth. But the best stories are often ones that go on a bit, allow for development, maybe take a surprising turn or two. You don't have as many stories like this as you do short ones, but surely you have such a tale in you; it might involve a trip or the passage of time. Let me put it this way: if there's a story that's good enough for you to have told a dozen times, you've already written the draft of a poem. And probably not the first draft either: we tend to compress or extend or change stories as we tell them and notice how audiences react, probably not even consciously. Got a good story? It might be the easiest poem you've ever written.

Prompts

IMPROBABLE SITUATION

You don't have to foresee the beginning and middle of your story. Just start it by putting someone or something into a setting where he or she or it shouldn't be. Once you let the bear into the kitchen, the story will write itself. Be patient and let that happen—don't get in the bear's way.

I BEAT YOU TO THE PUNCH

When you're reading or watching TV or a movie and a good story starts to get underway, stop. Instead of letting the story finish the way someone else planned, you finish it your way. Henry James did: once when someone at a dinner party started telling him about a governess trying to protect her charges from ghosts that only she saw, he stopped that person in mid-story and wrote *The Turn of the Screw*, one of the scariest ghost stories of all time.

One time I was reading a true account of a kidnapping, stopped and wrote my own version, then went back and finished the book. I was glad to see it ended differently than my poem did—and much less interestingly, I'd like to think.

Prompts

3.2

Getting Stabbed Kinda Takes the Fight Out of Ya

So what makes a good story good? The answer to that question will tell us something that we need to know about poetry in general, namely, how do we get people to listen to us? You've heard people (maybe you're one of them) who say, "I can't tell a joke," which probably just means they've never tried, never worked on their timing and the rise and fall that a good joke (or story or poem) needs. Certainly you've heard people who are no good at it try to tell a joke or story and rush the telling or dawdle or put in too many details or mess it up in a dozen other ways. But you also know people who are so good at spinning a yarn that it seems that everything out of their mouth is a story and a good one, too.

Let's turn you into just such a person. The poster boy for poets of every kind is the hero of Coleridge's "Rime of the Ancient Mariner." The idea is that an old sailor has suffered a terrible ordeal at sea, so of course he wants to unburden himself once he's back on land. The first person he sees is a guy going to a wedding and looking forward to a good time. Not a chance! The mariner's tale is too hypnotic. The poem begins this way:

> It is an ancient Mariner,
> And he stoppeth one of three.
> "By thy long grey beard and glittering eye,
> Now wherefore stopp'st thou me?
>
> The Bridegroom's doors are opened wide,
> And I am next of kin;
> The guests are met, the feast is set:
> May'st hear the merry din."
>
> He holds him with his skinny hand,
> "There was a ship," quoth he.
> "Hold off! unhand me, grey-beard loon!"
> Eftsoons his hand dropt he.
>
> He holds him with his glittering eye—
> The Wedding-Guest stood still,
> And listens like a three years' child:
> The Mariner hath his will.
>
> The Wedding-Guest sat on a stone:
> He cannot choose but hear;
> And thus spake on that ancient man,
> The bright-eyed Mariner.

Usually in poetry, we just think of a single person, the speaker. But notice here that the emphasis is placed on the listener. That's one built-in advantage that narrative poems have over other types. As long as everything else works, the narrative poem makes the reader feel that he or she is crucial to the poem's success. Ideally, the speaker will come across as someone who is telling a story they love to a close friend. There's an intimacy in such a telling, and it makes the reader feel important.

Immediately after the 2012 massacre at Sandy Hook Elementary School in Newtown, Connecticut, in which six adults and twenty children were killed, President Obama went to the school and met with the families of the victims. You'd think a politician would offer "thoughts and prayers" or some other trite formula as the aggrieved looked on mutely, but instead the president said, "Tell me about your son. Tell me about your daughter" as the parents described their child's favorite foods, television shows, the sound of their laughter. Hour after hour, the president listened. The parents told their children's stories, and for a moment, the dead lived again.

What's the difference between poetic voice and any other? Not much. When someone speaks, whether it's in a poem or a novel or on TV or sitting next to you in an airplane, either you listen or you don't.

That said, voice is hard to define. It's like love: everybody thinks they know what love is, but nobody seems to know how to describe or measure it.

EXPERT OPINION

Let's see what the experts say. I'm going to begin by quoting some novelists (I hope you realize by now that a good poet learns from everybody). I'd like to start with Gabriel García Márquez, who once said: "I learned a lot from James Joyce and Erskine Caldwell and of course from Hemingway . . . [but the] tricks you need to transform something which appears fantastic, unbelievable into something plausible, credible, those I learned from journalism. The key is to tell it straight. It is done by reporters and by country folk."

Márquez is not the first writer to say one should "tell it straight." Before him, there was Hemingway, and before Hemingway, there was Emerson, and before him, Montaigne. One reason Montaigne is such a good writer, says Emerson, is that he sounds like someone who's talking to the reader rather than dipping his quill in ink and setting words down on parchment.

According to Emerson, Montaigne's prose is the language of conversation transferred to a book:

> Cut these words, and they would bleed; they are vascular and alive. One has the same pleasure in it that we have in listening to the necessary speech of men about their work, when any unusual circumstance give momentary importance to the dialogue. For blacksmiths and teamsters do not trip in their speech; it is a shower of bullets. It is Cambridge men who correct themselves, and begin again at every half-sentence, and, moreover, will pun, and refine too much, and swerve from the matter to the expression.

So Márquez praises the direct speech of country folk, and Emerson does the same with blue-collar workers. Directness—simplicity—is just the start, though. If fine writing were just a matter of showering one's readers with bullets, then best-sellerdom would be every blacksmith's side hustle.

The voice we hear is one that will keep talking to us whether we want it to or not.

Jeff Lindsay is the author of the six novels on which the Showtime series *Dexter* was based. Here's what he says:

> Good writing does not come from emulating. . . . It comes from saying what you mean in a way that no one else can say it. F. Scott Fitzgerald is not Charles Dickens, and the difference goes far beyond time and place and subject matter.
>
> It is more than style, too. Style is the part that we can actually see, but it is just the surface. The real difference is underneath all that. It is a direct expression of who a writer is and why he writes.
>
> It is The Voice.
>
> Every writer must find a way of writing that tells the reader: This is me and no one else. The Voice can be idiosyncratic, but it cannot be obscure. It is a blend of style and content and intent and rhythm and pure personality. If it is done right, it is so intimately wired to you that it cannot be duplicated—although, paradoxically, the best Voices

> can be parodied.
>
> The annual Bad Hemingway Contest is proof of that. Anyone can string together a series of short and forceful words, like "Drink the good coffee. It is rich and dark." We all recognize it; that's Ernest Hemingway.
>
> But to put together enough of these words to make a novel, one that hits us with the sledgehammer force of *For Whom the Bell Tolls*? So far, only one person has turned that trick.

So to Lindsay, style, content, intent, personality, and rhythm are what constitute voice. He's right about all that, especially rhythm.

Here's what Virginia Woolf said in a letter to Vita Sackville-West on that very topic:

> Style is a very simple matter; it is all rhythm. Once you get that, you can't use the wrong words. But on the other hand here I am sitting after half the morning, crammed with ideas, and visions, and so on, and can't dislodge them, for lack of the right rhythm. Now this is very profound, what rhythm is, and goes deeper than words. A sight, an emotion, creates this wave in the mind, long before it makes words to fit it.

In a sense, everything is narrative. As you saw with the Wallace Stevens poem in Chapter 3.1, when we read a difficult poem or look at an abstract expressionist painting or simply find a shoe in the street, we start to tell ourselves a story about it. Then, if that story is good enough, we tell it to someone else.

But of all the components that flow into that single concept of voice, I'd say images are by far the most important. Why? Because they work on us like no other tool in the writer's toolbox.

Yes, I went on forever about images in Chapter 1.4, but that's because it's impossible to overemphasize their centrality to poetry. Even people who think they are immune to artistry respond to images. Remember what Emerson said? Even people who think of themselves as practical and commonsensical types stand taller and breathe faster when they see their country's flag.

I'd say that 62 percent of voice consists of images.

No, wait—make that 83 percent.

Another thing is that, if you get your images right, everything else that makes up voice more or less takes care of itself.

HOW IMAGES WORK

But how do images work, exactly? In an essay called "Your Brain in Fiction," Annie Murphy Paul says this:

> What scientists have come to realize in the last few years is that narratives activate many . . . parts of our brains as well, suggesting why the experience of reading can feel so alive. Words like "lavender," "cinnamon" and "soap," for example, elicit a response not only from the language-processing areas of our brains, but also those devoted to dealing with smells.
>
> In a 2006 study published in the journal *NeuroImage*, researchers in Spain asked participants to read words with strong odor associations, along with neutral words, while their brains were being scanned by a functional magnetic resonance imaging (fMRI) machine. When subjects looked at the Spanish words for "perfume" and "coffee," their primary olfactory cortex lit up; when they saw the words that mean "chair" and "key," this region remained dark.

What Paul says reminds me of what I've read about brain scans of people who are kissing. When a couple isn't kissing, their brains look like North Korea at night. But when their lips touch, look out! Suddenly we're in Times Square on New Year's Eve.

Paul continues:

> The way the brain handles metaphors has also received extensive study; some scientists have contended that figures of speech like "a rough day" are so familiar that they are treated simply as words and no more. [Recently], however, a team of researchers from Emory

> University reported in *Brain & Language* that when subjects in their laboratory read a metaphor involving texture, the sensory cortex, responsible for perceiving texture through touch, became active. Metaphors like "The singer had a velvet voice" and "He had leathery hands" roused the sensory cortex, while phrases matched for meaning, like "The singer had a pleasing voice" and "He had strong hands," did not.

As is sometimes the case, here science reassures us of something we already know, which is that readers like images. Why, though? I'd say it's because when the speaker in a poem or story or newspaper article is getting through to us, it's because he or she *is* us.

Without really registering it, suddenly we find the speaker's voice is inside our head, saying things we've always thought or want to think or are half-thinking without knowing we're half-thinking them, only the speaker is saying things so much better than we could. But since we're enchanted by the speaker's voice—since, like the wedding guest in Coleridge's "Rime of the Ancient Mariner," we "cannot choose but hear" when the old sailor begins his riveting tale—it's as though it is we who are doing the speaking.

In Proust's words, "Every reader, as he reads, is actually the reader of himself. The writer's work is only a kind of optical instrument he provides the reader so he can discern what he might never have seen in himself without this book. The reader's recognition in himself of what the book says is the proof of the book's truth."

When you're reading something good, it's like singing in the shower. It's still your voice, but it sounds a lot better.

But the speaker who has gotten into our head is not necessarily speaking in the voice of a genius or a prince or a queen or an atomic scientist. The voice that becomes ours is often that of someone who is as different from us as possible. He might be Márquez's farmer or Emerson's beefy teamster.

Or he might be a thug. Once I heard novelist Dennis Lehane speak on the subject of voice. Lehane had spent his younger years in a rough part of Boston but went to Miami to study writing. There he missed the sounds of his neighborhood, so when he went home for the holidays for the first time, he looked up some of the old gang.

When he asked one of his buddies how he was doing, the guy said, "I, uh—well, I got stabbed" and then "I don't know what you've heard, but getting stabbed kinda takes the fight out of ya."

Lehane spent the next ten minutes of his talk unpacking this sentence. First there's "I don't know what you've heard," as though getting stabbed is a common topic of conversation. Then there's not "it hurt like hell" or "I cried like a baby" but "getting stabbed kinda takes the fight out of ya." Finally, there's that little modifier "kinda," as though you're just, you know, *slightly* discouraged. If you'd been clubbed with a baseball bat, you might have been disheartened, and if you'd been shot, well, that would probably take the fight out of you altogether. But being stabbed just "kinda" takes the fight out of you.

That's voice.

In the introduction to his invaluable little book *The Art of the Voice*, Tony Hoagland writes that "in pre-1900s English poetry, the poetic voice tended to be rhetorically lofty, authoritative, wisdom-dispensing, and high-minded." As an example, Hoagland quotes the first four lines of Wordsworth's "The World Is Too Much with Us":

> The world is too much with us; late and soon,
> Getting and spending, we lay waste our powers;—
> Little we see in Nature that is ours;
> We have given our hearts away, a sordid boon!

The speaker here has a strong voice, says Hoagland, but hardly an intimate one. By way of contrast, he offers Eleanor Lerman's contemporary poem "Ode to Joy" with its conversational voice, one that sounds like an ordinary person speaking to another. Lerman's poem begins

> Four drinks after nine o'clock at the
> sports bar down by the river—the river
> that is commanded by Newtonian forces,
> or so they say. They also say that
> particles collide, but I've never seen

that happen. And then, of course,
there is the theory that giant lizards
are patrolling outer space in spiny ships.

Hoagland notes that Lerman's voice is attractive because it's educated yet unpretentious. And then he says, "As a reader, on some level you might ask yourself: am I going to continue reading this poem? And if so, am I going to keep reading because of the *story*, or the *voice*? Probably the latter."

If you think about some of the great conversationalists you know, the friend or neighbor or aunt that everybody just loves to listen to, and if you can pause for a moment and try to hear that person's voice in your head as you read this chapter, you'll probably be aware of the pace and timbre of that voice but also the little tics and whoops and hiccups that seem to pop spontaneously into a good speaker's speech. In the last chapter, I made much of the narrative commotions that can stop and restart a story in a way that makes that story all the more enjoyable. Something similar happens when you're listening to someone's voice.

THE MIND'S ANKLES

Take a look at this poem by Morgan Parker, and then I'll comment on a little trick she pulls off that works every time.

The Book of Negroes

1

You see the commercial on BET
while you're painting your nails.

The women are only crying.
The cabins are dull. You're trying

to text this dude. Negro, please,
why sleep when the world so bad.

Twisted golden butt in ash. You crazy.
D'Angelo. Slum Village. That good good

memory of skin. For him you would
be pumice shined to pearl.

He makes you wanna write your name.

2

This book is spit, cum, cloud cover.
We Definite people.

This book is about lying down quietly.
No one wrote the blessing of our ankles

in foamy water. We always emerge.
We sing because we cannot bear the heat.

We wear black. We cannot bear the heat.
We don't call the police. We fill bathtubs with

windchimes and lower them in the ground.
We Nothing left.

This book is uncorrected proof. You read it
on your eyelids. You sleep under it.

You give it away. You tear out whole chapters.
You say you read it but you didn't.

3

What to a slave is the fourth of july.
What to a woman is a vote.
What to a slave is an award show.
What to a slave is a story book.
What to a slave is fine china.
What to a woman is a canopy bed.
What to a slave is the hard sky.
What to a woman is the bottom of a glass.
What to a slave are flatlands from an aircraft.
What to a woman is a missed call.
What to a woman is the milky way.
What to a slave is a square technically it's perfect.

4

Summertime and the living is
extraordinarily difficult. The sunset

seems unimportant. It becomes
a calm. Sunglasses, white

wine spritzers. Would you hate yourself
less if you picked your fruit from trees.

You prefer friends to remain
in train stations. What side the mountain

is home. You were not invited
into the orange groves.

Sometimes you go outside
and control is possible.

Everybody has an opinion.

Everything rolls off your shoulders.

This poem tackles head-on the assumption that life is the same for all of us. It isn't. Even today, more than a hundred and fifty years after the Emancipation Proclamation, life is still radically different for the children of the slaves and the children of the enslavers. I was introduced to Parker's poem by Sam Anderson, who writes in the *New York Times* that "every culture is a vast carpet of interwoven references: clichés, fables, jingles, lullabies, warnings, jokes, memes. To be a part of that culture means that it only takes a few words, the tiniest head fake, to set your mind racing along a familiar track." But "one trick of art is to constantly invoke—and then manipulate and complicate—these familiar mental scripts. The artist sets your mind on a well-worn road, and then, just as you settle into that automatic groove, yanks you suddenly in another direction. It's the same trick as a crossover dribble. Great art is always, if you will, breaking your mind's ankles."

Parker does exactly that in "The Book of Negroes." Take a look at the first two lines of the poem's fourth section, where she hits us with a nasty crossover. Anderson continues:

> She invokes one of the most famous opening lines in American music—Gershwin's "Summertime, and the living is easy"—a cultural script so powerful that, even without music, even as just words on a page, our internal orchestras automatically swell, and we hear the mournful crooning of Billie Holiday or Sam Cooke or Janis Joplin or Billy Stewart or Bradley Nowell of the band Sublime—whichever version you happen to know best. The familiar melody unrolls, slowly. "Summertime, and the living is. . . ."
>
> Just as we reach that final, crucial word, however, Morgan replaces "easy" with its opposite: "extraordinarily difficult." It's a perfect little moment of comic whiplash. A negative in place of a positive. Two clunky Latinate words in place of the easy "easy." And it tells us, very clearly, that what's coming is not what we have been taught to expect.

Parker's poem is all over the place. And it's a big place: it's America, from its founding through yesterday. Poems like this need to be made memorable in some way, and if you do remember this poem, it's probably because you hear Morgan Parker humming "Summertime and the living is / extraordinarily difficult."

It shouldn't surprise anyone that an African American poet might take an ironic view of American history, which is too often celebrated as triumphant. Actually, it is, if you look at history solely from the point of view of the European settlers who imported one race to do their dirty work for them on the land they'd stolen from another. For that reason, you'll also find a skeptical take on European culture in poems like the one by Natalie Diaz in Chapter 3.4 and in this poem by Joy Harjo.

An American Sunrise

We were running out of breath, as we ran out to meet ourselves. We
were surfacing the edge of our ancestors' fights, and ready to strike.
It was difficult to lose days in the Indian bar if you were straight.
Easy if you played pool and drank to remember to forget. We
made plans to be professional—and did. And some of us could sing
so we drummed a fire-lit pathway up to those starry stars. Sin
was invented by the Christians, as was the Devil, we sang. We
were the heathens, but needed to be saved from them—thin
chance. We knew we were all related in this story, a little gin
will clarify the dark and make us all feel like dancing. We
had something to do with the origins of blues and jazz
I argued with a Pueblo as I filled the jukebox with dimes in June,
forty years later and we still want justice. We are still America. We
know the rumors of our demise. We spit them out. They die
soon.

Here Harjo dramatizes how hard it is sometimes just to be yourself, especially if you belong to a minority that has to kick constantly against stereotypes imposed by the majority. "We / were the heathens, but needed to be saved from them," writes Harjo, and then "thin chance."

See what she's doing here? If it were easy for Native Americans to keep themselves from being demonized, then "fat chance" would have been the right phrase, just as Morgan Parker could have said "Summertime and the living is / easy" in her poem if she'd wanted to smooth over the difficulties of belonging to your own ethnic group and yet, as Harjo says, be "still America."

When you think back through the poems in this book so far, don't you often find yourself visualizing them? Didn't you see the lovers in the meadow in Molly Fisk's "Cancer, again" and the pool players leaning over the table in the Harjo poem you just read and even the big mysterious figure Wallace Stevens refers to as the Emperor of Ice-Cream? When all is said and done, voice is mainly a matter of images. Tom Petty says, "A good song should give you a lot of images. You should be able to make your own little movie in your head to a good song." The same is true of poems.

Another musician, Trey Anastasio of Phish, says a Phish song is something simple at the beginning and end with a whole lot of notes in the middle.

Plug in "images" where Anastasio has "notes," and you've got the whole of Chapter 3.2 in just sixteen simple words.

The only thing I'd add is that, when you're writing, the images come first. When he says a song begins and ends simply, Trey Anastasio is describing the finished song, not the writing process. You discover your simple idea by playing with images, not the other way around.

Then you encrust that simple idea with all those chunky, crusty, chewy images the way the great artists of the pagan world and Judaism and Christianity and Islam stuck mosaic tiles onto the walls and ceilings of their patrons' villas and synagogues and cathedrals and mosques and statehouses for thousands of years.

When you stand below one of these masterworks and gaze up at it, it looks as though it's been there forever.

Talking Points

What poet/musician/story has a voice that, like the wedding guest, you "cannot choose but hear"? Offbeat examples will probably tell you more than mainstream ones. It's said that the most radical thing about Bob Dylan is not his politics or the lyrics of his songs but his voice, which can be raspy and nasal or just plain ordinary. Nobody ever accused Dylan of having the beautiful tenor of a Metropolitan opera star, but his voice is more memorable than many of theirs. Certainly he liberated hundreds of thousands of singers both professional and amateur. If a guy who sounds like that can sing, so can I.

Turn this last talking point on its head: what poet/musician/writer/ex-roommate/next-door neighbor has a voice you can't stand and why? If you want to stick with music, *Blender* magazine has a website called "50 Worst Songs Ever." Be prepared, though, because you might like some of them.

Prompts

THE END OF THE WORLD

In Chapter 3.1, I suggested that most of the narrative poems you write will be taken from your own life. But you can make up stories as well. Write down twenty events that would indicate the world is ending: pigeons freeze and fall from the sky, the ink on the page of the newspaper you're reading turns red, a beautiful stranger kisses you passionately, and so on. Pick the ten best, put them in an order that makes sense to you, and write your poem or story.

STRETCHING TIME

Take an event that ordinarily takes no more than a few hours: eating a meal, say, or watching a play or a ball game.

Now make it last forever. You and your dinner companions are getting older, but the food still keeps coming (and it changes as some dishes fall out of fashion and new ones are developed). Or the actors onstage die as new ones are born and take their place; meanwhile, the people in the audience around you change, too.

The Argentine writer Julio Cortázar wrote a story called "Weekend" in which one of those legendary traffic jams caused by vacationers returning to Paris turns into a permanent city of people who live in their cars, get married, have babies, and so on. Cortázar's story, like a lot of literature both new and old, has an absurd beginning that slowly turns into a poignant, knowing comment on human aspiration and frailty.

The main thing about narrative as opposed to other kinds of writing is that it has characters, that time passes, and that the characters change as time goes by. For the life of me I can't remember who wrote it, but I read a story once about a plane that never landed. One day a little boy wandered up to the cabin, the captain took a shine to him, and, as the boy grew older, he taught him to fly. Eventually the captain died, and his young pupil knew how to land the plane, but he wouldn't—all he'd ever known was life in the sky.

WORLD WAR IV

Everyone knows what World War III is going to be like: nuclear bombs, total devastation, starting over again as cave people.

So what about World War IV? When will it happen, who will the combatants be, what sort of weapons will they use, what will the big battles be, what will be the final outcome?

Or fast-forward through several conflicts and describe World War VII.

3.3

Furbelows, Lozenges, and Doohickeys

Recently somebody introduced me as a speaker who was going to tell the audience everything they needed to know about "furbelows, lozenges, and doohickeys." As I waited to take the stage, I was more than a little baffled, since I had no idea what she was talking about.

As it turned out, my introducer was referring to a poem I'd published a few years back and forgotten. In it I describe the stage of an opera production that featured a very ornate set, one in which the walls of the cardboard castle where the action would take place were studded with furbelows (a pleated or gathered piece of fabric), lozenges (not a throat candy but simply a diamond shape of any kind), and doohickeys (a nonsense word meaning doohickeys).

We'll continue talking about voice here, with particular attention to sound. People talk about the mind's eye, but the mind has an ear as well. The poem that seems to sit silently on the page is made of words we've heard a million times, and it's only naturally that we "hear" those words without really doing so.

Besides, the best poems work on both stage and page. If you're not doing it already, sooner or later you'll have a chance to read your poems to a live audience that will encounter them in no other way.

So let's give those poems the sound quality they deserve. When you finish reading your poem, you don't want your audience to gawp at you in bewilderment. You want them to laugh or weep or gasp or say "Yes!" or burst into applause or, and best of all, just sit back with a big satisfied smile.

Even reading you in private, a solitary reader in her easy chair with a cup of tea will hear your voice.

Let's make it the most appealing voice possible. Before long, we'll be looking at rhyme and meter and parallelism and anaphora and all sorts of formal qualities you can use in your poems, but for the moment, let's just shake it out and be silly. Think furbelow, lozenge, doohickey. Don't those words make you happy? Now you know what they mean, but you don't have to define them to like them. There's a childlike sound to those words, and even though we're all big strong grownups here, each of us has a child within, and that child's just waiting to be tickled.

CELEBRATION SONGS

A few years ago I wrote a book called *Little Richard: The Birth of Rock 'n' Roll.* Little Richard is the musician who taught me more about poem writing than any other. In 1953, the #1 Billboard song in both America and the UK was Patti Page's "How Much Is That Doggie in the Window." And then the world turned on its radio and heard the madman from Macon shout "A-wop-bop-a-loo-bop-a-lop-bam-bom!" When "Tutti Frutti" aired, it was, as Keith Richards of the Rolling Stones said, as if someone had flipped a switch, and the world went from black-and-white to Technicolor.

When my book appeared, the *Times Literary Supplement* of London called it "a hymn of praise to the emancipatory power of nonsense."

If genius is childhood recaptured at will, as Baudelaire said, then

Little Richard is a genius in the same way that few others are. In our culture, only a handful of artists have the ability to appeal to child and adult alike, that is, to actual children as well as the child who is still alive in the adult's heart. Van Gogh's an example. You can gasp in wonder at his work whether you're eight or eighty.

In Chapter 2.3, I talk about the early rock 'n' roll recorded in Cosimo Matassa's New Orleans studio and how a lot of those songs must have sounded nonsensical to the preachers and parents and principals of this world, though Cosimo just called them "celebration songs," that is, music that doesn't have a lot of sense to it but simply makes people happy.

I was born and spent the first twenty-one years of my life in south Louisiana, and you'd hear those kinds of songs all the time. You'd hear:

> Jockiemo fee-nah-hey
> Jockiemo fee-nah-hey
> If you don't like what the big chief say
> You gotta to jockiemo-fee-nah-hey

And if you were walking by a field or a railroad track where men were working or a kitchen where women were cooking, often voices would be raised in song, and the person with the best voice would be adding little embellishments, like this.

> Jockiemo fee-nah (hooray, Melinda)
> Jockiemo fee-nah (Jockiemo, Jockiemo)
> If you don't like what the big chief say
> You gotta to jockiemo-fee-nah-hey (one more time now).

It's a cliché to say that there were two kinds of black music in those days, a cleaned-up version for white listeners and an earthier kind for black audiences. I think that's wrong. I think the division is not black and white but adult and child. The difference is that no child wants to hear songs about making love, but both grownups and kids love the celebration songs.

Besides, I'm not sure those celebration songs are so innocent. In "Da Doo Ron," the Crystals sing, "And when he walked me home / da doo ron ron ron da doo ron ron." I'll leave what all that da-doo-ron-ronning means up to you.

Besides, to say a song is "childlike" is not to say it's trivial. Something that is childlike is not careless or trivial. Roland Barthes says a child artist works very hard; he "applies himself, presses carefully, rounds things out, sticks out his tongue."

UNCLE SAM WANTS YOU

And to say an artwork is fun doesn't mean that it can't be serious as well. To me, "Tutti Frutti" can be read alongside the Declaration of Independence. Both works say that we must declare ourselves free from America in order to fully and freely be part of it. To borrow some words from our best cultural critic, Greil Marcus, Little Richard "takes you off your feet and away from anything like home, makes home unrecognizable, unwanted, and then leads you back." Like the Declaration of Independence, "Tutti Frutti" bolstered us: the Declaration bolstered the citizens and soldiers who heard it read aloud in the streets of Boston and Philadelphia, and "Tutti Frutti" bolstered us teenagers hunkered over our little green plastic Westinghouse radios.

In *The Origins of Cool in Postwar America*, Joel Dinerstein says that a blues song often begins wordlessly in a moan or a stamp of the foot and then proceeds with a sigh or a hum as the performer tries to say something that "has no name in any language."

The poet Charles Simic lives in America, but he was obsessed with the blues as a boy in Belgrade at a time when you could go to jail for listening to American music. Of course—the Soviets and other despots don't like art, because they don't know what it means.

Ready for a poem or two? Okay, but I've got a couple more stories for you first. I want to make sure you're knocking all the old ideas you had about poetry out of your head and leaving room for the fresh ones that you yourself come up with.

Here's one. One of the greatest success stories in the history of pop music is that of the rise of Berry Gordy Jr.'s Motown Records. A huge part of the company's achievement is due to the attention Gordy himself gave to song lyrics. Here's Peter Benjaminson in *Mary Wells: The Tumultuous Life of Motown's First Superstar*:

> Gordy believed that lyrics were the key to capturing the attention of record buyers and making his records into hits. He rejected dream images or poetry for the songs his company released; what he wanted were stories, and stories written in the present tense, to capture the attention of busy listeners. Not "My girl broke up with me" but "My girl is breaking up with me."

One of Mary Wells's story-songs demonstrates the power of metaphor, which allows a listener to believe the statement that's being made and its opposite at the same time. "Two Lovers" describes a devoted boyfriend and then one who is callous and indifferent. The trick, of course, is that they're both the same guy. But if you're a young man, it's almost impossible to listen to "Two Lovers" and not think that *there really are two men in this song* and that beautiful seductive Mary is singing to no one but you.

Just as you have to stay loose and open to meaning when you read poetry, so you have to be that way when you write it. Dizzy Gillespie said, "I don't care too much about music. What I like is sounds." Here's the musician many say is the greatest jazz trumpeter of all time, yet he thought of himself as just making sounds.

Painter Marcel Duchamp said, "I don't believe in art. I believe in artists."

Once I was late to a chamber music concert. I'd got the time wrong, and I was arriving just as the musicians were packing up their instruments. I was so demonstrably crestfallen that the lute player came up to me and, with no preamble, said, "You know, the words and the music of a song don't have to go together." I said, "Excuse me?" and he said, "I can see you're upset, so I wanted to give you a little present, and that's it: everybody thinks the words and music of a song have to go together, but they don't."

What a gift! I've never listened to music the same way since. Like most people, and without ever really thinking about it, I figured words and music had to fit together as tightly as the pieces of a chair. But they don't. Listen to Willie Nelson sing "Blue Skies" and you'll see what I mean. The words say that life couldn't be better for the singer, yet his voice sounds as though he's at a funeral.

Comedian Andy Kaufman said that comedy doesn't have to be funny.

I hit you with a ton of ideas in the last few pages, and I wouldn't have done that in the first part of *The Knowledge* when you were learning the ropes, but by now your poet's mind is supple and well-formed and ready to grow even more. These are your ideas now, not mine. Change them, turn them inside out, combine them as you will.

That's what these poets did.

First, take a look at this poem by Yolanda Franklin.

Elegy for Shawn: Omega B-Boy Stance

1.

Black people love hip-hop!

Ever see a b-boy battle? I've got a burn scar from a cardboard
breakdancing mat on my inner right knee.

We make millions dubbing tracks for white folks.

Well, not millions for each of us, but you know what I mean.

A relevant definition of commerce: when Blacks make money from
white folks enhancing (t)heir rhythm.

Urban Legend: a cardboard break dancing mat will remain portable.
Wasn't true, so Shawn requested an 8X8 linoleum one for his

thirteenth birthday.

2.

Boys, boys, boys.

Every summer I had to fight: Gerald, Wendell, that big-ass-kid who stole that purse Gamma made me carry. The counterbalance of his tone arm spun like a slingshot double-dutch-tempo. Damn, I couldn't get a punch in; couldn't equalize control.

My battle record of copper pennies, twin scabs on my knees, reopened, bled down my shins faster than I could belt-drive away on one of their Huffy bikes.

Huffy bicycles are for boys; domestics are for girls.

Turntables: have you ever wondered why *Home*land Security isn't an office run by girls?

3.

Our Gamma didn't have a Maytag dryer. Since the summer I turned twelve, Tasha and I pinned the line to dry.

Double-wide = poverty.

Out North Ridge Road, Aunt T lived unhitched, in a double-wide like Gamma, but with cable and *Yo! MTV Raps*. Shawn used the remote control as a crossfader, channeled our commercial conversations to a cappella.

Poverty = inherited heirloom.

Gamma died in hers: Parliaments lit like birthday candles inhaled her.

Aunt T hitched, inherited a brick house on Nancy Drive.

4.

Nancy Drive's yard, the square footage of an LP, fade to the church congregation in chrome-camellias under a mourner's tent once used as shade for front-yard barbeques.

Aunt T: a scratched album cradled by Uncle Michael in the milk crate frame of the doorway.

This poem has everything in it: hip-hop beats, childhood memories, puns, images as sharp yet as nuanced as a black-and-white photo, history lessons drawn from music, culture, politics. It has everything in it but Shawn, for whom this elegy was written. He's only mentioned twice. Yet Shawn is the invisible center of this poem. Look at how complete this picture is of a threadbare yet idyllic world. It was their world, Shawn and the speaker's. Shawn may not be with us now, but he lived innocently and joyfully in a kind of paradise that has been made permanent in this poem, an Eden he shared with the speaker, and now the two of them share it with us.

This poem by Kyle Carrero Lopez also grows out of the speaker's childhood, though here the language is pushed even farther toward its limits. I've said before that you should read every poem out loud. This one you have to read out loud. If you don't, you'll miss its musicality.

(slang)uage

talked montclairian growin' up in jerz: chirp yerp in a dark park,
hear it called back: you good to cyph. whole people dubbed head
or mug—
that bougie teen $ynecdoche—chug too much queeze and you'll boot.
here i learn
'college fund' from white folk, then probe home on where mine went.
never fully

got our place in the quainter, browner part of town till then.
what luxe liberaltopia,

where kids with two mommies or daddies festooned the terrain.
even had queer friends young. jackson and ethan used to mop coats
from garden state they'd vogue down the streets in.
cat kitty cat-ca-ca-cat meow, 'burb-fag stunts the house down, sis!
codify this fuzzy hunty. we'd ki how gods might way up there,
radiant, skies-far from earthbound mess. the innocence,
the fuckery, none taught me the T on (white-run) gay space,
its paradox-forgery by thieves who can't see your work or you.
having grasped more i know this for sure: mixed up rainbow stripes
streak dark as ham's cursed kin.

witness i, _chievement g_p filler, croon problem-deepening theses
on heuristic, heteroglossic verse, conference floor field holler
set to hyfrydol tune. codify this fuzzy discourse, question
every line of questioning. concoct new insights on hume v.
hobbes in under one pg. my elders know next to nil of this
lexicon, but drop guillen's "sóngoro cosongo, songo bé" _nd bet
they'll feel it: lukumí drum sounds pound pound in our blood. jstor
won't give you rhythm. honestly,

qué sabes sobre black talk 'sides aave rules you got from schools?
do you really fuck with expressive culture? schoolyard roasts cut
my teeth. if they call you soft save the tears—if they say you got that
mushmouth
jaw, ask why they built like chuck e. cheese. o, word!? y'all may-I-speak-
to-the-ma_ager haircuts assume we might scrap cuz we yell or y'all get
spooked, but it's mostly grade zero serious. mammals stay perplexed
by mammals. some af-am fam be geeked at ceviche type blacks a_d
vice-
versa, but real talk: the bridge which fixes afro to –(suffix) may rotate
to a wall.

spanish chunks twist en mi mind's mix—too few sprinkled
to shut latinx snobs up. they call it our native speech. ¡jajaja! our?
yorùbá says hi, and nice try cuttin' her all the way out. on the plus,
foods in hispanophone kitchens taste richer when spoken.
zanahoria for carrot. melocotón names peach. many cubans
say fruta bomba for papaya. mitt romney once claimed
he loves papaya on miami cuban radio, unaware
it means pussy. que clueless, que jokes, when we speak
before we know.

Okay, maybe you should read "(slang)uage" out loud not just once but a couple of times. And possibly even a little faster than usual, because "(slang)uage" seems to glide by you like a car packed with rowdy teens who've got the radio turned way up, and as they do, you might give them the finger even as you secretly wish you could join them. This poem is defiant, raucous, deliberately irritating. Do I know why Kyle Carrero Lopez takes the "n" out of "ma_ager"? I do not. And I'm not going to worry about it. This is a poem made almost entirely of furbelows, lozenges, and doohickeys.

Ah, childhood. Where would poets be without it? I used to tell my own kids that they only had two jobs, which were to make good grades and not say "Yuck!" when I made them try a new food. There's a third job that every kid has that I didn't tell them about, and that's to be stupid. Good judgment comes from experience, and experience comes from bad judgment. Make mistakes, kids! You're supposed to. And then you're supposed to write poems about them.

This poem by Dzvinia Orlowsky is a sweet, affectionate, funny poem about a goofy, well-meaning dad and his adoring daughters.

Fack You

Father called us into our room, sat on the edge of one twin bed,
head lowered, then lifting up his eyes asked: *Have either of you ever*
heard of the word . . . "fack"? He pronounced it like he pronounced
"mashrooms,"—immigrant doctor ordering pizza at Fatbob's when

Mother came up short on chicken livers or tripe. He looked at us in disbelief, his now foul-mouthed daughters. A houseguest had overheard us—me—scream *fuck!* while driving the ping pong ball directly into the net, my sister spinning wildly on her heels, her *ha ha's* booming up from the dusky basement paneled with faux brick, a half-case of 16 ounce cokes already chugged between us. We ached to be *Greaser* girls of teased hive hair, the runs in their black nylons an arrow to their jutting hips as they slouched against the dumpster smoking Lucky Strikes behind the pizza joint, a secret society of popularity and sin waiting for Greaser boys to slink through, slicked hair and black Banlon shirts, flipping the finger to anyone who dared even walk past them—*Go Fuck yourselves you Fuckin' Mother Fucker!*—Instead we were Father's two angels carrying pails of water to a thirsty horse in our desiccated meadow, no shade in sight—and Father, always running late, making his rounds, dressed, always, in his Steve McQueen sky blue suit, revving his silver roadster T-Bird, a Hell's Angel patient coming in for an allergy shot, catching him instead napping on the gynecologist's table, his feet up in the stirrups, an open can of seven-up next to him. America had opened its arms. But he had not done his job. At day's end, in the parking lot surrounded by poppers pinging in shallow marshes, in a moment of freedom, we knew, forgiven, he'd put the blame on the *pleased-with-herself* houseguest warming herself like a fat August fly at our front window. *Fack her*, he'd whisper, fumbling for his keys.

There are so many endearing little details here. You start with "*mashrooms*" and go on to the two teens trying to be sexy without really knowing what that means. To their father, of course, they are something out of an Old World painting, "two angels carrying pails of water to a thirsty horse in our desiccated meadow." The father, by the way, is not the grumpy scold who is often portrayed in stories of this type but a hardworking doctor who also wants to be hip in his own way. And that Hell's Angel finding him asleep in the gynecologist's stirrups . . . priceless! It'd be easy to make a bland story out of all this: our father didn't understand us, but then he talked himself out of it, and now he does. But it's the furbelows, lozenges, and doohickeys that make this story memorable.

One more. Jessica Sorenson wrote this poem.

My Dad's Name is D. K. Sorenson, Jr.

Being the oldest of five children, Douglas K. Sorenson, Jr.
was often left in charge of the other, younger boys—
then it was Scott Sorenson, and then it was Steven Sorenson.
When the third son came into the picture, the two oldest boys
took the baby down the rain-soaked street to the closest Piggly Wiggly.
They stripped him naked and placed him in a shopping cart,
"June's not your momma," the two boys explained, "and you should wait here
for Mrs. Robinson to come get you. She's your real mother, Stevie."
And they left him there but somehow my Uncle Steve made it back home
and their mother never was the wiser because it had happened while
she popped down the street to a department store. It was 1956.
When the final two were born—well, they were John Strudwick's kids.
The Sorenson boys called them the Struddies. Altogether, June had four boys
and lastly a girl but she died very young. The doctors say it was meningitis
and the brothers will say it was just bad parenting. And what of Douglas, Sr?
In the words of my dad, he's referred to as Scott's effing father.

By the time Doug was seven, he would put on galoshes
and hike through Lake Michigan collecting crawfish in a bucket.
He traded these inland for a few cents to buy himself a box of cereal
and that would be his dinner for the next few nights. That same year,
he confirmed his new name, Douglas Keith Paul Sorenson, Jr. and still
he has the names, the guilt, and the alcoholic tendencies that back up his religion.

When Douglas turned seventeen, he was voted prom king at his high school.
The same year he moved out of the house, moved the heck out.
His buddy, Rudy, took him to that train station for an interview to work on the tracks.
They both had to pass an I.Q. test in order to prove fit for the job on the railway.
One question on the test he can still remember, "Betty is a blonde.
All blondes are dumb. Is Betty dumb?" Douglas is a blonde. Douglas got a job
with the station and Rudy didn't pass the written portion of the interview. He got an apartment
with the money he made while standing up telephone poles down the tracks through Wisconsin.
He claims that through all his time at the university in La Crosse, and still to this day,
he is in love with some girl named Annette. Well, my mother's name is Debra.

Once again, God is in the details. Almost any narrative poem can be reduced to two or three sentences that express the universal truth at its core. Here, that truth is that a lot of us struggle as we grow up, suffering from the smaller and larger problems others create for us even as we create problems for others and ourselves as well. With a little luck, though, things turn out okay—well, 93 percent okay, which is close enough. But Jessica Sorenson makes a brightly colored cartoon of the pesky siblings, the shopping cart, the crawfish, the telephone poles, and the inconvenient but forgivable fact that Douglas Sorenson, Jr. moans about his lost love Annette while his wife Debra shakes her head, thinks "oh, that Doug," and pops another casserole in the oven.

Have you noticed how many of these poems feature a subtle musicality based on repetition? In poetry, there's a word for that: anaphora. Anaphora just means the repetition of a word or phrase, often at the beginning of a line. You've seen an example in Chapter 1.4 in Christopher Smart's poem about his cat, each line of which begins with the word "for." Here's another poem that's propelled by this simple device, and this one's by Tara Betts.

Hip Hop Analogies

After Miguel and Erykah Badu

If you be the needle
                I be the LP.
If you be the buffed wall,
                I be the Krylon.
If you be the backspin,
                I be the break.
If you be the head nod,
                I be the bass line.
If you be a Phillie,
                I be the razor.
If you be microphone,
                then I be palm.
If you be cipher,
                then I be beatbox.
If you be hands thrown up,
                then I be yes, yes, y'all.
If you be throwback,
                then I be remix.
If you be footwork,
                then I be uprock.
If you be turntable,
                then I be crossfader.
If you be downtown C train,
                then I be southbound Red Line.
If you be shell toes,
                then I be hoodie.
If you be freestyle,
                then I be piece book.

If you be Sharpie,
then I be tag.

If you be boy,
then I be girl
who wants to
sync samples
into classic.

If you compare "Hip Hop Analogies" to Yolanda Franklin's earlier "Elegy for Shawn: Omega B-Boy Stance," you can see why I put so much influence on the similarities between poetry and music. But notice the differences: whereas Franklin's poem lifts off and circles and returns like improvisational jazz, "Hip Hop Analogies" is as tight as one of Mozart's fugues, in which one phrase ("If you be") is introduced and then interwoven with another ("then I be"). What a lovely idea: Betts is just speaking the truth that you can be one thing and I can be another, yet we become something so much bigger and better when we come together as one.

Another wonderful poem that uses anaphora is Eric Paul Shaffer's "Officer, I Saw the Whole Thing," which begins this way:

Officer, I saw the whole thing. I was standing there minding my own business,
when the sky cracked open like a blue Easter egg, and suddenly, I saw it all
was made of atoms and molecules and elements bouncing around like the
tiniest, infinitesimal, electron-microscopic drunks in the universe. Yes!

and goes on for many stanzas, each beginning with "Officer, I saw the whole thing" as the action gets wilder. And wilder. And wilder! I won't quote the whole poem here, but it's online and well worth the read.

OPEN-ENDED

Before we leave this chapter, I want to say something about the ends of these poems. In Chapter 2.4, we talked about the different ways to end poems, including one of my favorites, which is the ending that suggests the poem still might go on for a while. As long as everything else in the poem contributes to that effect, this is one of the most engaging ways to make your exit. The open ending means your poem is like a friend or relative who might be elsewhere at the moment but is still vital, still has life.

Many novelists and filmmakers keep their stories going by never really ending them. Take James Scott's *The Kept* as an example. Here a frontier woman returns to her farm to learn that her entire family has been slain except for one young son, with whom she sets out on the trail of the killers. The two of them end up in a town where the killers are, though neither group knows quite what to do about the other. The book ends with the mother and son sitting armed in their boardinghouse room as the killers approach and kick in the door. Your eyes bulging in anticipation, you turn the page, and . . . nothing. That's it. Story over.

On Amazon, just about every reviewer who commented on that ending hated it. One person titles her review "Worst. Ending. Ever." Another says, "When I got to the last page, I really thought I was missing pages in my copy." A third review consisted of just four words: "Does not end right."

I read *The Kept* four years ago. I'm still haunted by it, and I tell other people about it all the time. If you need to have your fiction wrap up neatly like a Dickens novel or a fairy tale, *The Kept* is not for you; there's no "they lived happily ever after" here. But much of the greatest art teeters on the edge of something that doesn't happen.

Think of God reaching toward Adam on the Sistine Chapel ceiling. It's an indelible image, yes? Would you be happier if they were hugging like two football players in the end zone? In life, we're always on the verge of the next thing; it's what focuses us, spurs our imagination, drives us forward.

Now hum your favorite pop song to yourself. It's a song that's stuck in your head precisely because of its mystery and allure. If you want certainty in your music, try the "Happy Birthday" song. And if you insist on disposable fiction so you can forget about it quickly and get back to your job or golf game, there's always "Cinderella" or "Snow White." But if you love stories that are indelible, that fire the imagination and make you feel more intensely alive than you've felt in a long, long time, read *The Kept*.

Open endings work even in non-fiction. The writer James Marcus told me that Robert D. Richardson's biography *Emerson: The Mind on Fire* is a book so good "it makes my teeth ache." James is right. And Richardson's book ends like no other biography I've ever read. Every other biography ends with its subject's death. Not this one. Of course, we are told of the day of the philosopher's passing, but then Richardson goes back to Emerson's final hours on earth, and the last sentences of the last chapter say: "As was his custom, he went to the fireplace and took his fire apart, setting the sticks, one by one, on end on each side, and separating all the glowing coals. That done, he took his study lamp in hand, left the room for the last time, and went upstairs."

As I say, if you get the beginning and middle of a poem right, sometimes the end just takes care of itself.

Talking Points

We're often told to "write what you know." A better idea is to "write what you knew." Tess Gallagher likens the act of remembering to finding money in the pocket of an old coat. So many great poems begin in memory, and for good reason. When something startling happens to us, it's imprinted immediately, but we haven't really processed it yet. That takes time. Think about something that happened five or ten or fifteen years ago and describe it in two sentences. Now sit quietly and revisit that memory, putting in the details as they come to you. And if they don't come to you, plug in details that are appropriate to the situation. Your memory can be pleasant, but it can be unnerving as well—indeed, the unnerving ones may lend themselves more to this kind of self-hypnotic treatment. When I was sixteen, I was driving along a Texas highway at night with some friends when we came across a terrible wreck. We watched boys our age die, and there was nothing we could do about it. For years, I wouldn't let myself think about what I'd seen. But as I matured, I acquired the skills to do so. I put together my poem about this incident over a period of weeks, sitting quietly and letting the images rise: the smell of blood and whiskey, the sounds the victims made, the headlights of the ambulance as it approached. Ironically, the more I remembered (or, without knowing it, probably invented), the better I felt. It was the details that gave me my poem and put to rest this terrible memory.

As the example of the wreck shows, neither our memories nor the poems we make of them have to end neatly. There just has to be a completeness about them, a realization that we have seen everything there is to see and that there is no more. Screenwriters know this, and what they know affects the season finale of many a series. Think of the endings of some series you've seen. Which are satisfactory and which not, and why? (An iconic example is the end of *The Sopranos*. Did Tony die or not or did something else happen, and does it matter?) You might also think about the end of a short story or novel or movie or poem in this same way.

Prompts

OPERA RECIPE

Write down everything that goes into an opera. Not a specific opera, just opera in general: a duke, say, a traitor, a castle, a dwarf, a mud hut, a river made of cardboard waves, a woman with blond pigtails and a Viking helmet, lots of swords, and two glasses of wine, one that is poisoned and one that isn't. Create your own scenario using these elements.

Don't know anything about opera? Big deal. Like a poem, an opera can be anything it wants to be as long as it has a beginning and middle and end. And as you see from the discussion in this chapter, it doesn't even have to have much of an end at all. Just accumulate a bunch of furbelows, lozenges, and doohickeys and get going.

JOB SITE

It goes without saying that if you've ever had a job, you've worked with some weirdos: the crusty old mechanic, the nurse with the tattoos who gave you all that advice about men (most of it correct, as it turns out), the crazy alcoholic pizza-delivery guy. Once you've spent some time with an eccentric, in a sense you've already got the first draft of a terrific poem. All you have to do is take out details that are inconvenient and supply ones that will turn life into art.

When I was a senior in college, I had a job one summer in which I installed appliances for Sears, and my supervisor was a guy who disliked me so much that he only said two things to me during that whole three-month period. This made such an impression on me that I got two pieces of writing out of it: I wrote not only a poem that appeared in a literary magazine but also an essay that was published in the *New York Times*.

DON'T KNOW MUCH ABOUT HISTORY

Go to the library. Ask the reference librarian where the history books are. Walk straight to them and grab the first one you come to, open it, and jab your finger at the page. This is the subject of your next poem. Is it the revision of the 1905 tax code? Grab another book. Or stick with this one: as you've seen a poem can be about anything, since its beauty lies in the execution rather than what the poem's about.

When you consider how many plays and films and poems and stories are about historical people or events, it's a wonder that writers don't think of history first. From *Macbeth* to *War and Peace* and beyond, history is behind thousands of works we call classics.

Of course, you don't have to write about kings and emperors and soldiers; sometimes the seemingly smallest events inspire the best work, which is the rationale behind the "grab, jab, and write" approach. And if you do write about a general, don't begin with his battlefield successes. Make him human first—start with his affection for his cat or his fear of women who carry umbrellas.

A LITTLE HELP FROM MY FRIENDS

This is a variation on the Grab and Jab School of Poetic Beginnings. And it'll save you a trip to the library: just grab whatever magazine or poem or story collection that's handy and open it at random. Wait, let me take my own advice . . . okay, I'm looking at a poem by Thylias Moss called "Lunchcounter Freedom" and the lines "I've made up my mind not to order a sandwich on / light bread if the waitress approaches me with a pencil." See what I mean? You've just been handed a character who is weird and savvy and funny as well as a poem or story starter that could go off in any of a hundred directions.

OVER AND OVER AND OVER AGAIN

Think of an event or occurrence, either historic (the first plane flight) or personal (that time you got on stage and realized you'd put on your skirt backward). Or a person: a celebrity (Marie Curie) or someone you know (your ex-best friend). Or just a text or phrase, something you saw on a bathroom wall or overheard on the sidewalk. Take your time. Write down three or four of these crunchy little nuggets, pause—take a breath, check your phone, whatever—and then pick the bit that has the most energy.

Now choose one of these three refrains. Feel free to vary the wording, of course, or come up with a refrain of your own, like a phrase from a pop song or some catchphrase only you and your buddies understand.

1. She just threw it out there.

2. What's the problem, officer?

3. He had the audacity to tell me that . . .

Begin to write about the subject you chose in step 1, randomly working in your refrain. Try for the Goldilocks Effect: don't use the refrain too often or too seldom but just as much as you need to and no more or less. Vary your refrain as needed (somebody who has a snootful might say, "What's the officer, problem?"). Write at least half a page. Pause again, and revise mercilessly. If this poem doesn't go anywhere, go back to steps 1 and 2 and try another option.

What the hell—try another option anyway.

3.4

Delivery Systems R Us

Many a poetry class starts out by teaching students scansion and meter and rhyme and all of the formal techniques that go into accentual-syllabic poetry. We're halfway through *The Knowledge*, and with a few notable exceptions (like Barbara Hamby's "Mambo Cadillac"), I've been showing you free verse rather than the kind that dotes on accents and syllables and other formal qualities.

Learning the old ways first is essential in some disciplines. A cook needs to be able to scramble an egg before he can make a soufflé, and a soldier should probably know how to load and shoot a rifle before she's put in charge of the heavy artillery. But too much rigor in the beginning is death to poetry. I've emphasized play all along, and that's what I've asked you to do up to this point, to play with words and make something of them the way a kid plays with sticks and boards to make a fort. You find your voice by savoring words and trying them in different combinations, not by pouring them into preconceived molds.

That said, it's time to look at some of the formal aspects of poetry, both because that information will help you make your way through poetry's rich history and because, now that you've got greater mastery over your voice, you're ready to see how formal techniques will add richness to your own work.

The first thing you need to know is that a formal constraint doesn't impose a limit of any kind. To the contrary, a formalism can push you toward newness and keep you from being lazy and doing something you've done a dozen times before.

The great choreographer George Balanchine said it's necessary to outline the steps a dancer must take because dancing is tiring, and if you rely only on instinct, you might just take a timid step forward when it's time to make a beautiful leap.

According to William Blake, "Truth has bounds, Error none." A more vernacular version of that is "the difference between stupidity and genius is that genius has its limits," but you get the idea. Following a recipe can result in a delicious meal, whereas winging it might have you dialing the nearest pizza franchise. You can bet the people who own the pizza franchise don't wing it. That's why they get dialed all the time.

You think nuns don't like being nuns? Joining a convent might not be for you, but look what William Wordsworth says on the subject.

Nuns Fret Not at Their Convent's Narrow Room

Nuns fret not at their convent's narrow room;
And hermits are contented with their cells;
And students with their pensive citadels;
Maids at the wheel, the weaver at his loom,
Sit blithe and happy; bees that soar for bloom,
High as the highest Peak of Furness-fells,
Will murmur by the hour in foxglove bells:
In truth the prison, into which we doom
Ourselves, no prison is: and hence for me,
In sundry moods, 'twas pastime to be bound

Within the Sonnet's scanty plot of ground;
Pleased if some Souls (for such there needs must be)
Who have felt the weight of too much liberty,
Should find brief solace there, as I have found.

We'll talk more about the sonnet form later, but you get the idea. As a statement on job requirements or prison life, this isn't much. But Wordsworth is talking poetry, not policy. He uses the metaphors of the nun, the hermit, the student, the maid at her spinning wheel, and the weaver to suggest that you can be awfully productive if you just sit in one spot and take care of business. Wordsworth even says prison isn't so bad, which is probably true for some people: jail time can provide structure and a chance to turn your life around instead of letting you roam the streets looking for trouble.

PROSODY, OR, METERS AND FEET

"Nuns Fret Not at Their Convent's Narrow Room" features one of poetry's most potent combinations of meter and foot, iambic pentameter, though, like all great poets, Wordsworth varies his meter when he needs to, never sacrificing sense on the altar of form. I'm always surprised when people say they find metered poetry too difficult to write and analyze. Perhaps it's the Greek names for the most commonly used measures that intimidate them, which is why I try to lock the poetic feet into my students' crowded memories with homey, one-word examples. Thus:

iamb (iambic) unstressed-stressed, as in "balloon"

trochee (trochaic) stressed-unstressed, as in "gavel"

anapest (anapestic) unstressed-unstressed-stressed, as in "overturn"

dactyl (dactylic) stressed-unstressed-unstressed, as in "avalanche" spondee (spondaic), stressed-stressed, as in "railroad"

Determining the number of feet in a line is a lot easier, since we might stress words on different syllables (my southern farm-girl mom used to warn me about coming to the attention of the "PO-lice"), because all you do is count. So if the line has only one foot, which is pretty rare, that's monometer. Two feet is dimeter, three trimeter, four tetrameter, five pentameter, six hexameter, seven heptameter, and a line of eight feet is octameter. So if a line is written in iambs, and if there are five iambs to that line, then that's a line of iambic pentameter.

Want to practice? Try scanning your own name. Mine is David Kirby, which, when voiced, becomes DA-vid KIR-by. The stresses are like the ones in GA-vel, right? Which is a trochee. And there are two of them, which means that my name is a line of trochaic dimeter.

I doubt that my or any parents had a certain meter and foot in mind when they named me or anyone else, but I have noticed that there are a lot of trochaic dimeters out there. So if you're Susan Casey or Bertie Andrews (or William Shakespeare or Herman Melville, for that matter), that's how your name scans. If you're Marie Laveau, that's a pair of iambs. Antoinette Wigglesworth Berthelot? Each of these names is a dactyl, like "avalanche." So taken as a whole, Antoinette, your name is a line of dactylic trimeter.

Now if you're carrying a lot of syllables around, you may have to do some tailoring to get your name to fit into one of these patterns. For example, "Aloysius Buford Beauregard Jones" is all over the place. But do a little trimming and you get "Al B. B. Jones," which is four spondees or a line of spondaic tetrameter.

But there's much more to Wordsworth's little poem than meter and foot and much more to the sonnet in general. The sonnet is *the* archetypal poem format, so much so that it's all but synonymous with "poem" in the minds of many. Traditionally, the sonnet poses a problem and solves it, making it a kind of little essay. Yet meter and foot make it musical as well, so you've got both argument and music together, and in just fourteen little lines.

THE SONNET

"Nuns Fret Not" is arranged in the form of a traditional Italian or Petrarchan sonnet, rhymed abbaabbacddccd (there's also a Shakespearean sonnet rhymed ababcdcdefefgg). There's usually a volta or turn in the middle, and you see one here when Wordsworth lays out his argument in general terms and then, with "and hence for me," applies it to himself.

While you're acquiring new vocabulary (like "volta"), let's look at enjambment. That French word is taken from *jambe* or leg, and to enjamb in a literal sense means to throw your leg over, though in poetry it means to continue beyond the end of the line without punctuating. Notice that the first seven lines of "Nuns Fret Not" end with a punctuation mark, but the lines that end in "doom" and "bound" don't. Those lines bleed into the next without interruption, which is why it's always a good idea to break up your poem by enjambing some lines. Otherwise you'll end up with a ba-BOOM ba-BOOM ba-BOOM sound that'll turn your poem into doggerel and give your reader a headache into the bargain.

As far as rhyme goes, it's fairly strict here: loom/bloom, bound/ground, and so on. In addition to strict rhyme, there's a kind called slant rhyme or near rhyme or half rhyme; examples are "lake" and "fate" (as opposed to "lake" and "fake" or "late" and "fate") and "mill" and "sold" (as opposed to "mill" and "sill" or "mold" and "sold"). You probably studied assonance (similar vowel sounds) and consonance (similar consonant sounds) in another class. That's all slant rhyme is. If you listen to rap, you know the great rappers push slant rhyme even farther, echoing "cavity" with "family" and "restless" "with "necklace." And so do the great poets: Cody Walker's long poem "Trades I Would Make" includes rhymes like these:

> A ticket to Loserdom for some booze or gum.
> A ticket to Nowhere for a stern warning: Don't Go There.
> Electronica rap for a quick, uh, nap.
> A punch in the ear for a buncha beer.

Wordsworth doesn't go that far here, but notice the subtle little variations that occur when he rhymes "cells" with "citadels" and "must be" with "liberty."

As with enjambment, the idea of slant rhyme is to throw the reader off a little, but in a good way. Your ear expects one sound, but you get one that's a little different, which is so much more pleasant than a lot of dull sameness.

Some fun, huh? Don't answer that. The study of technique can be a little dry, but remember, we're populating your toolbox at this point. The more tools you have, the more variety you can put into your own work later.

And having tools means you get to do what you want with them. The second the sonnet was invented, poets began goofing on it. Here's just such an innovation by Dorothy Chan. It's not one sonnet but three. And it's not about nuns, either.

Triple Sonnet for Studmuffins Wrapped in Bacon

I'd like to order a lover wrapped in bacon
        from your secret menu, because I'm a really
hungry Chinese girl at this drive-in—
        give me all meat, all man, 100% Grade A
all-natural cut with a side of sensitive,
        and don't forget the condiments in the bag,
and isn't this ideal? Having your cake
        and eating it too, or having your beefcake
and eating *him* too, or having your studmuffin
        feed you strawberry cake in the bubble bath
like you're both rich and happy with unlimited
        wardrobes and private jets, and I want to feel
like women with enviable thighs, in erotica
        winding up their men: she winds, he drools,

        she winds, he drools—her boy toy or man toy,
and I want to lean in for a kiss after telling

my lover about wrapping *him* in bacon,
because bacon tastes good on everything
from deviled eggs to mac and cheese,
and Heart Attack Burgers on secret menus:
three greasy patties and bacon bacon bacon,
a little melted cheese, and once I watched
an interview with a starlet who said how
melted cheese was her favorite food,
and no more beautiful words have ever
been spoken, and let food be your fantasy:
how children believe that the moon is made
of cheese or how adults want to live in houses

made of gouda, and in Hong Kong, my cousin
Janet recommends cheese hot pot with chicken,
and no, that's not the same thing as fondue
also known as the 2000s version of romantic:
dip your date in cheese, or take me back
to the drive-in, and let me order some #1s
of hunks of men on bread dipped in cheese
and some #4s of man sandwiches: cut
and chiseled to perfection with tomatoes
and special sauce, or what about some #5s
on the breakfast menu: studmuffins both sweet
and full of whole grains and buff buff buff,
and why is it that I start giggling when my love
and I start talking about food—pass the sauce,

please, I'm ready to eat you up, order *you* again.

That whirling noise you hear from the direction of St. Oswald's Church in Grasmere is the sound of Wordsworth spinning in his grave. It'll stop soon, though. Wordsworth and Coleridge turned the literary establishment on its head in their day when they began writing poems about nature and ordinary people instead of city life and drawing rooms. I'm not saying that Wordsworth saw Dorothy Chan coming, but now that he's got his teeth back in his head, I bet he's pleased.

VILLANELLES AND MORE

You can experiment with meter and foot all day long and never run out of combinations, but some of the poems that are the most fun to write and read rely more on repetition. Here are four types, beginning with the villanelle. A villanelle has nineteen lines. It only uses two rhymes. There are five three-line stanzas or tercets and a quatrain. The first and third lines of the opening tercet are repeated alternately at the end of the other four, and both are repeated at the end of the quatrain.

I know—that sounds more like algebra than poetry. In practice, though, it's a pretty simple formula. Consider this villanelle by Julie Kane:

Kissing the Bartender

The summer we kissed across the bar,
I felt sixteen at thirty-six:
as if you were a movie star

I had a crush on from afar.
My chest was flat, my legs were sticks
the summer we kissed across the bar.

Balancing on the rail was hard.
Spilled beer made my elbows stick.
You could have been a movie star,

backlit, golden, lofting a jar
of juice or Bloody Mary mix
the summer we kissed across the bar.

Over the sink, the limes, as far

as you could lean, you leaned. I kissed
the movie screen, a movie star.

Drinks stayed empty. Ashtrays tarred.
The customers got mighty pissed
the summer we kissed across the bar.
Summer went by like a shooting star.

The best part about writing a villanelle is that once you've written that first tercet, you can go down the page and plug in the first and third lines where they'll appear in the stanzas that follow and build the poem around them. And just like that, you've got most of your poem written. You just have to follow through.

Because it keeps returning to its beginnings, the villanelle is especially suited to a treatment of those knotty problems we all have that just keep buzzing around in our brains like angry wasps. See, for example, this poem by Amy Newman dealing with the tricky business of trying to fool ourselves that we're over someone when we really aren't.

The Letting Go

Somehow I managed to let go of you.
You said you loved me deeply, but it was
not true, not true, not true, not true, not true.

The bees make sweets from pollens they accrue,
but I'm forgetting you with each day's buzz,
somehow. I managed to let go of you.

Regret's a dark, sweet nectar I fly through.
I'll make of it a honey labeled Was
Not True, Not True, Not True, Not True, Not True.

Let's inscribe those two words as a tattoo,
red inks indelible as my heart thaws.

Somehow I managed. To let go of you,

I'm pouring water on this crazy glue,
this airtight seal, whose lifetime guarantee's
not true. Not true, not true, not true, not true!

my heartbeat says. Oh fuck its point of view,
insistent muscle, pumping out red laws.
Somehow I managed to let go of you.
(Not true, not true, not true, not true, not true.)

If you liked the villanelle, you'll love the sestina, which is like a villanelle on steroids. At first glance the formula for the sestina is more daunting, but in a way, it's even easier to write. A sestina has six six-line stanzas followed by a three-line envoi or concluding stanza. Each line ends with one of six words that is repeated in a certain order. The envoi must also include the end words, but since there are only three lines in the envoi, one of those words must go in the middle of each line. The pattern looks like this:

1 2 3 4 5 6
6 1 5 2 4 3
3 6 4 1 2 5
5 3 2 6 1 4
4 5 1 3 6 2
2 4 6 5 3 1
(6 2) (1 4) (5 3)

Here's a sestina by Sandra Beasley.

Sestina Inviting My Sister to Become a Pirate

We wake to breakfast in a burning house,
Mom cussing. Our eggs have embers in them.
Fly the black flag on this family again.

I'll wear the eye patch, you will thread a ring
through your ear. Now, let us head out to sea.
Let all the Atlantic try to douse us.

You have to remember that they love us.
Burying a hatchet's harder than razing a house,
and raising a child is hardest. The sea
can lift bottle, barrel, ship. But for them
to keep this marriage afloat will take ring
and pulley that could raise Atlantis again,

with God shouldering the rope. Once again,
pegleg life is better balanced for us.
Parents? We'll take parrots. Choose a skull ring
set with rubies, grog-soaked night-jigging, house
boys to swab the deck. Fellow mates. To them,
it's clear we were always meant for the sea.

Monsoons, I know. We could go down at sea.
Captains blue- and black-bearded, drunk again,
might mutter that we're just wenches to them,
prod us with swords. But I'd rather see us
walk a plank than back into this damn house.
So what if Dad has lost his wedding ring?

So what that his story has a familiar ring?
Oh, my darling buccaneer, don't you see?
Burying a hatchet's easier than burying a house,
burying a treasure easier again—
all the same day's worth of digging to us.
If their smiles glitter like doubloons, let them.

But then lock the chest tight. We can love them
in the leaving, as galleons love moorings
of harbors they may yet come home to. But for us,

for now, no X can compete with the sea,
cross-stitching white caps again and again.
I believe a dank cabin beats a house

ablaze. I believe we can beat them, that the sea
offers vows sacred as rings. I won't ask again.
Join us. I'll wait in a rowboat, by the lighthouse.

Like the villanelle, early on the sestina becomes an engine that generates itself. Put a lot of care into that first stanza, because you're going to be seeing those last six words a lot. Once you've got stanza one the way you want it, just go down the right margin and write in the six end words using the order in the formula. Then all you have to do is go to the start of every line in the left margin and write across till you're done. Don't worry about the envoi just yet. In my experience, once the body of the sestina begins to cohere, the envoi will take care of itself.

The pantoum is a form contemporary poets have gotten a lot of mileage out of, even though it goes back quite a way. The pantoum originated in Malaysia in the fifteenth century as a short folk poem, typically made up of two rhyming couplets that were recited or sung. A pantoum can be any length as long as it's made up of four-line stanzas in which the second and fourth lines of each stanza serve as the first and third lines of the next. This form was popularized by Charles Baudelaire and Victor Hugo in the nineteenth century, and it gained popularity among American writers after John Ashbery used the form in his 1956 book *Some Trees*.

Here is a pantoum by Arthur McMaster.

Mortgage

Here is the small yard my father prepared;
he, raking and hoeing away the hard stones.
Here is the grass that finally grew,
and the tools we used, and we broke, and repaired.

He, raking and hoeing away the hard stones,
my father entrusted his lawn to my care,
and the tools we used, and we broke, and repaired.
As the family grew, we remodeled that home.

He, having entrusted his lawn to my care,
I might well have paid his work more heed.
As the family grew, we remodeled that home.
My mother got sick; one son went to war.

I might well have paid his work more heed,
mindful of all the work he had done.
My mother got sick; one son went to war.
I finished at college—had earned my degree.

Mindful of all the work he had done,
I might well have offered to visit him more.
I finished at college—had earned my degree,
but I got busy. I wanted my fun.

I might well have offered to visit him more:
watch the Yankees together. Drink a cold beer!
But I got busy; I wanted my fun.
Here is the small plot the workers prepared.

The last line of a pantoum is often identical to the first. But notice the tiny change Arthur McMaster makes and the huge difference that results. The first line refers to the "yard" the speaker's father prepared. The two grow older, and the son becomes neglectful. How poignant, then, that the last we see of him is the son standing at his father's grave, at the "plot" the worker prepared.

Let's look at one more of these formal delivery systems, and then I'll give you a looser pattern to work with. I've heard the word "ghazal" pronounced every way under the sun, but I'll go with the simple version that a lot of people use, "guh-ZALL." The ghazal is of Persian origin, consisting of five or more couplets linked by the repetition of a closing word or phrase, as in this example by Patricia Smith.

Hip-Hop Ghazal

Gotta love us brown girls, munching on fat, swinging blue hips,
decked out in shells and splashes, Lawdie, bringing them woo hips.

As the jukebox teases, watch my sistas throat the heartbreak,
inhaling bassline, cracking backbone and singing thru hips.

Like something boneless, we glide silent, seeping 'tween floorboards,
wrapping around the hims, and *ooh wee*, clinging like glue hips.

Engines grinding, rotating, smokin', gotta pull back some.
Natural minds are lost at the mere sight of ringing true hips.

Gotta love us girls, just struttin' down Manhattan streets
killing the menfolk with a dose of that stinging view. Hips.

Crying 'bout getting old—Patricia, you need to get up off
what God gave you. Say a prayer and start slinging. Cue hips.

If you're feeling a little strapped in by all of these poetic forms, why don't you do a few shoulder rolls and loosen up with the abecedarian? You actually know this form already, or at least you mastered 90 percent of it when you were in the first grade. The abecedarian is a poem where each line begins with a letter of the alphabet in their proper order: a, b, c, and so on. But the trick is to do that as skillfully as Natalie Diaz does in "Abecedarian Requiring Further Examination of Anglikan Seraphym Subjugation of a Wild Indian Rezervation" so that the reader doesn't realize what you're doing till halfway through the poem, if then. The poem's subject is the imposition of European religious beliefs (in, among other things, "Anglikan seraphym" or angels of the type who figure in the Anglican tradition) on Native Americans.

That's a weighty topic, but Diaz's colloquial speech is so jumpy and quick-paced that it doesn't give you enough time to really ponder the poem till you're done with it. You'll see when you read the full poem online.[4]

PARALLELISM

Now not all poems are as formal as the sonnet, villanelle, sestina, pantoum, ghazal, and abecedarian are. In fact, most aren't. But the opposite of form is not chaos. No doubt there are a lot of poems that sit well with you without your being able to say why, and many of these are likely to come from a tradition called parallelism. Parallelism is as old as the Bible and comes up through Blake and Whitman and Ginsberg. It's probably what underlies most of the poems being written today: not "free verse" in the sense of chopped-up prose but variations on the Old Testament-based Hebrew poetry shaped by the repetition of not stressed and unstressed syllables but parallel ideas.

This parallelism takes three forms. It is (1) synonymous when the original and the subsequent thoughts are identical; (2) antithetical when the original and subsequent thoughts contrast; and (3) synthetic when the one is developed or enriched by the other.

Here, for example, is an example of synonymous parallelism from "Song of Myself":

> I celebrate myself, and sing myself,
> And what I assume you shall assume,
> For every atom belonging to me as good belongs to you.

And antithetical parallelism:

> A child said What is the grass? fetching it to me with full hands;
> How could I answer the child? I do not know what it is any more than

4 For full poem, visit link: https://bit.ly/abecedarianND.

he.

And synthetic parallelism:

Do I contradict myself?
Very well then I contradict myself,
(I am large, I contain multitudes.)

This, too, is a kind of formal poetry, though it's not metered. If its very openness leaves a lot of room for error, that same openness can yield some breathtaking results. These days, a lot of poets are like a kid on the edge of a pond who's trying to skip stones across the surface. Some of the stones land just a few feet away, sending up an impressive rooster tail of water and then vanishing, while others splash only a couple of times and sink. But some stones skip six, seven, eight times, the way they're supposed to. Ping, ping, ping: they disappear in the darkness that swallows the water, the opposite bank, the woods beyond. And maybe some of those seeming clunkers are actually deliberate change-ups intended to vary the rhythm of the skips or at least provide a little relief to the kid's shoulder which aches like a son of a gun, yeah, though it's worth it to finally make that one perfect toss and hear that one stone splash off into the distance, ever more faintly.

Then there's the priamel. A priamel consists of a series of alternatives that serve as contrasts to the real subject of the poem, which is revealed at the end. Sappho used this device in the sixth century BCE, and so did the authors of the Bible:

> Some trust in chariots, and some in horses: but we will remember the name of the Lord our God. (Psalms 20:7)

and

> And Jesus said unto him, Foxes have holes, and birds of the air have nests; but the Son of man hath not where to lay his head. (Luke 9:58)

This is an example of a contemporary priamel by Betsy Rupp.

We Don't Believe in That

Momma says she doesn't believe in otters
who live in Crooked Lake because she's
never seen one in real life, she believes
they're salty creatures, even though my
Aunt Saundra took pictures of one sunning
itself on her dock just to prove Momma
wrong, but that's not all that surprising
because she was raised by Mamaw who
never believed that you could leave a building
from a different door than the one you
came in from because that's how demons
catch you in their fiery fishing nets, which
might explain how Momma ended up with
Daddy who says that he doesn't believe in
the state of Missouri because who'd make
some guy named Louis a patron saint of
anything since one of them, can't remember
if it was thirteenth or fourteenth, was a bit
of a shit king, and my brother thinks Daddy's
on to something and said he doesn't even
believe there's land there, just a landing pad
for Steven Hawking's black hole and added
on that he doesn't believe anyone actually
lives in Canada other than moose, but I haven't
paid too much attention, I have to keep
reminding the ghost who lives under my sink
that I don't believe in him, no matter how often
he steals my cereal bowls and steak knives.

ALL DELIVERY SYSTEMS WORK

Let me wrap this chapter up by saying that while forms like the sonnet and the sestina call attention to themselves immediately, the best often don't. When form is used subtly, you're likely to be half or all the way through and thinking, "Hmm, there's something going on here," and then it hits you. That may or may not have been the case for you when you read "Mambo Cadillac" in Chapter 1.5, but if it was, that's at least partly because Barbara Hamby invented her own form instead using one that had been handed down.

The most important thing is to realize that every poem has its best form, and it's the poet's job to find it. Even sprawling, spacey poems have a form that either works or doesn't. The Mishkan T'filah is a book of prayer used by Reform Jews, but it also contains some practical advice that applies to both fire building and poetry: "What makes a fire burn is / space between the logs. . . . It is fuel and absence of fuel together that makes the fire possible." A poem is doing its best work if it has the right sprawls and spaces, and if not, it isn't. A big irregular poem by William Blake or Allen Ginsberg or Frank O'Hara may be all over the place, but every bump and lurch and outgrowth looks deliberate.

Go back for a moment to the epigraph by Mark Strand that begins *The Knowledge*. There Strand talks about poetry as witnessing. Witnessing takes the form of words, but the words have to arrive in a way that appeals to the reader. In Howard Nemerov's *Contemporary American Poetry*, Jack Gilbert says that

> Poetry, for me, is a witnessing to magnitude. It is the art of making urgent values manifest, and of imposing them on the reader. It is the housing of these values in poems so they will exist with maximum pressure, and for the longest time. It is the craft of doing so in structures that are a delight in themselves. And it is the mystery of fashioning poems in such a way that the form and the content are one.

Everything either looks right or it doesn't. Wine comes in 750-milliliter bottles: can you imagine what it would be like if you said, "I'll have the Chianti" and you got a thimbleful one night and a gallon the next? Movies last about two hours, symphonies consist of four movements, we order a dozen oysters, the second half of a play is slightly shorter than the first. With exceptions, married people limit themselves to one spouse, because trial and error suggests that's the right amount. Or one spouse at a time, I should say. The airlines tell us to have one carry-on bag, one personal item. I could go on like this forever.

Every poem has the right or wrong dimensions and symmetry. Poems are short, so it's easy to tell when they need something more or have too much content or are just right, as Goldilocks said. Again, trial and error is the key here. And customer satisfaction: sometimes I'm asked why my poems look the way they do, and I always say, "Because editors like them."

Judgment is subjective, but when I look at a free-verse poem, I want to feel as though the poet is in charge. There is nothing bad or good about a poem that is loose or tight. Part of my cross to bear as a poet is putting up with people who say a poem is not a poem if it doesn't rhyme. I've got news for them: there are terrible rhyming poems, and there are sublime poems that don't scan or rhyme at all.

Unless you're writing a sonnet or sestina or villanelle, you're not going to know what your poem is going to look like until you've written it. Novelist Kazuo Ishiguro says this, and it applies to poets as well: "You can think of me like an early aviator before airplanes were properly invented. I'm building some sort of flying machine in my back garden. I just need it to fly. And you know how odd some of those early flying machines looked? Well, my novels are a bit like that. I put them together out of anything I can think of according to my thinking to make the thing fly."

All delivery systems work. The question is, which one works best?

Talking Points

You can do this on your own, but it'll work best with a handful of people. What you want is for one of you to find a poem that most readers won't be familiar with. That person should make the words of that poem into one big block of prose. The rest of you will turn it into lines and stanzas and give it the form that best delivers what the poem wants to say. Now it's time for a beauty contest. Lay everyone's rewrites out on a table and decide which ones work and which don't and why.

Since you're already working with some others, divide them into two groups. Have one group locate two examples of very formal poems, one that works well and one that doesn't work at all. Have the second group do the same with two free-verse poems. Make enough copies of the two pairs of poems for each person to have one and discuss.

Prompts

BACKTRACK

At this point, you'll learn the most by looking through the poems you've written already and reshaping them in terms of one of the formal strategies covered in this chapter. You might want to select one new delivery system and go from start to finish, although you may get more mileage from taking one of your older poems and trying to start it three or four different ways before going ahead with one.

As an alternative, riffle through your bits journal and see which bits might lend themselves to a sonnet, a sestina, a priamel, and so on, and which want to be free verse.

KID STUFF

Speaking of the kind of thing you might find in your bits journal, at different points in your life you and your friends would play certain games obsessively: you'd get your Barbies together for cocktail parties or launch (or try to launch) model rockets or throw eggs off bridges at passing cars. These activities must have meant a lot to you—why? Why did you start, why did you stop, what happened in between?

Because you did these things over and over, this might be a topic that would lend itself to a repetitive form like a villanelle or pantoum. Then again, you never know what will happen till you try, and maybe a sonnet or free verse would work better. If a poem lands, it doesn't matter how it got there.

LOST LETTER

Make a list of words and phrases without an "e": aardvark, banana, cassowary, dog food, flippant, golliwog, sandal, and so on. Write down as many of these as you can and then construct a poem from them. You can also do this same exercise with words lacking the other vowels.

Sound tough? French novelist Georges Pérec wrote an entire novel called *The Disappearance* that doesn't have a single "e" in it.

3.5

It's Called the Renaissance, You Know

Writers, musicians, and other artists are often asked, "Who are your influences?" That's a question that's impossible to answer. So many writers and artists have preceded us that it's very difficult to pinpoint where their work has seeped or trickled or flooded into the work of others, especially if that work is ours. We're too close to it to be able to tell. Every writer I know, myself included, has had someone say, "James Dickey wrote a story similar to yours, didn't he?" or "Your character reminds me a lot of Oedipus," to which the writer can only say, "Wow—I guess you're right."

In this chapter I want to talk to you about enriching your voice through a process that's hard to analyze but easy to put into play. I want you to cultivate your sense of this world's richness in a way we haven't talked about in depth yet. You have so much at your disposal: your memories, your present life, the ideas and images that come to you out of nowhere, and now the great words of the past, the ones that

Keats said were written by "the mighty dead." How will you use them?

One of my books of literary criticism is about foreign influences on U.S. fiction in which I identified a minimum of sixteen different ways in which influence might work: there's direct influence, of course, but then one writer might influence a second who influences a third, for example, or a writer might be influenced by one culture's notion of a central figure in a second culture.

And sometimes influence is startlingly direct. "Lady and gentlemen," said composer Dimitri Tiomkin in his 1955 Academy Awards acceptance speech, "because I working in this town for twenty-five years, I like to make some kind of appreciation to very important factor what make me successful to lots of my colleagues in this town. I'd like to thank Johannes Brahms, Johann Strauss, Richard Strauss, Beethoven, Mozart, George Gershwin, Jerome Kern, Wagner, Tchaikovsky, Rimsky-Korsakov. Thank you."

Ukrainian-born Tiomkin had won for Score of a Dramatic or Comedy Picture (William A. Wellman's *The High and the Mighty*), but he's also remembered today for one of the shortest and funniest speeches in the history of the Oscars. The host that evening was Bob Hope, the comic who served in that role a record nineteen times. But the next day, the headline in *Variety* read "Tiomkin Tops Hope."

The fact is, we're all influenced by someone else, whether we know it or not. John Maynard Keynes said an economist who says he is not influenced by other economists is influenced by a dead economist he has forgotten about. I suspect that's true for football coaches as well. There are only so many players and so many yards on the field and a limited number of ways of moving the ball. The play you just called? I bet somebody else called it before you did.

So how much are we influenced by other writers? How much should we be influenced? How much can we hint at or echo, and how much can we steal outright?

The pros seem to think it's okay to mug anybody. Henry Fielding said that "we moderns are to the ancients what the poor are to the rich," so that "Homer, Virgil, Horace, Cicero, and the rest are to be esteemed among us writers as so many wealthy squires, from whom we, the poor of Parnassus, claim an immemorial custom of taking whatever we can come at."

Yet thousands of college students get their knuckles rapped every term for not acknowledging their sources.

IT'S OKAY TO STEAL

In *The Art of the Voice*, Tony Hoagland says, "The truth is, a writer's voice is made from other writers' voices. Pieced together, picked and chosen, stumbled into, uninformed: influence seems like an involuntary series of contagions that eventually turns into a sort of vessel, or transportation system."

How strange, writes Hoagland, that "we should fervently believe in the 'originality' of our writing, when it is clear that the self in words (like the self in life) is comprised from the intermingling, overlapping, crosscurrents of so many others." Even better, "the remarkable news is that this pastiche of voices results in the incarnation of a new poet, a new hybrid distillation of voice, capable of telling the story of experience in new, valuable ways."

Charles Wright makes the same point in a little essay titled "Improvisations on Form and Measure," which ends, "Only technique can tell us what we don't know. The content's a given we've heard before."

T. S. Eliot advised us long ago that immature poets imitate whereas mature poets steal. The quote often stops there and is met with a ha-ha from a listener who is amused to think of the greats as light-fingered cutpurses rather than venerable rhymesters.

But Eliot goes on. The entire statement reads this way: "Immature poets imitate; mature poets steal; bad poets deface what they take, and good poets make it into something better, *or at least something different*."

I italicize those last five words because that makes your job and mine easier. We don't have to improve on Milton or Emily Dickinson—fat chance! We just have to do something they didn't think of.

I heard Mark Strand read at the Miami Book Fair once, and during the Q&A part, someone asked Strand what inspired him. Nothing, he said, adding that he noticed that people who claim to be inspired are always inspired the same way.

I was talking about all this with one of my grad students recently, and he said, yeah, if you don't work others into your writing, you're relying on sensibility alone.

From time to time, someone will walk up to me and say, "I wrote a poem, David." That sentence is never uttered by a poet. That'd be like a barber saying, "I cut hair today." No, it's always uttered by a relative or neighbor or colleague in the chemistry department. And it's always "a poem," the poet's first and only, and it's implied that it's a pretty darned good poem, too. Why else would he be telling you about it?

I want to say that's a little like saying, "I built a submarine today" or "I got up and ran a marathon this morning—why waste my time training?" But that would end our friendship, so I always smile and say, "Lay it on me."

Fully half the time, the poem I'm handed uses iambic tetrameter and an AA rhyme scheme and sounds like Joyce Kilmer's "Trees":

> I think that I shall never see
> A poem lovely as a tree.

Now your neighbor or relative or colleague probably doesn't think his or her original thoughts are influenced by anyone else, but they are: not by Joyce Kilmer but by the pop singers and rap artists whose rhymes and rhythms are as ubiquitous as the air we breathe.

That's because the majority of those tunes also use the AA scheme and are written in iambic tetrameter's musical cousin, the 4/4 time signature. Just as there are four stressed syllables in a line of tetrameter, there are four quarter notes to a bar of music in 4/4 time, as you'll see if you look at some examples.

Consider these lines from Taylor Swift's "All Too Well":

> Oh, your sweet disposition and my wide-eyed gaze
> We're singing in the car, getting lost Upstate.

Or these from Kendrick Lamar's "Wanna Be Heard":

> Can you relate to my story? Can you follow my dreams
> and admirations that I had ever since I was thirteen?

One consequence of all this formal similarity in the musical world is that a lot of songs are going to sound alike (go to YouTube, type "similar songs" in the search window, hit the enter button, and you'll see what I mean). And here is where my blood pressure starts to rise. Anyone who has ever listened to two pieces of music knows that one is very likely to have some relation to the other. There are only seven main musical notes. As the saying goes, even John Coltrane failed to discover the key of H. Yet every year, musicians are sued by other musicians for plagiarizing. Judges and juries who can't tell the difference between a piano sonata and a couple of trash bins falling off a garbage truck have found one musician guilty of ripping off another.

The most infuriating case of someone being sued successfully for musical plagiarism involves George Harrison, whose "My Sweet Lord" was alleged to be taken directly from the Chiffons' "He's So Fine." Yes, the first three words of both follow the same descending chord pattern, but after that, the songs diverge completely. Yet the tone-deaf judge who pronounced on the matter in 1976 found them "virtually identical."

An interviewer once praised Sting for composing such original songs as "Roxanne" and "Every Breath You Take," and here's what Sting said in reply: "I don't think there's such a thing as composition in pop music. I think what we do is collate. It's like folk music. It makes copyright a bit interesting and difficult. I'm a good collator." Interesting, huh? We'd probably never identify the wellsprings of songs by Sting or any other musician, but that's not important. What matters is that the joy he takes in playing with earlier sources is what keeps him productive.

Music critic Elijah Wald says, "One could see the early Beatles as a summation of all the trends of the previous few years wrapped in a particularly attractive package. 'I Want to Hold Your Hand,' their first hit in the United States, had the hand-claps of the girl groups, the melodic sophistication of the best Brill Building compositions, a rhythm perfectly suited to the new dances, and the loose energy of the surf bands—one reviewer tagged it 'Surf on the Thames.'"

But what do you expect? The act of discovery and appropriation and revision has been going on for millennia. It's not called the Naissance, you know. The Roman poets, sculptors, and architects took from the Greeks, and Michelangelo, Leonardo, Brunelleschi, and the other European masters took from both.

Before he enrolled in the Writing Seminars at Johns Hopkins University, novelist John Barth studied jazz at Julliard. Barth's musical background may help explain why he channeled Fielding, Sterne, Smollett, Cervantes, Rabelais, Voltaire, and other masters of the picaresque novel to arrive at the narrative voice for his masterpiece, *The Sot-Weed Factor.* "At heart I'm still an arranger," Barth once told an interviewer. "My chiefest literary pleasure is to take a received melody"—a classical myth, a biblical scrap, a worn-out literary convention or style—"and, improvising like a jazz musician within its constraints, re-orchestrate it to present purpose."

SOUL SIBLINGS

John Barth just might be an exception, though. Most of us don't know what we're doing, which is probably a good thing—they don't call it "the paralysis of analysis" for nothing. So when it comes to grappling with the immensity of our literary past, instead of having my students tell me who their influences are, instead I ask each of them to identify and write a five-hundred-word report on three soul siblings, artists who are more like family members or neighbors or roommates than ancestors.

The students will name mostly recent U.S. poets, of course, but I encourage them to think of at least one poet who is not living and/or non-Anglophone, and they may include a "wild card," if they like: a visual artist, singer/songwriter, medieval mystic, and so on.

The results are astonishing. Let me give you some actual examples to show you the range of what I get in these soul sibling reports. Some of the responses are fairly conventional (Richard Brautigan, Allen Ginsberg, Mark Strand), while others mix it up (one recent student listed Betina Hershey, Tammy Houtz, and Marc Kelly Smith, none of whom I'd heard of).

The best threesomes include (and this is an actual example) a mix like this one: Cher, Jennifer L. Knox, and Shakespeare, that is, a diva, a wacky aunt, and a boss. An all-indie-musician or all-classics list suggests a range of relationships that's just too narrow.

Every time I collect these soul sibling reports, I make up a handout with everyone's choices so the students can be reminded of poets and artists they haven't thought of in a while and, like me, discover new ones. And then every few years, I combine my handouts and make a master list to see who's in and who isn't.

Over time, there's so much overlap that you could make a tip-top poetry syllabus out of the repeats, since these include, and again I'm basing this list on actual names my students have given me, the ancients (Dante and Shakespeare), modern classics (Eliot and Williams), women poets (Plath and Olds), poets of color (Komunyakaa and Dove), international voices (Neruda and Lorca), and such "stand-up" or "kitchen sink" poets, as they've been called, as Allen Ginsberg and Billy Collins.

But I've resisted that impulse to teach from such a master list. For one thing, my soul siblings and yours are almost certainly going to be very different people: you might see yourself sitting on a curb with Kim Addonizio waiting for a club to open while I'm out on Fire Island playing volleyball with Frank O'Hara. Too, over time, choices tend to move toward the center, and if you assigned the names that show up on these lists again and again, you'd just end up with the people you already know.

Besides, what I like about these lists are the wild cards. How else am I going to discover medieval French poet Guillaume de Machaut and American labor organizer, folk singer, storyteller, and poet Utah Phillips?

Really, the soul sibling exercise is just a way of handling the influence issue by turning it into Influence Lite. Sort of takes the pressure off, doesn't it? Instead of worrying about being dominated by some towering figure from the past or, worse, feeling inadequate because you're not being influenced by anybody, now you can just hang out.

We're told to keep our friends close and our enemies closer, but don't worry about your soul siblings. They'll always have your back.

And they're going to be there whether you know it or not. The day after Dimitri Tiomkin gave his Oscar acceptance speech thanking all the musical artists who had shaped his work, fellow nominee Franz Waxman, who, like Tiomkin, had fled Europe during the rise of the Third Reich, was appalled at Tiomkin's seeming hubris and told him so. Tiomkin listened patiently and said, "I don't know why you're so annoyed, Franz. I don't hear any influences of these great composers in your music."

One effect of working your way through your possible soul siblings is that you're likely to stumble across phrases you can use as epigraphs. An epigraph is the little quote from another source that writers place at the head of their own work as a starting point. The Bible and Shakespeare have probably furnished poets with more epigraphs than any other source, and in the prompts section below I'll urge you to ransack them for some weighty words you can then adapt to your own ends. After those two venerable repositories of knowledge, I'd say more poems are inspired by the daily paper, which makes the world's journalists soul siblings to us all. Let's close out here with a poem by Catherine Pierce that starts with a provocative quote from the *Washington Post* about a government move that may have been triggered by either a bureaucratic snafu or an alien invasion. Which of those options are you rooting for? Yeah, I thought so. Me, too. And Catherine Pierce as well.

Please Let It Be Aliens

"A solar observatory in New Mexico is evacuated for a week and the FBI is investigating. No one will say why."—*Washington Post*

Let it be a silver disc, a foil zeppelin

blipping across the radar, a blot
in front of the sun
and then gone.
Let the word *intergalactic*
be paired at last with *espionage*.
Let uniformed men stride briskly
down long corridors, let astronomers
pace and calculate.
Let there be phone calls and code words,
an envelope unsealed
by trembling hands,
and let the light become strange,
the radio signals scramble,
the dogs whine skyward.
Let there be a great silver crack
down the sky of our surety,
and flames, and fear
borne of wonder. O, let it
be aliens for once, instead of another
threat from our own sad-sack planet,
a call-from-inside-the-house twist
we all see coming.
Let us believe,
though it seems impossible,
that someone still wants to claim us,
someone still thinks our poison-
green world worth wanting.

Talking Points

Think. Think hard. Look for a poem of yours that might stand up to a close examination and then ask yourself who that poem's ancestors might be. You might have used a subject that recalls one of Neruda's, only the voice in this poem sounds more like Lorca's voice. And those dashes—think you might have borrowed them from Emily Dickinson? Look, too, at the poem's measurements, its overall length as well as the lengths of its lines and stanzas, not to mention its use of tabs and diagonals and other unusual typographical features. Who used these things before you did, and how are you varying them and making them your own? This is a great exercise to do in a group or just with a friend if you swap poems, look at them for ten minutes or so, and then report what you see.

Who are your soul siblings? The best way to go about identifying the ones who are most important to you is to jot down a list of six or eight candidates and put it aside. Later, another name or two will come to you. When you think you have all the finalists you can muster, pick the three most important. And you don't have to make it a final choice, but do entertain the possibility of a wild card, a street performer or cellist or grade-school teacher or crazy uncle who is not a poet at all but who shaped your poetic practice.

Talking Points

Prompts

INSTANT ANCESTOR

Open the Bible or the plays of Shakespeare, jab your finger at the page, and use the sentence your finger lands on as an epigraph.

Say you pick these lines from the Book of Jeremiah: "yet will I not leave thee wholly unpunished." This could be the prelude to a comical list of your own woes, the dozen little injuries you suffered through recently, from having noisy neighbors overhead to getting nothing but junk mail. It could also function as an understated introduction to a real tragedy: on an otherwise ordinary day, for example, somebody loses a loved one to a terrorist's bomb.

Or say you happen upon these lines from *Richard II*: "My comfort is that heaven will take our souls / And plague injustice with the pains of hell." This sounds like a real invitation to list all the terrible things ("pains of hell") that should befall either your enemies or those of a character you invent. If you don't have any enemies, invent them, too.

Prompt

3.6

The Beautiful Theremin Player

One more thing before we move on to the final section of *The Knowledge*. This isn't a chapter, by which I mean a chapter-chapter with talking points and prompts. It's just a shirttail.

Here's how you create vision in poetry. You create vision by not creating vision.

Let me leave that with you for a minute. I'll get back to it.

First, I want to tell you a story. Four years ago, I was at a party in a large midwestern city. It was the dead of winter, and sixty people were crowded into a room designed to hold twenty. The guests were all artists—poets, painters, filmmakers—and they served themselves liberally from the bar.

Among them was a woman who played the theremin. The theremin is the only instrument that the player doesn't touch: he or she moves his or her hands toward and away from two metal antennas, one determining pitch and the other volume. If you think of the Beach Boys song "Good Vibrations," you'll get the idea (it's that woo-OOO-ooo sound). The theremin player was striking to look at. She was curvy and had bright red hair that sprang from her head.

She played beautifully as well, and as she played, the man standing next to me told me that the year before, he'd been at a similar party—icy weather, arty people, lots of drinks—and the beautiful theremin player said that if nobody looked, she'd disrobe and play the theremin in the nude. I said, "But people looked, right?" and the man said, "Nobody looked." I couldn't believe it. "They didn't look?" I said. And he said, "From where I stood, I could see everybody. And nobody looked."

It's the Lady Godiva story, isn't it? Lady Godiva was troubled by the crippling taxes her husband levied on the citizens of Coventry. He said he would lower the taxes only if she rode naked on horseback through the center of town, which she did, though first she asked the people to stay inside and not look, though one man, named Tom, couldn't resist opening his window to get an eyeful. (For his pains, he was struck blind, whence the name "Peeping Tom.") Anyway, Lady Godiva finished her ride, and true to his word, her husband lowered the taxes. This is what we call a win-win situation: the townspeople are saved from onerous taxation, and Lady Godiva gets credit for saving them. She does so by taking a great risk, but sometimes that's what you have to do if you want to make your mark in this world. After all, the legend of Lady Godiva was first recorded in the thirteenth century, and look, we're still talking about her today.

Let me leave you with the beautiful theremin player for a minute. I'll get back to her.

When I say you create vision by not creating vision, I mean that you take the reader up to the brink of vision, and if you do that right, they'll see it, which is something you can't make them do otherwise.

Here's a poem by Emily Dickinson about the gradual revelation of God's beauty:

He fumbles at your Soul
As Players at the Keys
Before they drop full Music on—

He stuns you by degrees—
Prepares your brittle Nature
For the Ethereal Blow
By fainter Hammers—further heard—
Then nearer—Then so slow
Your Breath has time to straighten—
Your Brain—to bubble Cool—
Deals—One—imperial—Thunderbolt—
That scalps your naked Soul—

When Winds take Forests in the Paws—
The Universe—is still—

The gears shift perceptibly in this poem: "Then nearer—Then so slow." But suddenly it's as though a car careens over a cliff; there's an explosion, the dust settles, and silence returns, though the world's been changed utterly. That gap before the last two lines speaks volumes to me; Dickinson was fond of regular stanzas, especially quatrains, or single long ones. Here, though, she pauses as a composer would before a final chord. One almost hears the inhalation of breath that takes place in the gap between the crash of the thunderbolt and the stillness that follows.

Dickinson belongs to that great tradition of highly charged erotic writers who are celibate. St. Teresa of Avila is another. Some of the most beautiful passages in St. Teresa's writings are the ones in which she talks about Christ's gradual revelation of himself to her. During one prolonged visitation, she says she first sees Christ's hands, which are ravishingly beautiful, and then, a few days later, his face, and after that, his body, which shines more brightly than the sun: "It isn't a dazzling radiance but a soft whiteness and infused radiance, which delights the eyes so much, they're never tired by it. . . . This light is so different from what we're used to that the sun's brightness seems very dim by comparison. . . . Afterwards, we don't want to open our eyes again."

In sculpture, Gianlorenzo Bernini's statue of Teresa and the angel conveys this ecstasy, though the moment Bernini captures doesn't show the climactic moment. The angel is smiling as he prepares to thrust his arrow into the ecstatic saint. It's up to us to imagine what happens after that.

In Chapter 3.3 I mentioned two prose works that stop short of their actual endings, James Scott's novel *The Kept* and Robert D. Richardson's biography *Emerson: The Mind on Fire*. So that's five examples of what might be called narrative brinkmanship from five different media: a Dickinson poem, St. Teresa's memoir, Bernini's statue, a contemporary novel, and a biography of Ralph Waldo Emerson.

You create vision by not creating it. Octavio Paz described his poetry as "the apple of fire on the tree of syntax." That's what you give the reader, your imagery and your syntax. Those are to the reader what a compass and a walking stick and a hat to keep the sun off and a canteen are to the traveler. You give readers the necessary tools, you point them down the path, and you let them create the vision.

Back to the beautiful theremin player. I asked the man who had been at the other party why nobody looked at her as she played her instrument in a state of undress. "For one thing," he said, "we had promised we wouldn't. But the main thing is that the music was so wonderful. Nobody wanted her to stop."

FOUR: YOU GRAPHOMANIAC, YOU, OR EVERYTHING I HAVEN'T SAID YET

4.1

Graphomania: The Basics

I began *The Knowledge* by telling you where poems come from and how they operate on us when we read them. That was to ground you in this often tricky but always satisfying profession. Then I told you what I know about writing poetry, beginning with the basics and moving on to some more advanced strategies. In this final section, I want to talk less about the nuts and bolts of writing and more about the writing life. There'll still be talking points, but if you're working with a group, by now you've broken the ice and have plenty to say to each other, and if you're working your way through this book by yourself, at this point I bet you're pretty darned good at having conversations with yourself. There will still be prompts, including ones that you may find more challenging than earlier ones. And you're ready for that, too, if indeed you are a writer.

Are you? If you've stayed with me this far, of course your answer is "yes." So let me put it another way: do you *have* to write the way you have to eat, drink, and sleep?

As often happens, the other day I was talking to someone I'd just met and she asked me what I did. When I said I was a writer, she said, "I used to write, but lately I haven't been able to." When I asked her what she used to write about, she said, "Oh, nothing. . . ."

She's not a writer. Writers write. Now like anything else, you can take writing too far. Someone who writes compulsively is known as a graphomaniac, which is not what you want to be. Graphomaniacs carry pen and paper with them at all times and scribble things down when they should be talking to others and enjoying themselves. I haven't been able to verify this, but I was told that a former governor of my state used to carry different color index cards around with him and record everything on those cards: the blue cards were for committee meetings, the green for social interactions, the pink for leisure time, and so on. Every time he completed a card, he'd give it to an aide, who'd file it with all the cards of the same color. Somewhere in the basement of the capitol, there are boxes and boxes of these cards that detail every occurrence in our governor's daily routine: who said what to whom, what dressing so-and-so had on his or her salad, and so on.

That's true graphomania, and if it sounds just a little restrictive, remember that while this guy was writing down everything, he was able to keep his day job. Remember, too, that we're all on one spectrum or another and while there are people who are compelled to write too much, there are many of us who have to write, not all the time, but regularly.

That's me, and I'm thinking that it might be you, too. If so, we're not graphomaniacs, but we do have graphomaniacal tendencies. Having a particular disorder can be terrible, but having its tendencies is not bad at all and, in fact, can be quite productive. Thus it's not good to have an obsessive-compulsive disorder and wash your hands a hundred times a day or fill your house to the ceiling with old newspapers and empty food containers. But a lot of successful people have obsessive-compulsive tendencies. Take Noah Webster, the lexicographer. If he hadn't had OCD tendencies, how else could he have put his dictionary together in a day when there were no computers and not even typewriters? If he was as nitpicky as I'm sure he had to be, I wouldn't be surprised if he made his wife and children miserable. But if you use the dictionary as much as I do, you have to be grateful to Noah Webster for wanting to see everything lined up and in the right order.

So while a graphomaniac would have to write down everything as they talked to you, I would say that a person with graphomaniacal tendencies is someone who gives events their maximum reality by writing about them. During a thirty-two-day train trip across Russia with my wife, Barbara, I had a lot of new information to organize and a lot of time to organize it in, and the only way I could do that was by writing about it. Staring out the window of my compartment was better than TV: there were wild horses racing across meadows, camels loping through the sand, people bathing in their underwear in the chilly rivers of Siberia.

But I was happiest when I watched a while and then wrote a while. Moreover, I found myself getting unhappy when I wasn't writing. Usually when we travel, I'm walking the streets and going to plays and museums and talking to people and dining in nice restaurants, but on this trip we spent many a day just in that one rail compartment. At one point, we were on the train for two and a half days without getting off. If I hadn't been able to write during that time, I would have been very hard to live with. And Barbara, too: one advantage of being married to a writer is that you never have to stop writing to entertain them, because when you're writing, usually they're writing, too.

Now you don't have to travel all 5,009 miles from St. Petersburg to Beijing to find out whether or not you have to write to live. But if someone has trouble writing, it may be that they're not a writer. A lot of people want to write but can't. Maybe they should be doing something else. I even know people who've had a fair amount of success in publishing their work and then stopped writing and now seem bewildered that they can't get back to it.

You're not one of those people. You're a writer—no doubt about it.

AN EAGLE'S EYE, A LADY'S HAND, A LION'S HEART

What exactly does "you're a writer" mean, though? By this point in *The Knowledge*, you should have absorbed everything you need to know to make a life for yourself in poetry. And while we're not done yet—there's always more to learn, believe me—now is a good time to widen the lens and take a broader view of the writer's life.

As he was readying himself to write his great poems, John Keats trained as a doctor, notably with Sir Astley Cooper, senior surgeon at Guy's Hospital in London. And Sir Astley Cooper said that a surgeon should have three attributes: "An eagle's eye, a lady's hand, and a lion's heart." When I read that, I thought, boy, the next time I need a surgeon, I want to make sure my mine has an eagle's eye, a lady's hand, and a lion's heart. And then I thought, wait—to what profession do these attributes *not* apply? In what line of work would you not need to have a great eye for detail, a certain delicacy of execution, and the courage needed to bring you through when you're tired or discouraged?

While I'm a poet first and foremost, I've written a lot about writers, including writers who are very different types. The author from whom I learned the most about writing is Herman Melville. In many ways, Melville was the archetypal writer: neither the genius nor the mouthpiece that some people think an author is but one who was lucky and unlucky, stable and unstable, blessed and cursed. Primarily, Melville was eccentric in both the figurative and the literal meanings of that word. That is, he was a little odd psychologically—more than a little, perhaps—but also he spent much of his life on the margin of everything that might be considered conventional.

What I've learned from writing about other writers, and from Melville most, is that successful writers have two traits in common, no matter how different they may be otherwise. The first is that they never give up. The second trait, and it is closely related to the first, is that they adapt.

Melville wrote novels, stories, essays, and poems both short and book-length. A member of the next generation of American writers that I've also written about is Henry James, who wrote fiction of every possible length but also biography, criticism, plays, reviews, travel essays, and art criticism.

As different as they are, what we see in both Melville and James is dogged persistence matched with a consummate versatility. In some instances, a writer will move deliberately from one genre to another, though in others they have no choice. James, for instance, was literally hounded from the theater after the failure of his play *Guy Domville*. The audience booed him lustily. James went into something like shock for a while and then wrote movingly in his notebook on January 23, 1895: "I take up my old pen again—the pen of all my old unforgettable efforts and sacred struggles. To myself—today—I need say no more. Large and full and high the future still opens. It is now indeed that I may do the work of my life. And I will."

And he did: in less than a decade James published what many consider his three greatest novels, *The Wings of the Dove*, *The Ambassadors*, and *The Golden Bowl*, works built largely around scene, dialogue, and other dramatic conventions he mastered during his "failed" foray into the theater. (Incidentally, late in life James tried again to write plays, though with little more success than before.)

But even more than James, Melville demonstrated throughout his career an aggressive resistance to discouragement. When he found one door closed to him, he looked around until he found another that was open. He's actually one of the best American poets of the nineteenth century, and if he hadn't written those big fat novels, we'd still remember him for his poems. But his only truly popular books were essentially travelogues, and his great uneven masterpiece *Moby-Dick* was largely ignored by a world that was not ready for it. Yet during the decades of public silence that followed the realization that his fictions were no longer marketable, he wrote the poems that alone would have guaranteed him a permanent if minor position in U.S. literature. And as he lay on his deathbed, he was writing *Billy Budd*, one of the finest short fictions of his or any time.

Obviously, the two traits characteristic of great writers, persistence and adaptability, are common to successful people in any field. But there's one other trait common to great writers only. Yes, they are (1) persistent and (2) adaptable, but they're also (3) passionately devoted to literature.

It is this third trait that makes a successful person into a successful writer, just as one might expect successful orthopedic surgeons and corporation presidents to be persistent and adaptable people who are devoted, not to literature but to their own fields of endeavor. Successful writers are necessarily neither more brilliant nor luckier than other people but more persistent, more adaptable, and better-read, that is, more familiar—in a literary sense, at least—with the entire geography of the human mind and heart. I can't think of any writer who would disagree with me, for these are the things that, consciously or half-consciously, drive us all.

Let's assume you want to keep that drive going for a while. It's probably a little early for you, but if you end up loving writing as much as I do, sooner or later you're going to be thinking about a career and how to sustain it.

I have one word for you: obscurity. Obscurity equals longevity. Neil Young has had one of the longest careers in the music business, and here's what he says: "I know that the sacrifice of success breeds longevity. Being willing to give up success in the short run ensures a long run. If you're really doing what you want to do." In *The Shape of Things to Come: Prophecy and the American Voice*, cultural critic Greil Marcus says that's why Neil Young "scatters terrible concept albums among dissonant masterpieces and craven, comfort-food crowd pleasers."

Great musicians, like great poets, don't worry if what they're working on doesn't seem promising. Remember what I said in Chapter 2.2 about the "slump songs" that Barry Mann and Cynthia Weil wrote and how some of those slump songs became hits?

In other words, diversify. You're going to bore yourself to sobs if you do just one thing. At least be binary. If you're a scientist, when you're not chasing quarks, learn how shoes are made, and make a pair. If you're a poet, when you're not writing poems, write cookbooks. If you spend your life setting goals and fulfilling them, you're going to walk a very narrow path. Be passionate instead. Be lively. Have fun.

EVERYTHING HAS TWO HANDLES

While you're at it, take your time. Use your negative capability: in an 1817 letter to his brothers George and Thomas, Keats speaks of "Negative Capability, that is, when a man is capable of being in uncertainties, mysteries, doubts, without any irritable reaching after fact and reason—Coleridge, for instance, would let go by a fine isolated verisimilitude caught from the Penetralium of mystery, from being incapable of remaining content with half-knowledge."

You want to finish that poem, sure, but you won't get anywhere being irritable.

Walter Benjamin's ideal Parisian is the flâneur or "loafer" of whom it is said, "the whole point of the flâneur's wanderings is that he does not know what he cares about."

Don't ever stop wandering, even if you've been to the mountaintop and back.

After he had finished his masterpiece, here's what Melville wrote in a letter to Hawthorne: "Lord, when shall we be done growing? As long as we have anything more to do, we have done nothing. So, now, let us add Moby Dick to our blessing, and step from that. Leviathan is not the biggest fish; —I have heard of Krakens."

The Stoic philosopher Epictetus says, "Everything has two handles, the one by which it may be carried, the other by which it cannot."

It might—it almost certainly will, and no doubt it should—take you a while to find the right handle.

Consider this poem by Josephine Yu as an example of a topic picked up by the right handle.

The Thing You Might Not Understand

when I tell you the man whose children I babysat in college
cornered me on the deck after the party and copped a feel

is how his eyes looked drunk, glassy and sad,
and how his smile tilted apologetically but his body

was straight and formal, as if we were dignitaries shaking hands,
or how he held my breast as gently as I cupped his daughter's head

the first time I washed her in the kitchen sink,
rubbing the cradle cap from her hair with baby oil,

palming warm water over her head, pale silk strands
swirling like fine crackling in the glaze of old porcelain,

the veins of her eyelids a faint calligraphy on vellum,
the extant manuscript that would reveal, if we could translate it,

a treatise on forgiveness, or canticles maybe,
a tune we sometimes hum, unaware, under our breath

as we walk to the mailbox, or fill a birdfeeder with seed,
or lower a man's hand and lead him back into his house.

There are so many other handles by which this topic could have been seized. The easiest way would have been to make it a poem of outrage or one that spoke out against sexual molestation. The man's actions were outrageous, and no human being should treat another this way. But we know that already. I wasn't there when she wrote it, but I bet Josephine Yu said to herself, I don't want to just shout into the echo chamber—what can I say about this situation that's new?

What Yu gives us is a poem of great tenderness, understanding, and forgiveness. The greatest part of it is given over to the baby, the washing of it and the realization that it, like all human beings, is a book wanting to be read. When the speaker gets around to the drunk, pathetic husband toward the poem's end, she reads him for what he is: not so much a dangerous person as a sad one, someone whom we should handle with a kindness that is almost automatic, with a gesture as unthinking as a stroll to the mailbox or the filling of a bird feeder.

We love the speaker for her honesty. She warns us from the get-go:

the title and the first line say that it may be hard to understand why she does what she does rather than calling the cops. But we do understand. And we love her for her generosity more than we hate the man for his thoughtless vulgarity.

Talking Points

Think of people you know who have different abilities and who have surprised you by the choices they've made. The nineteenth-century French painter Ingres liked to play his violin—badly—for visitors instead of showing them his timeless artworks, from which practice we get the expression *violon d'Ingres*, meaning "an activity other than that for which one is well-known." It's said that every athlete wants to be a rapper, and every rapper wants to be an athlete. I know a guy who was so good at tennis that he won the state championship in his age bracket, but he hated it, and one day he walked off the court and never returned. Think about someone you know who has triumphed or failed in the pursuit of something they should or shouldn't have tackled in the first place. What does this tell you about human nature and our potential for self-understanding?

Your turn. Turn the lens on yourself. Conduct a ruthless self-inventory. What do you (1) love to do that (2) you're good at? Loving something and being good at it are usually the same thing, but as you see from the example of the tennis player, not necessarily. The idea is for you to test your commitment to the life of writing, but this is a great exercise for its own sake. By the way, some of the most interesting people I know are those I call a Writer Plus. I've had friends who published books while working at a lumberyard and as a tool-and-die maker. I have one right now who runs a six-hundred-acre cattle ranch. Oh, and he paints, too.

Life's going to throw stuff at you, and you're not always going to see it coming. Josephine Yu's poem suggests that there's more than one way to handle the unexpected. What examples do you have? You may or may not end up writing about an issue that had an unexpected resolution, but as with the other talking points in *The Knowledge*, the idea is for you to flex your mind and get yourself ready to write on this or any other subject.

Prompts

FUN WITH NUMBERS

Write the numbers 0 to 12 on slips of paper, draw one out, and jot down everything you associate with that number. Say you pick 2: there's two-timing someone, Tuesday, snake eyes in a dice game, twins, two's company but three's a crowd, and so on.

Or if your number is 3, you might think of the Three Stooges, the third rail on subway tracks (the one that'll electrocute you), the Holy Trinity, the movie *The Third Man*, three strikes and you're out, two's company but three's a crowd, and so on.

Take your time and accumulate as many of these as you can. Then choose the ones you want to write about and the sequence you want to put them in.

TIME'S ON YOUR SIDE

You often hear that writers should write what they know. Maybe a better way to put that is that writers should write what they remember.

This is an exercise involving memory, and it works this way. Imagine that it's late in the day, and you're in a building that's very familiar to you: the art museum, the natural history museum, the elementary school you went to when you were a child, the department store where you used to work when you were a teenager. Suddenly you notice you're the only one around. Then you hear the click of a door closing—you've been locked in! Now you have to spend all night there.

Take your time—you've got all night, after all—as you go from exhibit to exhibit or desk to desk or floor to floor, reacting to what you see, feel, remember. Wait for the forgotten details that will tell you what you want to say.

THREE OUT OF SIX AIN'T BAD

As they come to mind, write down the names of six places you've lived in or visited. Select three, write a stanza or paragraph on each, and work out the connection in a poem.

Or let these be three places in the past of someone who is either the protagonist or a secondary character in a story you now begin to write.

FOUR ELEMENTS

Select one of the four ancient elements: earth, air, fire, water. Now think of four contemporary examples of each: for example, fire might be fireflies, firecrackers, your high school coach's fiery temper, and jalapeño peppers.

Write a stanza on each and work out the connection in a poem. Or let these things be part of the thinking of a character you develop in a narrative poem.

4.2

Four Tricks of the Trade

Let's assume you have all the hallmarks of a creative genius. Let's say that you are persistent, adaptable, devoted to literature, and also at least intermittently sane. Does this mean that you will be a great writer? Of course not, although it is doubtful one could become a great writer by any other means. At some point in the discussion of art, rational inquiry ceases, and observers from every discipline agree only on what cannot be said.

Ben Dorsey used to work for Johnny Cash, and he had a bunch of suits that Johnny had given him, and one day Ben was walking down the street in front of the Grand Ole Opry, and this guy comes up with a guitar in his hand and thinks Ben is one of the stars because of the fancy suit, so the guy says, "How do you get started in this business?" and Ben says, "Ain't but one way, hoss. You start at the bottom, you go right to the top. Don't mess with that in-between shit." Sure, it'd be nice if things worked that way, as they do in the movies, though not in life. Maybe you've noticed.

The legendary Nashville musician Chet Atkins said, "A long apprenticeship is the most logical way to success. The only alternative is overnight stardom, but I can't give you a formula for that."

If I've used a lot of references in *The Knowledge* to genres other than poetry—fiction, music, opera, television, painting, and so on—that's because, as I say in the foreword, there are basic principles underlying art of every kind.

One of these common principles, at least from the point of view of every artist I know, is that we want to get our work in front of other people. To you and me, two writers who want to share our work with others but are aware that the competition is ferocious, that means dealing first with an editor.

Let's begin by remembering that the editors of the world are not our enemies—they love writing passionately or they wouldn't be the underpaid, overworked people they tend to be. And the ones I know are pretty open-minded. They don't care what you write as long as you write it well. They're simply looking for the best work out there. In fact, they demand it.

But they're overwhelmed, like a thirsty person trying to get a drink of water from a fire hydrant. Let's imagine an editor is sitting in his office and looking at a stack of, say, twenty submissions from twenty writers, and it's not even lunchtime yet. How are you going to make your work stand out? How are you going to get that editor to put the other writing aside and give your work a good, close read?

As a writer, teacher, contest judge, and, mainly, a fan of writing, I read dozens of works of all kinds every day, hundreds every month, and thousands every year, and I can tell you this: a poem or story or essay either engages my interest immediately or it doesn't. Too, a work also either sustains that interest or fails to.

THESE TRICKS REALLY ARE SIMPLE

How? There are actually four very simple tricks of the trade that every writer should know and that any writer can use to write what he or she wants to. So let me tell you what they are, and then I have a couple of surprises for you.

I can best illustrate my points if we look at a poem of mine first. It's a shortie, but I wrote one draft after another as I struggled with some technical aspects that I thought might help get my poem across.

Fallen Bodies

The night of the Franklinton game
the bus breaks down, the seniors cry
because they will never play football again,
and we all go home with our parents and girlfriends.
Billy Berry lies in the back of my father's Buick,
covered with bruises, unable to lift his right arm,
and tells stories he swears are true:

that apple seeds cure cancer,
that a giant dove hovered over the van
the night his church group
came back from Mexico,
that Hitler left Germany by submarine
after the war and established a haven
in Queen Maud Land, near the South Pole.

The air comes in through windows
that won't quite close
as we drive up the dark highway to Baton Rouge,
through towns where tired old men
sell peaches on the corners of used car lots
or doze in diners that sag by the roadside,
spacecraft cooling in the Louisiana night.

Using "Fallen Bodies" as our text, let's look at the four tricks of the trade that will make your poem stand out from all the others.

1. **The Hook**. What catches the reader's attention and makes this poem different from all others? The answer is something concrete and slightly mysterious; in this instance, it's a broken-down bus and a bunch of unhappy high school football players. Immediately you get a mental picture and then you ask, "What next?" The hooks that operate throughout a text were discussed in Chapter 2.3, but the hook that comes first is the most important: once your reader has started reading, almost nothing will stop them.

2. **The Voice**. We looked at voice in Chapter 3.3, but let's take another gander. What vocabulary (formal or streetwise), sentence length (long, short, mixed), and tonal qualities (wistfulness, confidence, horror, humor) do you want to use to get the effect you desire? In "Fallen Bodies," the voice is world-weary; look at all those negative words and phrases like "breaks down," "cry," "never," "bruises," "unable," "cancer," "won't quite," "dark," "tired old," "used," and "sag," not to mention the word "night," which occurs in the first and last lines of the poem and one other time as well. Yet this voice is also thoughtful: there are only three sentences in the poem, and each is packed with ideas and images, as though the speaker has composed his thoughts very carefully. So the overall effect is of a world-weary yet philosophical observer.

3. **Saturation**. The first draft of a piece of writing is usually a skinny draft. As I write this chapter, I'm also judging a poetry contest, which means reading 250+ poems by today's poets. Already I'm seeing some standouts, but the fact remains that too many of the poems are just flimsy. These poets set up enticing premises, but they don't follow through. In 1709, John Dennis wrote a play called *Appius and Virginia* that called for thunder, so he invented a noise machine that was a lot more popular than his play. *Appius and Virginia* was canceled. But when Dennis returned to the theater to see *Macbeth* and real-

ized they were using his sound effects for the storm scene, he cried, "That's my thunder, by God! The villains will not play my play, but they steal my thunder." First drafts are usually, um, *okay*, though they lack zip, energy, pizzazz—thunder, in a word. Fatten your draft with detail. Make noise, poets! Throw in some crashes and lightning bolts. The details in "Fallen Bodies" speak for themselves, from the capsule picture of the defeated team to the outlandish story of Hitler's submarine voyage to the portraits of the old men in the car lots and diners.

4. **The Big Idea**. Whenever I use that phrase, I always capitalize the first letters of the words to remind myself that the Idea must always be Big. A pretty poem can still be a trivial poem, so make sure your poem deals with something of consequence. That doesn't mean you should be obvious about it. You'll want to present your argument by means of images rather than editorial statements. In the case of "Fallen Bodies," I wanted to say that, even in defeat, one can still see that the world is filled with strange wonders, and this realization can be consoling in itself. Hence my final image: not chrome-and-glass diners per se but spacecraft that seem to come from another dimension, as if by magic.

And that's it. Once you gather your materials, you figure out the best way to start, you decide what voice you want to use, you saturate your writing with plenty of details, and you arrange everything so your Big Idea will emerge. You can test this scheme on other writings, your own or someone else's. My guess is that your favorites will all have the four elements I've outlined above and that the ones that don't work quite as well will be lacking in one or more areas.

FEED YOUR POEMS

Before we leave this list, I want to take a closer look at the third item, saturation. It's not that it's more important than the other three, but as I say, a lot of the poems I see are undernourished. I know one problem student poets have to face is that usually they have to hand their instructor a poem a week, which doesn't give them a lot of time to develop their work. But you can do that later. Excuse me—you *have* to do that later if you want your poem to grow up strong and healthy.

These two poems will illustrate what I'm talking about. This first one's by Lawrence Raab.

Permanence

I can't remember how old I was,
but I used to stand in front
of the bathroom mirror, trying to imagine
what it would be like to be dead.
I thought I'd have some sense of it
if I looked far enough into my own eyes,
as if my gaze, meeting itself, would make
an absence, and exclude me.

You look into your own eyes in a mirror
and that's all you can see.
Until you notice the window
behind you, sunlight on the leaves
of the oak, and then the sky,
and then the clouds passing through it.

This is one of those short poems you can talk about forever. What thinking person hasn't asked themselves what death is like? That's what the speaker is doing here. The question can't be answered, of course, but something happens that may be better than an answer. When the speaker stops being so self-absorbed, the poem opens up, and we see light, a tree, the sky, and clouds, each in motion, each in proportion to the other. The Big Idea here is that there always was and always will be a world, one that we are a part of, a world that is constantly changing, and so it is only natural that we change, too.

The second poem is also by Lawrence Raab. Oh, wait a minute—it's actually the same poem. Rather, this version is the original and complete one. As you see, what I did above was to cut the six middle stanzas in this eight-stanza poem.

Permanence

I can't remember how old I was,
but I used to stand in front
of the bathroom mirror, trying to imagine
what it would be like to be dead.
I thought I'd have some sense of it
if I looked far enough into my own eyes,
as if my gaze, meeting itself, would make
an absence, and exclude me.

It was an experiment, like the time
Michael Smith and I set a fire in his basement
to prove something about chemistry.
It was an idea: who I would
or wouldn't be at the end of everything,
what kind of permanence I could imagine.

In seventh grade, Michael and I
were just horsing around
when I pushed him up against that window
and we both fell through—
astonished, then afraid. Years later

his father's heart attack
could have hit at any time,
but the day it did they'd quarreled,
and before Michael walked out
to keep his fury alive, or feel sorry for himself,

he turned and yelled, *I wish you were dead!*

We weren't in touch. They'd moved away.
And I've forgotten who told me
the story, how ironic it was meant
to sound, or how terrible.

We could have burned down the house.
We could have been killed going through
that window. But each of us
deserves, in a reasonable life,
at least a dozen times when death
doesn't take us. At the last minute

the driver of the car coming toward us
fights off sleep and stays in his lane.
He makes it home, we make it home.
Most days are like this. You yell
at your father and later you say
you didn't mean it. And he says, *I know.*

You look into your own eyes in a mirror
and that's all you can see.
Until you notice the window
behind you, sunlight on the leaves
of the oak, and then the sky,
and then the clouds passing through it.

Some difference, huh? I love that almost forgettable phrase "like the time" in the first line of stanza two. It triggers a series of little explosions that are like the booster rockets that send a payload into space: the fire, the window, the heart attack, the thoughtless thing Michael shouts at this father, the sleepy driver who almost kills us but doesn't.

The abridged version of Lawrence Raab's poem I gave you first is thoughtful almost the way a greeting card or a kitchen sampler is. But remember what Tom Petty said earlier about a good song giving you lots of images and how you can make a little movie in your head from your images? That's what Raab does in his poem's middle. And the good news is that those images don't even have to be detailed. We see the boys jump back as the chemistry experiment goes wrong. We see their relief when the fall through the window leaves them unharmed. We see the rage in Michael's face as he shouts at his father, and we see the love in his face and his father's as they make up, just as we see the relief in our own face—and we might hear an audible "Whew!" as well—when the sleepy driver misses us. So, yeah, let's hear it for saturation. A poem has to start right and end right, and with few exceptions, it needs to be chunky and crunchy and chewy in the middle.

EVERY WRITER USES THESE TRICKS

And now for the surprises I promised earlier. The first you've probably guessed already, which is that my four tricks of the trade, which are intended to help students write the poems of the future, are also characteristic of the great poems of the past. Take Dante's *Inferno*. It begins with a guy getting lost in the woods at night: what a hook! Then there's the poet's voice, which ranges from comic to angry to pitying to devout but is, for the most part, simply awestruck at all the bizarre figures in the underworld. As for detail, if giants and harpies and dragons aren't enough, not to mention some of the greatest celebrity sinners of all time, there's Satan himself, frozen in the ice of Hell's basement. And while there's more than one Big Idea (after all, it's a Big Poem), certainly the immortality of true love is the greatest of these.

The second surprise is that the four tricks of the trade I've described as essential to any good poem are also indispensable to any piece of good writing. For example, a good novel has a good hook. (What would *Moby-Dick* be without "Call me Ishmael"?) Each hit song has an unmistakable voice; you could play "Somewhere Over the Rainbow" loud and fast, but the version most people remember is the wistful one that Judy Garland sang. Every good play is saturated with details: if *Macbeth* didn't have all those witches and sword fights in it, it would just be a dull treatise on Scottish politics. And each of these has its own Big Idea: pride, nostalgia, ambition.

The fact that these four tricks have always characterized every good piece of writing, regardless of its genre or the period it was written in, is especially good news, since it means that if you use them in your own writing, you will, in effect, marketproof your work against any changes in editorial taste that may occur.

Talking Points

By yourself or with others, think of the last thing you read or saw or listened to: poem or story or article, movie or show episode, song. How'd it do in terms of the four tricks? Did it hook you from the start? When the answer to that question is no, usually the hook is the second or third thing in the text, so move it up to the top. Now what about voice, saturation, Big Idea? How do they work in your example? How would you make them work even better?

Now do the same with something you've written recently. And prepare yourself to do it each time you write something new. Measuring your poems against this four-point checklist won't harm them, and it could do them a lot of good.

Prompts

THE CHURCH OF TERRIFYING MATHEMATICS

Create three columns of words. In the first, put monumental buildings (museum, church, institute). In the second, put adjectives (improbable, terrifying, reverse). The third list will consist of fields of study (architecture, mathematics, evolution).

Now pick one word from each column, so that you end up with the Museum of Improbable Architecture, say, or the Church of Terrifying Mathematics, or the Institute for Reverse Evolution. Let this place, its people, and their work be the subject of what you now write.

This could end up being an abstract poem if you're not careful, so as you go, be sure you work in the Four Tricks of the Trade. Likewise with the next prompt.

LITERARY LARCENY

Take a quote from a work of prose or poetry, famous or not, and extend it. For example, *Moby-Dick* begins, "Call me Ishmael." Your poem or story would begin the same way and continue, "No, not that Ishmael," and go off in its own direction.

Less famously, William Carlos Williams wrote, "It is difficult / to get the news from poems / yet men die miserably every day / for lack / of what is found there." Well, what *is* there in poems that sustains life? Williams doesn't say, so you might as well.

A second version of this exercise involves using this same line or another and then writing everything that "comes before" so that your work ends with that line.

Now try this exercise a third time (with either of the lines you've used so far or a third) so that the borrowed line occurs almost unnoticed. You'll want your reader to skim right over "I heard a fly buzz when I died" and be two or three lines farther along before saying, "Hey, that's from Emily Dickinson!"

4.3

What Producers Do and Why You Need One

Have you noticed that people you don't really know that well are often more helpful to you than friends and family? It's because they pull you out of a context that was useful up to a point but has lost its usefulness, and they can do that because while you and those who are near to you are invested in that context, they aren't, which means they're free to do or say whatever they want. In his extraordinary study *The Structure of Scientific Revolutions*, Thomas Kuhn notes that scientists work with a paradigm that constitutes normal science until that framework is replaced by a new and different one that addresses the original idea in a totally different way, his example being the switch from the Ptolemaic to the Copernican view of the universe. This is where the term "paradigm shift" comes from, and Kuhn's finding is literally a paradigm shift in itself.

Einstein said "we can't solve problems by using the same kind of thinking we used when we created them."

Oh, that's right. *The Knowledge* is about poetry, not science. Okay, here's Emily Dickinson then: "The Mind is so near itself—it cannot see, distinctly."

No matter which authority you cite, the fact remains that writing is a solitary profession, but you don't want to go it alone. Indeed, you can't: someone's got to tell you when you're at your best and when you're not.

I'm a music journalist as well as a poet, and just as I turn to others to tell me if a poem is doing its best work or not, I often pillage the music world for insights into the poetic process. Let me tell you a few stories that will show you how you can get the most out of your work with others.

A lot of pop songs traffic in masculine self-pity. Poor, poor pitiful me! shout the miserable millionaires who live lives a hundred times more splendid than anything you or I could dream of. But self-pity sells as well as anything else if you package it right. Case in point: Neil Diamond's "Solitary Man" is the ultimate ode to masculine woe, yet what gives the song backbone are the trombone salvos at the end that lend the singer's teary utterances a bracing mariachi air. Those horns may have been Neil Diamond's idea, but I suspect it was his producer who said, "This is nice as it is, but it sounds a little wimpy—how about mixing a couple of trombones into that final chorus?"

Now let me ask you this: Who is Merry Clayton? Few people know, yet everyone recalls the beautiful voice that sings the cutaway chorus in "Gimme Shelter." Clayton tried to have a solo career because everyone said, "Who's that amazing singer!" But little came of it. Merry Clayton is the best part of the song, but she isn't the song.

Four hundred and fifty years ago, Montaigne said, "Raisins are the best part of a cake. But raisins are not as good as a cake."

Merry Clayton added the raisins to the Rolling Stones' cake. But she's not the cake.

As with the trombones in "Solitary Man," what we know about the addition of Merry Clayton's voice to "Gimme Shelter" tells us everything we need to know about the role of a producer. No less an authority than Mick Jagger himself says, "The use of the female voice was the producer's idea. It would be one of those moments along the lines of 'I hear a girl on this track—get one on the phone.'"

"Gimme Shelter" is about seeking shelter in a dystopian world that's about to be ravaged by an approaching storm. Mick Jagger does his best to convey terror, but the fear doesn't hit home till Merry Clayton's higher-pitched second vocal track kicks in. Her voice cracks a couple of times under the strain of her hyperemotional delivery, and at one point you can hear an amazed Mick Jagger say "Whoo!" as though he's stepping out of the song to comment on it and then jumping back in. In Mick's case, "Whoo!" is another way of saying "that producer was right."

In 1968, somebody gave me a ticket to hear Jimi Hendrix at Hunter College. He started off with "Purple Haze," the last line to the first verse of which is "'Scuse me while I kiss the sky." That's an appropriately druggy line, but a lot of people thought it crossed another boundary and that Hendrix was saying "'Scuse me while I kiss this guy."

Every published version of the lyrics of "Purple Haze" includes the correct phrasing. But on the night I heard him, when he got to that line, Hendrix turned stage right, pointed at bass player Noel Redding, and said, in a very clear voice—and even though the music was thunderously loud, the instruments always go silent at this point so the singer can be heard—"'Scuse me while I kiss this guy."

The audience went nuts. Of course it did! Kissing the sky is a gauzy image at best. You can't see it, so how can you react to it? Whereas the in-joke of one man smooching another sent us all into a state of childlike glee. Clearly Hendrix knew he could set his audience on fire in the first verse of the first song by playing off a silly misapprehension. Did a producer tell Hendrix to make that change? Doesn't matter. It worked.

When the Detroit band Alice Cooper auditioned for producer Bob Ezrin, Ezrin listened to their music and said he would produce their album but that they had to relearn everything and develop a "signature." Told that no one in the band knew what he meant, Ezrin explained: "When you hear the Doors, you know it's the Doors, and when you hear the Beatles, you know it's the Beatles. When you hear Alice

Cooper, you could be any psychedelic band."

So the musicians set up in a barn north of Detroit and practiced ten hours a day until they developed a distinctive sound. For better or worse, their nearest neighbors were patients at a psychiatric hospital, and when that captive audience roared its approval, the band knew (or at least told themselves) that they had a good song.

Alice Cooper was one of the few local bands that made it out of Detroit in those days. There were musical acts who got to the national stage—Bob Seger, Ted Nugent, Grand Funk Railroad—but too many young Detroit musicians just wanted to get together and jam and play gigs and score dope and, when the band they were in fired them, find a "revenge band" and take up where they left off. But without guidance, most of them were not able to move up to the next level. By equating creativity with anarchy, they put a limit on how creative they could be.

Remember, two hundred years before Alice Cooper cut their first record, William Blake had it down cold: "Truth has bounds, Error none."

In the 1960s, when producer Clive Davis was getting his start at Columbia Records, that label's stars included Dinah Shore and Rosemary Clooney Then this crazy new sound called rock 'n' roll came along, and suddenly Clive Davis and his associates had to come to terms with a culture that was turning from martinis and fedoras to pot and Afros. "I knew what the problems were," Davis said, "but I didn't yet know how to fix them." He made a few tentative moves, but his Saul of Tarsus moment didn't come until a few years later when he signed a band called Big Brother and the Holding Company and their lead singer, Janis Joplin.

Goodbye, Dinah. See you, Rosemary.

Not so fast, though. First there had to be some changes. The original version of what would become one of Joplin's biggest hits, "Piece of My Heart," ran longer than four minutes, which meant its radio play would be limited. Too, the chorus wasn't repeated often enough to become the irresistible hook in the version we know today.

Davis put it to Joplin plainly. Without a hit single, Big Brother's first album might sell two or three hundred thousand copies. With a radio hit, it would do twice that, maybe more. Deep-dyed in her generation's skepticism toward The Man, Joplin wasn't pleased with the suggestion, but she went along with Davis's idea to cut the song's length by half for radio play and repeat the chorus with its "come on / come on" hook. (Go back to Chapter 2.3 if you need a refresher on hooks.) "Piece of My Heart" went to number twelve on the charts, and the *Cheap Thrills* album rose to number one, selling more than a million copies.

From there, Clive Davis went on to produce hit after hit. And not: much of his memoir *The Soundtrack of My Life* is the story of artists who ignored his advice and those who took it. As Davis explains it, if Laura Nyro, Loudon Wainwright III, Gil Scott-Heron, Jeff Healey, Taylor Dayne, and Curtis Stigers haven't had the same careers as Simon and Garfunkel, Santana, the Grateful Dead, Rod Stewart, Dionne Warwick, Whitney Houston, and Bruce Springsteen, it's because the members of the first group didn't listen to suggestions offered by Davis that might have propelled them to the stardom of the second.

In a telling anecdote, Davis recalls bumping into John Lennon in a coffee shop and asking him what new music he liked. Apparently the former Beatle had forgotten that he and his then-novice bandmates got their start by copying the music of America's black singer-songwriters, covering songs by Chuck Berry, Fats Domino, and Little Richard until they were savvy enough to write their own. Because Lennon replied, "Clive, let me ask you a question. Do you think Picasso went to the galleries to see what was being painted before he put a brush to canvas?"

The answer, of course, is yes: Picasso's earlier paintings are shaped by artists as diverse as Paul Cézanne and the African mask makers, and even in late life he incorporated the work of Velázquez, Delacroix, and Manet into his own. If you put any Beatles song up against a solo effort by John Lennon, you'll see why it's a good idea to learn from others.

LET'S PUT ON A SHOW

I hope I've shown you how important it is to have a good producer if you're a musician and, by extension, a poet. Now let me give you an example of how this process works in the theater.

A few years ago, I saw a production of Chekhov's *The Cherry Orchard* starring John Turturro and Juliet Rylance as the characters Lopakhin and Varya. In Chekhov's play, a family of penniless aristocrats is about to lose its estate, which includes the cherry orchard of the title, because it must be auctioned off to pay the mortgage. Since the family can't live together anymore, everyone must go off to a separate fate. In an ironic twist, the estate is bought by Ermolai Alexeyevitch Lopakhin, the grandson of a serf who is now a wealthy businessman. The eldest daughter of the family, Barbara Mihailovna, called Varya, loves Lopakhin, who seems to be attracted to her. Were he to marry her, of course, the family could stay on their estate.

In the final act of the production I saw, Varya is telling Lopakhin that she has lined up a job as a housekeeper unless something changes. Lopakhin either doesn't get it or he doesn't care. Varya is packing, and as she turns to look for something, Lopakhin is talking about the weather, how it's sunny but cold. A voice at the door calls him, and he goes out, never to return, as Varya sits on the floor and weeps.

Not much happens. You could almost say nothing happens. But in this production of *The Cherry Orchard*, as Varya turns to look for something, a silent but crucial gesture changes everything. Lopakhin gets down on one knee, just like a man who is about to propose. When the actress playing Varya turns around and sees him, a look of surprise, delight, and fear comes over her face. And what does Lopakhin do? He delivers the weather report, and when he says "there's three degrees of frost" and then falls silent, tears leap from her eyes.

It's one of the most profoundly moving scenes I've ever seen in the theater. Remember what I said in Chapter 1.5 about emotions under pressure? Here the two characters all but detonate. Yet here's the thing: there is nothing at all in the stage directions to say the scene should be played this way. The credit here goes to the director or whoever it was who said, "John, try it this way. Say the lines, but say them haltingly, and as you do so, sink to one knee as though you're going to propose. And Juliet, you'll be answering John as you should, but your heart will be breaking, and you'll let your body say everything the words can't."

In medicine, a second opinion is a good idea. In art, it's essential.

But this doesn't mean you have to do exactly what your producer or director or teacher or writing partner says you should do. I'm talking about collaboration here, not dictatorial orders from one person and blind obedience on the part of the other. I make a point of telling each of my students that if we call their poem A and my response B, what I expect to get back from them in a few days or a week is something we'll call C, which might or might not take my B into account. More often than not, I get back M or X, that is, something that started out as A and then, after it encountered B, became not C but something radically different. In fact, when I look at a student's revision of a poem, half the time I detect no presence at all of my reaction to it, though I know that reaction was a catalyst as the poem evolved into its final form.

What's really exciting to me is watching a young poet write one poem and then another and then ten and thirty and forty until he or she develops an artistic signature, a look on the page as distinctive as someone's handwritten name. What's equally exciting is to watch that signature change. As with Thomas Kuhn's scientific paradigms, the best writers become the self they were meant to be, and then they became someone else. Indeed, they should. Recently I was wondering why some of my favorite poets no longer appealed to me as much as they used to, and then I realized that they were still writing good poems, but it was the same good poem over and over.

Once an artistic signature starts to work, it can be repeated over and over, but it can also enable the artist to grow and try new things. Jim Morrison of the Doors said, "You give people what they want or what they think they want and they'll let you do anything." Actually, later in their career the Doors were known for angering and confusing their audiences, with Morrison himself snarling at his fans and baiting them. Of course, the Doors had already established themselves with bouncy pop hits like "Hello, I Love You" and "Light My Fire," so they could afford to be offensive. As a result, the band appealed to heartland teens but also to listeners who were looking for something edgier, and it's because of their more developed work that they have a place today in the Rock & Roll Hall of Fame.

THE GOLDEN ARCHES

Okay, let's see. Einstein, Emily Dickinson, Mick Jagger, Michel de Montaigne, Jimi Hendrix, Janis Joplin, Anton Chekhov, Jim Morrison . . . in my discussion of how essential second opinions are, have I left anyone out of my catalog of notable artists and thinkers? Of course! Ray Kroc! Why didn't I think of him first? (Slaps forehead.)

Ray Kroc is the entrepreneur who took the tiny one-store McDonald's operation nationwide. He is also responsible for the success of the Filet-O-Fish sandwich, even though initially he opposed adding it to his all-meat offerings. He grudgingly took a bite of the prototype and said it was okay but it'd have more flavor if the sandwich included a slice of cheese. Sales took off. Kind of like adding a bracing trombone flourish at the end of a sad song, yes?

Poet, your Ray Kroc is out there. Find him.

When you do, he will probably not be a hard-charging businessman but a poet like yourself. Unless you're paying someone to be producer, the best way to get good poetic advice is to offer it in return. When you and your partner swap poems, use the following checklist to get the most out of your exchange. You can use this as you talk about individual poems, but I'll add some points to make this checklist useful to you if you and your partner are looking at multiple poems or even putting a collection together. (Like a lot of the smart ideas in *The Knowledge*, I got this one from Barbara.)

Discussion Points for Poem Exchange

Format

- Do lines meander or are they controlled?
- Do lines end with significant words?
- How are stanzas divided, by subject or formally (that is, as couplets, tercets, etc.)?

Language

- Search poems for abstractions and be merciless (except, of course, in places where only an abstraction will do).
- Find places where a simile or metaphor or heightened language of some kind would make the poem more interesting.
- How does the poem end—with an image? If not, you might want to suggest one.

Overall

- Is every poem clear—is it clear enough? Is it too self-explanatory, too mysterious?
- Is it the right length? Does it need an "extra act"? Would it read better if it were compressed?
- Does every poem have an effective title? Remember, a title is a line as important as any other line in the poem.
- Are the poems in the best order? For example, does the sequence begin with a bold poem, make its way through the quieter ones, and end with a bang?
- What title do you want to give these poems? Make it a title that pulls all the poems together.

Talking Points

Think of the person you haven't seen in ten years who taught you that one small thing that made a world of difference: the teacher who repositioned your pencil in your hand so you could write cursive, the camp counselor who showed you where to kick the ball to land it in the night, the stranger you were talking to at a party who said the only way to cook a steak is to braise it slowly in the oven and then sear it quickly in a cast-iron skillet. I think of the police officer I was talking to at a club one night who said the secret to crowd control was never to draw a line in the sand and always give the party in question options ("either your friends can take you home now or I'll have to run you in"). I talked to this gent for five minutes twenty years ago, yet I use his two guidelines every time I teach.

How about you? What are your add-a-slice-of-cheese-to-that-sandwich life hacks? You'll never know what impact they've had on strangers, but you wouldn't keep saying these things if they didn't work. My wife is a gardener, and every time she plants a bush or tree, she goes to Capital City Seafood and buys a mullet or other cheap fish to throw in the hole first.

Prompts

LOVE-LOVE

Find the perfect reader for your poems. Take your time. Finding a perfect reader is like finding a perfect tennis partner. You don't want someone who thrashes you every time, nor do you want to play tennis with someone you're a lot better than. If you're going to do this more than once, you want to play against a partner who wins one or two games out of most matches just as you do something similar. You could even say that finding a perfect reader is like finding a romantic partner. Doesn't your mother or some other wise person in your family say something along the lines of "there are a lot of fish in the sea, and most of them should stay there"? She's right. In poetry as in love: try out a number of possible partners before you sign on the dotted line. By the way, if you do find the perfect poetry partner and discover you're also crazy about each other, marry that person. (I did.)

PLAYS WELL WITH OTHERS

There are so many ways to write collaborative poems that one could compile a separate anthology of examples. Here are three suggestions for collaboration that you can try with at least one partner and as many as you like. (1) Using any prompt in *The Knowledge*, write separate poems, then combine the best features of each of them to produce a single poem. (2) Write a line of poetry, fold the paper so the next person can't see what you wrote, and continue till the poem is done.

Go back and edit fiercely. The French Surrealists practiced this way of writing, which they called Exquisite Corpse. (3) Think of a fixed number of items that go into each line of a poem. Write yours, let others write theirs, and combine. The New York School poets Kenneth Koch and John Ashbery wrote a sestina called "Crone Rhapsody" in which every line included the name of a flower, a tree, a fruit, a game, a famous old lady, and the word "bathtub."

4.4

The Hot Potato Effect

Prose is words in their best order, said Coleridge, and poetry is the best words in the best order. No poet would disagree with that. But when you're putting poems together for a class portfolio or a chapbook or a full-length collection or a live performance, the question of order can get tricky.

The obvious choice is frequently the wrong one. Too many poem collections start out with a modest and shy piece, as though the poet is already apologizing for taking up the reader's time. It's like an inaudible knock: when I have my door open for office hours but am engrossed in reading, sometimes I'll hear a faint noise repeated and look up to find a student saying something along the lines of "I knocked, but I didn't want to disturb you." Or say you're in a crowded room and you see a person you're really drawn to. Are you going to stand twenty feet away and mumble or walk over with your hand out and tell them your name?

Start big. That's one more lesson we can learn from musicians. Almost every concert begins with a loud, fast song. That pace is kept up for a half hour or more; then the band segues into ballads and slow songs. The show ends with a rave-up, though, and often the encore is a surprise of some kind: a crazy experimental song, a long-forgotten hit, a piece by another band altogether.

Whether you're simply writing a twenty-line poem or compiling a chapbook of sixteen pages or putting together a collection of a hundred pages or more, do the same: start big, slow things down, speed up again, and surprise your reader at the end.

In other words, exercise what Emerson identified in General Masséna as his "powers of combination" (Chapter 2.2).

Jack White, best known as a founding member of the White Stripes and for his solo work but also as a member of the Raconteurs, the Dead Weather, and, as you're reading this, probably several other bands that hadn't been formed when I began this paragraph, is known to admonish a drowsy audience for its torpor—"for not participating in the two-way experience of rock & roll," as music writer William Giraldi says. In contrast to European audiences, White thinks that "American audiences are so pampered, feel so entitled, that a concert for them is like a night at the movies," as though they are saying, "I bought my ticket, juggler, now entertain me as I repose."

On the night Giraldi is writing about, Jack White mocks the concert crowd just that way, asking if they think they're at a movie. Most people are seated except for a teenager in the stands who is upright and animated. "I'm proud of you, boy," says Jack White, and then tells the stage manager to give the kid every piece of White Stripes merchandise he can lay his hands on, and "minutes later, the manager can be seen hauling a cache of presents up to the first tier."

Here Jack White is closing the gap between artist and audience in a way that's hardly typical. If you look at concert footage or see a photo of some kids losing their minds at a club, you might get the idea that the artist-audience transaction is a one-way street, that a more or less indifferent group of musicians gets up on stage, and a pack of idol worshippers appear out of nowhere to howl, mosh, and spill beer. From

Beethoven to Beyoncé, it's as though the gods are in the footlights, and we fallen mortals in the pit.

But if you talk to people who write songs and play in bands, as I do, you get a totally different picture. Every band I've ever talked to (and the ones I was in briefly) proceeds by trial and error; they try out songs, musical styles, attire, and personnel and adjust as they go. There is in the exchange between artist and audience a shock of recognition as the audience looks at the artist and sees what it can be, just as the artist looks out at the throng of ecstatic faces and thinks, "As you are, so I was—who am I now?" In the exchange that takes place between artist and audience, both agree not to answer these questions but to ask them.

It's this exchange between speaker and listener, between writer and reader, between singer and audience that is at the heart of any art. Bob Mould of Husker Dü espouses what he calls the hot potato theory: "It's like inspiration is a hot potato you pull out of the oven and then toss to someone else. So we listen, we become fans, we become inspired, we create, and somehow the work we create eventually finds its way back to the ones who inspired us."

What is an audience? Here's a story that will define the word "audience" for you. Producer Butch Vig played a tape of his latest find to a few friends; it would become an album called *Nevermind* by a little-known group called Nirvana. The little audience didn't know that the album would go on to sell thirty million copies, introduce alternative rock to a mainstream audience, and be named by *Rolling Stone* as one of the most influential albums of all time. They just liked the rawness and intimacy of Kurt Cobain's voice, Dave Grohl's thunderous drumming, the amateurish passion of the guitars, the catchy hooks.

When the tape ended, there was silence. And then someone said "play it again."

That's what an audience is. The concept of audience has never changed and never will. The first time a couple of cavemen beat rocks together while a long-haired cave mama shouted her version of the hunter-gatherer blues, her listeners either shrugged and crept back into the shadows or said "play it again."

A DEFINITE MAYBE

If you're not ready to put a book of poems together, by now I bet you're at least ready to send a manuscript to a magazine. I'll say more about that in the afterword to *The Knowledge*, but for the moment, let me send you to any of the helpful websites that list presses and journals looking for work, including the New Pages, Poets & Writers, Authors Publish, and Entropy sites (I use the latter regularly). Most magazines ask you to send three to six poems.

So let's say you're looking at your poems and find ten that look as though they stand a fighting chance. Now winnow that down to, say, four poems. Remember that the editor who will be looking at your work may have seen another two hundred poems that day, so how are you going to snooker them into choosing one of yours?

Call me superstitious, but here's what I'd do. Yes, each of your four poems is a gem or it wouldn't have made the cut, but you can't help having favorites. I'd say lead with your second-favorite poem of the bunch. Then comes your third-favorite, then the one that barely squeaked into the final four, thus putting your absolute top favorite surefire they-can't-say-no instant classic of a poem in the final position.

Why? Because I see the editor reading the first poem and saying, "Wow—really good!" and feeling a little skeptical about the second and wondering by the third poem if they were right to love the first poem so much and then leaping up and shouting, "Hallelujah!" when they read the masterpiece that is poem number four.

Does this method work? I can give you a clear and decisive "maybe" in response to that question. I haven't kept records, but I'm pretty sure that a lot of my number four poems have been taken over the years. Actually, I'm even more sure that the second or third poem has been the one that was chosen, and I can guarantee you that the next time you're around a group of poets talking about their publication records, you'll hear at least one of those poets say, "And they took the poem I liked least, the one I threw in at the last minute to fill out my manuscript."

You may recall that in the chapter on delivery systems (Chapter 3.4) I suggested that using a set form like the sestina or ghazal is, since you have to follow a template, a way to make yourself write the poem. The same goes for the order you put your poems in before you send them out. Use my template or come up with your own, but whatever you do, send those poems out.

Talking Points

Think of the concerts you've been to in the last year. How'd they start? What happened in the middle? How'd they end? You can do the same with an album. If it's a group whose work you're familiar with, appoint yourself producer and move songs that are in the wrong position to the right one and take out songs that don't work and put in songs that do.

Do the same with a collection of poems or, even better, six collections. How do they begin, continue, conclude? Does a particular collection go from start to finish or is it in sections? If the latter, how does the sectioning work? Should there be more sections, fewer, none? What changes, if any, would make the collection you're holding work even better than it does already?

Prompts

CHAPBOOK

A chapbook is a wonderful middle stage between a single poem and a full-length collection. There's no set length, but typically a chapbook runs roughly 16–32 pages. The term comes from "chap," which derives from an Old English word for "trade," and so-called chapmen would lug boxes of the affordable, pamphlet-sized texts around town and sell them on the street. Sometimes poets will publish three or more chapbooks, pull them together, make whatever changes are needed so the whole is coherent, and publish that as a full-length collection.

In the last chapter I suggested that you find a perfect reader for your individual poems. If you've been lucky there, put together a chapbook and show that to your perfect reader. If you go to the Entropy website that I mentioned earlier, you'll find a variety of presses that specialize in chapbook publication.

SEND-OUT PARTY

You can put together a manuscript of three to five poems and send them to a magazine any old time, but it can be a lot of fun to get together with a handful of poet-pals and make an evening of it. I'll leave the drinks and snacks up to you, but you use this opportunity to research markets, lightly edit each other's work, and put together some packets of poems.

When you use Entropy or one of the other market sites I suggested earlier, you'll see that almost all magazines permit simultaneous submissions these days, meaning you can send the same poems to two or more magazines with the understanding that you'll alert the editor of one magazine if the poems are taken by another.

Just keep good records. The format for a submissions log is something else you and your poet-pals can discuss. Keep it simple: mine just has the name of the magazine(s), the date, and the poems submitted. If the send-out party is at someone else's house, make sure you clean up the mess before you leave.

ENTERTAINMENT TONIGHT

There's nothing more fun for a poet than to read their own work to an audience. Unfortunately, it's not always the other way around. There's nothing more hideous and squirm-making than to sit there in your folding chair while someone who hasn't worked on their presentation mumbles or rushes through their poems while you're wishing you were someplace else—anyplace else, actually.

But just as you can work with one or more friends to put together a chapbook or magazine submission, so you can do the same as you plan your reading. Show the others the fifteen to twenty poems you're choosing from, let them suggest the ten or twelve that might work best in public, and put them in the right order (as with a single poem or group of poems, make sure you start and finish big).

At this point you'll want to go off by yourself for a half hour or so and write some sentences you'll use to introduce your poems as a whole and then as comments on each separate poem. I know, I know: there's always someone out there who'll tell you that "the poems should speak for themselves." Don't listen to that person. A good poem takes a while to digest. You'll help your audience digest your poems and avoid upsetting their poetry stomachs if you say a few words about each before reading it: "This poem is about something that happened to me when I was five," say, or "Have you ever wondered if there's life on other planets? This poem asks that same question." Remember, poetry isn't sacred. It's too important for that. A poetry reading is showbiz as surely as an arena rock concert is or a Broadway play. When you face an audience, don't set your poems up as holy objects to be worshipped from afar. Sell them.

And when you read those poems, take your time. The greatest lesson I've learned about acting is from Levon Helm's memoir *This Wheel's on Fire*, where the singer is talking to Tommy Lee Jones when they're driving to the set of *Coal Miner's Daughter.* Having never acted, Levon is nervous, but Tommy Lee tells him that acting is two things: not saying as much as you usually say, and not saying it as fast. I haven't watched a film or TV show or video or home movie or given a poetry reading the same way since.

A few years back, my wife, Barbara, was invited to give a poetry reading at the 92nd Street Y in New York with Billy Collins. She went up a day early to practice, and as I approached the hotel room door the next afternoon, I heard a faint murmuring. When I knocked and she let me in, I saw she had moved the furniture around and built a stage of sorts and had spent that whole day going through her reading again and again. Billy is one of the great poets and readers of poetry ever, but when the reading took place at the 92nd Street Y the next evening, Barbara did as fantastic a job as he did. As a trailing spouse and a poet myself, I took a lot of pleasure in hanging back and seeing people who weren't as familiar with her work as they were with Billy's rush up to Barbara afterward to say, "My god, that was magnificent!" and simply, "I love your poems."

[illegible]

[illegible] as an arena rock concert or a Broadway play. [illegible] in demand [illegible] don't see [illegible] agents [illegible] to be [illegible] from [illegible] them.

And when you read these memoirs, take your time. The greatest lesson I've learned about acting is [illegible] in his memoir [illegible] the [illegible] is talking [illegible] Tommy Lee Jones [illegible] the set of *Coal Miner's Daughter*. [illegible] is nervous [illegible] Tommy Lee telling him [illegible] as much as you usually [illegible] TV show or video [illegible]

[illegible]

[illegible]

[illegible] Those are [illegible]

4.5

Be Generous to Everyone, Especially Yourself

Occasionally I'm asked what quality matters to me most in a poem. More than anything else, I look for generosity. Earlier I mentioned that I start my day with the four poems that the services I subscribe to send me. A lot of them are dandies, and all of them feature language that's organized intelligently, but many of the poems I get first thing in the morning lack cohesion. It's just statement, statement. Statement, statement, statement. They're smart statements, but they don't exactly fly into your heart.

It's a little like watching an experimental movie or a piece of music where you get a scene or a few chords and then there's a pause and you get something else and you're sitting there trying to figure out how the whole thing hangs together. Something is missing—a certain something-ness, you might say.

The poets who write these kinds of poems seem to be holding something back, whereas others give us everything we want and more.

Shakespeare is the greatest writer for exactly that reason. Nobody gives us more. I love Dante, Blake, Keats, Whitman, and Ginsberg for the same reason. But there are plenty of generous poets writing today: Amy Gerstler, Lucia Perillo, Sherman Alexie, the aforementioned Barbara Hamby. This time last year I fell hard for Jack Gilbert, a poet I had admired up to that point but hadn't come to appreciate fully. I got so involved with his work that I began to write poems like his. I'm serious. If you saw what I'd written, you wouldn't think it's me.

Here are some poets I plan to teach in the near future, many of whom I'm discovering for the first time: Craig van Rooyen, Patricia Smith, Heidi Shuler, Lynne Knight, Albert Haley, Ishmael Reed, Fatimah Asghar, Gregory Corso. The great thing about living poets is that you can call them up and tell them how wonderful they are. In Chapter 3.3 there's a poem called "Fack You" by Dzvinia Orlowsky. When I saw that poem, I wrote Dzvinia to say how much I liked it, and now we have a nice little correspondence going. So don't be shy. You can locate anybody on the Internet these days, and when you find somebody whose work you love, tell them so. You'd be surprised at the friendships that develop. As I heard the poet Laure-Anne Bosselaar say once, the best thing about poetry is the friends it brings us.

I always tell my students that when you write a poem, you're making a gift for someone. It's not for you—what fun is it to buy presents for yourself and open them and say, "Oh, a present!" Your poem begins with you, but it's for somebody else. The poem isn't your reward. Your reward is the delight that readers take in it. We've all gotten lousy presents. When you get a real stinker, you say, "Oh, gee, thanks" and put it aside. But when you get a good one, you're so excited. And the person who gave it to you is happier than you are.

Yes, do be generous. Who's the greatest writer, the one we can learn the most from? I've already named him: Shakespeare. And he's the greatest because he's the most generous. Here's the speech between Oberon and Puck in Act 2, Scene 1 of *A Midsummer Night's Dream* in which Puck is sent to fetch the herb that will create the delicious mayhem in the play:

OBERON
My gentle Puck, come hither. Thou rememberest
Since once I sat upon a promontory,
And heard a mermaid on a dolphin's back
Uttering such dulcet and harmonious breath
That the rude sea grew civil at her song
And certain stars shot madly from their spheres,
To hear the sea-maid's music.

PUCK
I remember.

OBERON
That very time I saw, but thou couldst not,
Flying between the cold moon and the earth,
Cupid all arm'd: a certain aim he took
At a fair vestal throned by the west,
And loosed his love-shaft smartly from his bow,
As it should pierce a hundred thousand hearts;
But I might see young Cupid's fiery shaft
Quench'd in the chaste beams of the watery moon,
And the imperial votaress passed on,
In maiden meditation, fancy-free.
Yet mark'd I where the bolt of Cupid fell:
It fell upon a little western flower,
Before milk-white, now purple with love's wound,
And maidens call it love-in-idleness.
Fetch me that flower; the herb I shew'd thee once:
The juice of it on sleeping eye-lids laid
Will make or man or woman madly dote
Upon the next live creature that it sees.
Fetch me this herb; and be thou here again
Ere the leviathan can swim a league.

PUCK
I'll put a girdle round about the earth
In forty minutes.

Isn't that wonderful? Oberon's speech makes me deliriously happy. He could have simply told Puck to "bring me such-and-such an herb." But no: Oberon tells a story involving a mermaid, a dolphin, the moon, Cupid, and a dozen other elements. He didn't have to, but he did. What a gift!

Some writers look at the objects of this world and put a coat of paint on them so that they appear a little different, and that passes as art. But Shakespeare never gives you a new version of what already exists. He doesn't depict reality. He creates reality. It's the difference between someone going to a store and buying you a piece of furniture or disappearing into their workshop for weeks and making one for you that's more beautiful than anything the store could offer. Which gift pleases you more?

Because Shakespeare spends so much time woodshedding, the result is a heightening of language fueled by desire, fear, anticipation, all the emotions that arise when you're on the brink of a new experience. In his introduction to *The Essential Shakespeare*, Ted Hughes writes about the Elizabethans' obsession with "the fortissimo eloquence of inner lives magnificently tortured." What those audiences wanted, writes Hughes, "with a kind of greed, was the language of more and more affecting and awesome emotions, more and more harrowing situations, more irresistible, stunning, hair-raising eloquence."

REMEMBER, START SMALL

Sometimes the easiest way to be generous is to simply sustain a simple premise, as in this poem by Katrina Papouskaya.

Welcome to the Office

Osmond, who sits over there, has a lot of crumbs in his keyboard

because he eats his lunch
at his desk, and he always eats a ham and Swiss on rye sandwich while watching the latest
NFL game. He claims he is watching a training video if you ask, and his headphones are
plugged in, so no one can technically say otherwise, but we know he is not.

The girl who's got pigs decorating every crevice of her cubicle is Loreta. Loreta loves pigs,
and the girl with cubicle opposite hers, Marietta, loves cows. Marietta drinks her
morning coffee from a cow mug with four udders at the bottom that serve as legs keeping
the heat from touching our very impressionable office desks (pen scratches rarely come off).

Marietta goes to church and is nice to everyone. Marietta also had an ex-boyfriend
who ended up murdering the girl he dated after Marietta. We don't talk to Marietta about it, but
sometimes you can find her crying over the phone in the stairwell to her mom.
We aren't sure what she's crying about, and we never ask. Best to keep busy.

Sandy sits over there in the cubicle across from hers. Wear the proper office attire
around Sandy. No bra straps must show. Make sure your blouses are completely opaque.
If you don't follow the proper office attire, Sandy will tell the boss. You don't want Sandy to tell
the boss. The boss will call you privately into their office and tell you

that there are men in this office, and would you please wear a blouse

that isn't quite so tight
around your bosom. You can't help that a button popped one time. Never mind that it was
your favorite blouse. You will never be able to wear it to this office again. In that corner
sits Clarkson. Clarkson will roll his eyes at whatever the supervisor tells him to do

but the supervisor will smile and pretend not to have noticed it. He will tell you you don't seem
confident in the job even when you are. Don't suggest changes to his process. Sometimes
changes will make sense, but he won't make them. He will use informal text speak
in emails. You will wonder why he can get away with it and why you have to refrain from

using contractions and only allow one smiley in an informal email per month. He will complain
about the pay and tell other employees "no" with an attitude. No one will say anything to him.
You will not be able to do the same for fear of appearing bitchy. You will be right. You
will look bitchy. Don't be bitchy if you want to keep this job. Be proper and polite at all times.

Tuck in your blouse. Make sure your pencil skirt is not too tight. If your boss sees
that your pencil skirt is too tight, she will call you into her office. You do not want to be called
into her office. The boss wears pencil skirts and blazers that are appropriate. The boss
has an essential oils diffuser in her office that helps her sinuses. When you go into her office

to ask for something and she is busy, she will smile and nod but you will know from her tone
that she is busy. Do not linger in the office if she is busy. The boss used to be a party girl
in college. She always jokes about her "former days" and you aren't sure what that means
except that sometimes she will crack an inappropriate joke. The boss sneaks

into your section's small birthday gatherings to eat the cheesecake. Always invite the boss to
these parties and let her eat the cheesecake. Carmen is here, far away from your cubicle. Carmen
wears feathers in her hair and sometimes bandannas. Carmen will become
your closest friend, so it is a shame that you sit on opposite ends of the office. Carmen will

sometimes come to your desk and your supervisor will tell her to not sit on your counter
because the counters in this office are rickety. What she is trying to say is that Carmen
has to leave. Your supervisor does not like the mingling in this office. You and Carmen will
gossip about your supervisor and the boss during your half hour of lunch. Always go out

to lunch outside the office. You do not want to be overheard. If you are overheard, the boss will
call you into her office. You do not want to be called into her office.

We've all had jobs like this. We've all had jobs of which we can say "the job stinks and the boss is a jerk and my coworkers are slackers except for one or two I really like." But one of the best things a poem can do is take a universal situation and stipple it with so many particulars that we can truly relate, truly feel we are not alone in a world of tedium. The more we see—the more Katrina Papouskaya lets us see—the more the scenario becomes comical, that is to say, tolerable. "Welcome to the Office" is one more example of Ted Solotaroff's observation that a poem helps us to organize and partly comprehend our experience.

PLEASURE FIRST

No matter what or how we write, the important thing to remember is that all your audience wants is pleasure. In his memoirs, composer John Adams describes how he wandered for years in the desert of atonalism and then detoured through the wilderness of music based on an aesthetic of randomness and anarchy. In California in the 1970s he built a synthesizer and began playing electronic music at "happenings." He liked to use ambient sounds, and once recorded the buzz of flies hovering over dog feces.

One day in 1976, while driving across the hilly Californian landscape, he listened to some Wagner on the car cassette player. He was seized by the sheer expressive power of the music. "This was not just music about desire," he says. "It was desire itself." Here's the full quote:

> What Wagner cared about was making the intensity of his emotions palpable to the listener. His harmonies, restless and forever migrating toward a new tonal center, moved between tension and resolution in an uncanny way that constantly propelled the listener forward. The melodic leaps, always singable, gave shape and direction to the churning harmonic movement beneath. This was not just music about desire. It was desire itself, and the emotional and sensual power it possessed was inescapable. Wagner's music was grounded in enormous technical and intellectual sophistication, but its overriding effect was something that, I realized, had been absent from my avant-garde experiments: a sense of ravishment.

Adams is describing his conversion experience here. After his flirtation with overly cerebral music that got him nowhere, he wrote such full, rich works as *Nixon in China* and *The Death of Klinghoffer* that won him audience acclaim as well as a Pulitzer Prize and five Grammys. See? Generosity pays.

As you are generous to others, be generous to yourself. Among other things, this can mean going down new paths. Once I had established myself as a poet, I began to get requests for my poems but also for statements about poetry: essays, reviews of poetry books, and so on. Okay, but after a while, enough was enough. I was tired of being monolingual, so I decided to learn another language. Literally: at a time when a lot of people think about retiring, I started taking guitar lessons and spending as much time with musicians as I could. From there, I started going to clubs and shows and writing about them for magazines and newspapers. As of today, I've gotten two books and dozens of articles and reviews out of this new life of mine.

So music writing became a new part of my life and will continue to be. Ten years ago, I didn't know I was going to be doing any of that. There's no telling what I'll be doing ten years hence. Whatever it is, it'll be in addition to poetry. I can't think of anything I want to do more than to write poems that other people want to read. Like the Osip Mandelstam I refer to in this book's foreword, I want to live not for poetry but through poetry.

A Facebook friend, Cary Bertoncini, posted this recently:

> Poetry makes me better at doing my day job: teaching. Poetry makes me a better father, husband, lover, friend. Poetry is how I am—it's the way I see the world around me, the way I make my cup of coffee in the morning, the way I see miracles in the little cat feet impressions in the snow outside my apartment in Korea and the way I carry on conversations with the azure-winged magpies outside my apartment here in China. Poetry changes the air I breathe, the way I eat my food, how I see my baby dancing with his mother's bra on his head. Poetry makes life more worth living by making everything in life more alive, more real, more immediate, more essential.

This time last year, I was standing at a hotel room window in Valparaíso, Chile, looking out at a ship in the harbor. The person in the room next to mine may have been looking out at the same ship and thinking, "A merchant vessel." What I saw was a shipful of poems. They were clambering over the side and heading my way.

Talking Points

What song or movie or famous painting could have used more of what made it distinctive in the first place? Or less? A lot of visual artworks are criticized for being too Minimalist. Do you agree? Plays are sometimes shortened depending on the audience; a standard *Hamlet* runs for close to three hours, but there's a two-hour version as well. There are editions of *Moby-Dick* with the "extra" chapters removed, but I think they give Melville's novel an encyclopedic fullness that celebrates life's richness as opposed to Ahab's mean and narrow view.

Look at your earliest poems. I wouldn't be surprised if they were skimpier than the ones you're writing now. I'm not necessarily recommending that you add to those poems now, because it can be hard to plug back into an energy whose time has come and gone. Besides, your early poems might be just fine. Or maybe you were too generous in those days. I don't always agree with the idea that less is more, but sometimes the best gift is a simple one.

Prompts

THE FOUR SEASONS

List the four seasons on a piece of paper, leaving room between them. Associate a food with each one and also a person: not someone you know but a person with summer characteristics, say. Associate a kind of music with each (samba with summer, Beethoven with late fall) as well as a book, a color palette, and an activity (picnicking in spring, napping in the dead of winter).

Keep developing your four stanzas or paragraphs until you get a complete picture of either a season you want to concentrate on or a full year.

INERTIA

Make a list of things that move: the sun, cars, people in general, your Uncle Bob. Now make a list of things that don't move: trees, mountains, skyscrapers, a favorite dress that's hanging in your closet right now.

From the first list, pick a moving object, make it stationary, and describe the results—a world in which the sun shines all the time, say. Or have Uncle Bob stand motionless in front of his open refrigerator for decades as the world around him changes and he stays the same.

Now do the same with something from the second list. You could do a lot with a world in which skyscrapers slide from city to city, visiting (or perhaps warring with) each other and crushing (or perhaps gracefully skirting) the things that get in their way. Or imagine that dress of yours going out for a night on the town.

This is one of those exercises in which you'll create much more than you'll use. Most likely, you'll find you want to concentrate on an item from one of your lists. Or it could be that your two items will start to relate to each other in some way that you couldn't have foreseen. Either way, keep the material you don't use in a notebook or computer file; you never know when it might prove handy.

OVERDETERMINATION

In Chapter 2.2, it was pointed out that Freud gives writers one of the most useful terms in their vocabulary when he talks about "overdetermination" in dreams and, by extension, works of art. An ordinary event is determined: you touch a hot stove, you get burned. But a dream is overdetermined; it may include a childhood memory, a recent occurrence, one or more anxieties or desires, and so on. The same is true for artistic creations. No good writing is monolithic; even TV sitcoms have a plot, a subplot, and several incidental episodes.

Write as many sentences or lines of poetry as you can that are overdetermined by creating a formula you'll reuse every time (in Chapter 4.3, there's a reference to a poem of this type, John Ashbery and Kenneth Koch's "Crone Rhapsody"). Let there be a color, a city, and an artist's name in every line, say ("Cleveland was mauve the day Picasso came"). Or a U.S. president, a food, and a method of transport ("Eisenhower ate bagels on the Paris metro"). Or a religious group, a sport, and a form of currency ("The Jains are playing jai alai with the rupiahs they found").

Obviously this is one more of those exercises where you'll want to take your time, surprise yourself, create much more than you'll end up using, and save the rest.

THE HAPPIEST YEAR OF YOUR LIFE

Write down quickly as many of your favorite things as you can: a food (kiwis), an activity (going to the movies on hot summer afternoons), something you like to see (an ugly, happy baby), a favorite article of clothing (that shirt you've had for ten years). Avoid generically pleasant activities (watching a popular TV sitcom); instead, be specific and personal. Let your list sit for a while. Then add to it and keep doing this until you can't think of anything else.

Now imagine that you enjoyed all these things a year ago, the happiest year of your life. Choose the things you want to write about and the order you want to follow and get started: "That year we went to the movies every afternoon, and as we left the theater, we blinked in the sunlight and moved slowly, like people waking up after a long sleep. And then we bought kiwis. . . ." This could be a very long poem. It should also be a lot of fun to write.

4.6

No Atheists in Foxholes

A former student says she wants to get back to writing, so I say write about some childhood memory. I'm doing the same thing, I tell her. I'm writing a poem about my brother's invisible friend Stephen. Once my parents pulled the car over because my brother saw Stephen waiting by the side of the road. We made room for him in the back seat, and he got in, my parents in front and the three boys in the back, one of them invisible. My brother was thirty-two at the time. Just kidding: I should have said my brother's invisible childhood friend.

I told my former student to send me what she had in a week. Two weeks went by. Then I got this: "I wrote down brief overviews of 27 childhood memories. No poems, but lots of good fodder and things cropping up that I hadn't thought about in years."

A few days later, this: "Your support the other week has helped me push through my big creativity block. I have co-written my first-ever song and have plans to write one a month toward the end of making an album with a friend."

Shortly after that: "I am also collaborating with an amazing artist near here, writing a series of poems based on his drawings. I will have five by the middle of the month and thirty by sometime this year so we can send it out as a fine arts book."

See what happens when you put yourself out? What happens doesn't have to be what you thought would happen. That sure wasn't the case here. In Chapter 1.4 I quote Palestinian poet Taha Muhammad Ali as saying that writing poems is like playing billiards, that you aim over here to strike over there. My former student just wanted to write one good poem and ended up with enough work to keep her busy for the next two years.

You can call her process reflecting or recalling or journaling or woodshedding or whatever you want, but I call it praying, not in the narrow sense of getting down on one's knees but in the broader one that a lot of religious orders practice, namely prayer through action. Monks and nuns spend a lot of time in church, but they spend more time clothing and feeding the poor, and the world is a better place for it.

In the summer of 1825, young Ralph Waldo Emerson took a break from his theological studies to work on his Uncle Ladd's farm near Newton, Massachusetts. There he met a laborer known to history only as "a Methodist named Tarbox" who told Emerson "that men were always praying, and that all prayers were granted." The idea of constant prayer was not new to Emerson, writes his biographer Robert D. Richardson, but Emerson "first felt its force for real life" there in his uncle's fields.

What is prayer? In its simplest form, prayer is an address to a deity. But in his essay "Self-Reliance," Emerson says that "prayer is in all action": in the farmer kneeling to weed his field, for example. And clearly Emerson means mindful action: no farmer wakes at midmorning and says, "Gee, I wonder what I should do today?"

So when I say my ex-student prayed, what I mean is that she acted but in a mindful and determined way. She kept praying—kept writing—and the result was not the one poem she wanted when she wanted it but songs and, later, an entirely different set of poems. So her prayers were answered in a way that was different from what she expected but in a very satisfying way. And they were answered not because she asked once but because she kept praying.

Emerson's sense of prayer as mindful action appeals to my students here at Florida State, especially as graduation nears and the world of work beckons. In this job market, you can say of poetry classrooms what is said often of foxholes: there are no atheists there. My students are prayerful, though in the Emersonian way, which is to say they pray by doing, because they know that before they find their place in the world, they have a journey ahead of them.

When you go to an airline website to plan a trip, you're asked whether you want a one-way or a multicity ticket. You have the same two options when it comes to your life's journey as well, because some travelers fly like an arrow to their target while others stop in a few other places before they reach their final destination. I was a one-way passenger. I started teaching at FSU when I was twenty-four and never left. Why leave Eden? Stay away from the apples and the talking snakes and you'll be fine, I figured.

But as many and maybe more travelers take the multicity route. Take my student Joanna, who double-majored in creative writing and theater. After a brief stab at the bohemian life of the New York playwright, she decided against that and took the law-school admissions test. She was admitted and set her sights on a lifetime of legal work.

But then Joanna realized that what she really wanted to do was help others. Her next stop was an adjunct position at a local community college. From there she went on to teach ninth grade, where she found herself mired in local bureaucracy and school politics. She could do more good by moving beyond the local level, she figured, so Joanna got a master's in higher education administration and is now in a doctoral program that she loves, preparing for a life of teaching and research devoted to improving outcomes for students at all levels.

Ben is another multicity traveler. He wrote a master's thesis under my direction, a collection of poems, but was also the lead singer of a band that signed with a major label and started touring. Ben tired quickly of the lifestyle and decided to become a teacher. However, teaching freshman comp as an adjunct at three different schools took its toll as well, so Ben enrolled in an online Ph.D. program in technical communication and is now a professor at a big state university in the Midwest. Which doesn't mean he forgot the work he did with me. "I wasn't able to find my identity as a scholar until I made connections with what I'd done in the past," he says. "Once I saw those connections I realized that I am still a poet and strive for the poetic, but that training informs my work in ways I never expected."

Another former student, Laura, is what I call a one-way traveler: she knew what she wanted from the beginning, which was to get into trade publishing. Like Joanna, she wrote a creative undergraduate thesis, and like her, Laura headed to New York, where she juggled unpaid editorial work at a small press with a magazine job and took literature classes at night.

Then came her big break. Laura became a publisher's assistant at a major press. At first that meant fetching coffee and answering phones, and then her responsibilities increased, and now she's a book editor with a great future ahead of her. "With every project I work on, titles that I acquire, and young agents I connect with," Laura says, "I feel this goal becoming more and more tangible." Already, she says, she has an office "with an actual door."

All three of my former students are living fulfilled, creative lives because they practiced prayer in the Emersonian manner: not kneeling to ask for something but through mindful action. And as Tarbox promised, their prayers were answered, if not always in ways they foresaw.

Oh, I should have mentioned that there's a third choice when you buy an airline ticket. In addition to one-way and multicity, there's round trip. But that's the thing about praying the Emersonian way: there's no such thing as a round trip. You never end up where you started. Tarbox knew that. He wouldn't have known what an airplane was, but he knew that all prayers are answered, that every life is transformed, even if you don't know when or how. All you have to do is keep praying.

SPEECHES, LETTERS, AND MORE

Prayers are as old as any other human artifact, and many a poem takes the actual form of a prayer. Let's look at one of those and then consider some other templates, some common forms (tests, applications, licenses, notices, summonses, transcripts, receipts) that are part and parcel of our daily lives. The poem-as-prayer I have in mind is this one by Gerard Manley Hopkins.

Pied Beauty

Glory be to God for dappled things—
For skies of couple-colour as a brinded cow;
For rose-moles all in stipple upon trout that swim;
Fresh-firecoal chestnut-falls; finches' wings;
Landscape plotted and pieced—fold, fallow, and plough;
And áll trádes, their gear and tackle and trim.

All things counter, original, spare, strange;
Whatever is fickle, freckled (who knows how?)
With swift, slow; sweet, sour; adazzle, dim;
He fathers-forth whose beauty is past change:
Praise him.

A prayer of praise, "Pied Beauty" celebrates everything that is "freckled," that has more than one color or that changes color as the sky does or a coal fire. The world's kaleidoscopic beauty is the gift of its creator, says Hopkins, who was a Jesuit priest, but you don't have to be a believer to love this variety-is-the-spice-of-life idea as well as the poet's succinct and masterful handling of it.

A prayer is a type of speech, but so is a speech. Most speeches are pretty humdrum. Some really soar, like Martin Luther King Jr.'s "I Have a Dream" speech. And then plenty of poems are speeches as well. Allen Ginsberg's "America" is an address to our splendid, confused, and deeply flawed (just like all the others) nation. Like a lot of speeches, this one is meant to motivate and includes lines like these:

> America when will you be angelic?
> When will you take off your clothes?
> When will you look at yourself through the grave?
> When will you be worthy of your million Trotskyites?
> America why are your libraries full of tears?
> America when will you send your eggs to India?
> I'm sick of your insane demands.

Walt Whitman was Ginsberg's poetry parent, and he, too, used the speech template frequently. In this short poem, Whitman addresses not an entire nation but one of its less fortunate citizens.

> To a Common Prostitute
>
> Be composed—be at ease with me—I am Walt Whitman, liberal and lusty as Nature;
> Not till the sun excludes you, do I exclude you;
> Not till the waters refuse to glisten for you, and the leaves to rustle for you, do my words
> refuse to glisten and rustle for you.
>
> My girl, I appoint with you an appointment—and I charge you that you make preparation
> to be worthy to meet me,
> And I charge you that you be patient and perfect till I come.
>
> Till then, I salute you with a significant look, that you do not forget me.

By the way, a speech doesn't have to be a speech-speech. Ginsberg's "America" has all the earmarks of a big, noisy public address (and there are fabulous recordings of him doing just that), but Whitman's poem is clearly an interior monologue. The last line is a tip-off that the speech has taken place entirely in his head. Poor Walt was too shy to actually say anything.

A template closely related to the speech is that of the letter. Both are forms of address, the first spoken and the second written to a person or persons. Or an insect, if you are Emily Dickinson.

Bee! I'm expecting you!
Was saying Yesterday
To Somebody you know
That you were due—

The Frogs got Home last Week—
Are settled, and at work—
Birds, mostly back—
The Clover warm and thick—

You'll get my Letter by
The seventeenth; Reply
Or better, be with me—
Yours, Fly.

In our day, one of the most hilarious and brainy uses of the letter template is by Amy Newman, whose *Dear Editor* is entirely composed of cover letters to editors that begin with something like

Dear Editor:

Please consider the enclosed poems for publication. They are from my manuscript *X = Pawn Capture*

and end with a similar kind of boilerplate language:

Thank you for your consideration, and for reading. I have enclosed an SASE, and look forward to hearing from you.

Sincerely,
Amy Newman

Every published poet in the world has written just such a letter many times, and it's a form that almost never varies. But Newman's letters do. As *Dear Editor* goes on, the letters get longer, needier, and more deliciously demented. Well into the book, you'll encounter a letter like this.

20 November

Dear Editor:

Please consider the enclosed poems for publication. They are from my manuscript, *X = Pawn Capture*, a lyrical study of the history of chess as my grandfather misrepresented it to me because he loved to tell his stories or, if you like the sound of this better, because I was too young to comprehend his indifference to me. In any case I preferred more my grandmother's understanding of a story, how her calendar was full of images of needles and flames and rushes of wheat, all standing for the way a young girl was left to fend for herself when the Romans decided to make a saint of her. We would sit in front of the stove while something proceeded though its permutations in order to be consumed by evening, and she'd speak of Saint Panacea's stepmother, Margherita di Locarno Sesia, who stabbed the little girl with a spindle because she was so pure, and I would imagine *Rapunzel, Rapunzel, let down your hair*, and castles of stone hewn out of quarries and bright-stepping horses with braided manes.

While the ashy length of my grandfather's cigar would measure the evening's disappointments by increments, the part of my brain built for learning and memory was focused on the strength of the hair follicle required for a healthy man to climb a high tower braced only by the golden length of her hair. If I could have transferred these thoughts to that part of the brain that processes motivation and emotion, or reading or language, I could write how Rapunzel felt as she supported the king's son's weight up the tower, only partially reeling from the stress on the outer root sheath and the dermal papilla. And all the unhappiness that follows in that story is because her mother, one enchanted evening, was hungry for wild ferns.

Thank you for your consideration, and for reading. I have enclosed an SASE, and look forward to hearing from you.

Sincerely,
Amy Newman

Talk about going down the rabbit hole. Earlier I showed you poems by Lawrence Raab (Chapter 4.2) and Katrina Papouskaya (Chapter 4.5) that are masters of development, poems that take banal occurrences (looking into a mirror, working in an office) and expand them until they become microcosms. Those poems go out into the world. This one goes in as the speaker becomes loopier and more unhinged in a way that, as very particular poems do, becomes very universal. We laugh at this poor miserable person right up to the point where we become aware of our own insecurities and start thinking "oh, jeez, she's talking about me."

Another template you can have fun with is the instruction manual. Here's a poem by yours truly that tells you how to get the most mileage out of that balky appliance, your body.

How to Use This Body

Remove clothes and put to one side.
Body will look awkward, which is normal.
Arrange body on sheets, adjust temperature,
and turn out lights.

At this point,

any number of things can go wrong:
phone can ring, vase or book can fall
from shelf, memory can quicken, love can beat
its wings against the window, and so on.
In that case read to body, give body

hot drink or bath, return body to bed,
and repeat steps two through four (above).
After several hours, remove body from bed
and wash.

Put body into clothes again.
Feed and love body. Do not cut, shoot,
hang, poison, or throw body from window.
Keep body from drafts and solitude.
Write us if you are happy with body. If so,
could we use your name in our next poem?

As you can probably guess, I'm a light sleeper. If you're an artist of any kind, that's actually an advantage. A bank teller or a deep-sea diver with insomnia can only read or watch TV till the sun rises, but a poet who can't sleep should think of her wakefulness as an opportunity to grab pen and paper and steal a march on the competition.

And since you're up anyway, consider that, for every poem in the world, there are at least as many and probably more forms and templates and patterns of one kind or another. The sky's the limit. You could write a poem that's a standardized test or an imaginary country's national anthem or its constitution. You could write a poem that is a set of architectural plans: with their neat corners and stanza breaks and other gaps of one kind or another, don't a lot of poems look that way already?

Talking Points

If you're a churchy person, I'm sure you have a very clear idea of what prayer is. If you're not, you probably thought that prayer was something other people did that wasn't particularly useful to you. Either way, you might look at prayer differently now if you think of it as mindful action. How has prayer-as-action played out in the lives of people you know? In your own life? Consider as well prayers that have been answered that shouldn't have. Be careful what you ask for, as the old saying goes, because you just might get it. I think of a friend who wanted a life in the arts but was afraid she wouldn't be able to support herself, so she got a degree in accounting. She ended up as an auditor for the Internal Revenue Service and spent years meeting mainly with frightened people who weren't criminals but just didn't understand the tax code. (Who does?) She quit the IRS and managed the books for an alternative newspaper for a while, and when she was in her fifties, she applied to and was accepted by an MFA program that allowed her to do what she had wanted to do all along, only thirty years later. I guess delayed gratification is better than none, but, yeah, be careful what you ask for.

Prompts

DOES IT SMELL LIKE BRIMSTONE TO YOU?

Traditionally, prayer is directed to God, but there's a long tradition of people trying to sign up with The Other Team. Goethe's Faustus made a deal with the devil. Bluesman Robert Johnson is said to have done the same, and before him, the Italian violinist Paganini (more on him later). The idea's always the same: a mysterious stranger grants our wish, and we get the job or the riches or the sweetheart we asked for, and then one day, there's a knock at the door, and it's someone we haven't seen for years, and he says, "Remember this?" And he points to the bottom line. And there's your signature.

This scenario has so many possibilities that you can't possibly go wrong. Outline three or four, pick the one that has the most promise, and go to town.

GIVE A SPEECH

Give a speech. Tell somebody off. Write a letter to someone you love, even if you don't know such a person at the moment. Concoct a recipe. Conduct a survey. Write a review of your parents' child-rearing practices or the history of the world to date or your own poetry. Script a movie. Interview anyone on any subject. The more questions you ask, the more answers you're going to get, and if you get too many, you might end with two poems. Or pray, bearing in mind that you can pray to anyone or anything: your landlord, a pop star, a plate of fettucine

Alfredo, yourself.

4.7

The Seamless Life

A couple of summers ago, Barbara and I were traveling through the South looking for outsider artists. Someone told us we needed to go to Pinkville, Alabama, and see Charlie "Tin Man" Lucas. How will we know where to find him, I asked, and the man I was talking to said, Oh, you'll know.

So we drove to Pinkville, which is not exactly a metropolis, and found ourselves on a dirt road with a lot of empty lots and crashed-out farm equipment. Before long, we came to a complex of farm buildings surrounded by trees, in one of which there appeared to be—well, let's call it a pterodactyl, though it seemed to be made largely of a couple of old Dodge Dart hoods welded together.

We parked, and to the side of the main house, we could see a herd of deer whose legs consisted of those big springs they used to have at the bottom of elevator shafts in case the cable broke. Everywhere, there were dinosaurs, people, birds of all kinds made of rusty metal parts that used to belong to now-obsolete machines.

As we poked around, I became aware of a man who was tending to this thing and that, the way people do on farms. After a while, he came over, and we chatted about farm topics: the weather, how prices were going, and that kind of thing. Then he asked us if we wanted to look into one of the outbuildings at something that he'd been working on. That's when I realized I was in the presence of Charlie "Tin Man" Lucas himself.

In my freelance writing, I've interviewed sports figures, musicians, and chefs, among others, many of whom had to be handled with kid gloves. They made me feel as though they were doing me a favor—if they would talk at all, that is. With Mr. Lucas, it was as though time didn't matter. He'd been working before we arrived and would be working after we left. Who's to say whether he might make something better during the time he spent with us or maybe make something better later, not because of our conversation with him but simply because he'd left his work for a while and went back to it refreshed?

Mr. Lucas is a businessman—no mistake about that. His work is in museums, and he sells to collectors. (Back in Pinkville, the guy behind the counter at the gas station chuckled and told me that "Charlie's prices go up when a car with New York plates rolls into the yard.") But pleasure comes first for him. You don't say "I think I'll make a deer out of rusty elevator springs" because you think there's a huge market for that kind of thing in Montgomery or Tuscaloosa.

Earlier today I took a break from *The Knowledge* to have a cup of coffee and read the *New York Times*, where I saw an article about English rocker Jarvis Cocker, who, like a lot of artists, has his thumb in many pies. One of his projects was a TV series in which he traveled around and interviewed outsider artists much like Charlie Lucas. Cocker says this about them:

> There's a guy called Leonard Knight who built Salvation Mountain, a big, kind of psychedelic mound in the Salton Sea. There was also a guy in France who covered his house in broken crockery.
>
> My question was always, "Why did you make this?" And they never

> had an answer, which was frustrating. But eventually it clicked. It had never crossed their minds to ask why. They got so much pleasure that they couldn't stop.

Charlie Lucas leads a seamless life, it seems to me. He'd work, talk to someone, work, get a cup of coffee and look at his mail, work, take a walk in the woods, and do this all day long without fretting about what he'd done, was doing now, or needed to do later. It's a way of living that probably is as productive for an artist as the stop-and-start method is. Certainly it's a less anxious way. As I looked in my rearview mirror at the magical realm Charlie "Tin Man" Lucas had built from the fragments of the broken world we all live in, it seemed like the only way.

The seamless life: I can't say I live it every day. But I'm trying.

Isak Dinesen said, "I write a little every day, without hope and without despair."

Henry James said, "We work in the dark—we do what we can—we give what we have. Our doubt is our passion, and our passion is our task. The rest is the madness of art."

E. L. Doctorow says, writing is "like driving a car at night: you never see further than your headlights, but you can make the whole trip that way."

In other words, b + T = P.

AFTERWORD, OR, SEVEN SHORT BUT POWERFUL EPILOGUES

Just as there is no end to poetry or the streets we navigate or the world itself, so is there no end to *The Knowledge*. "Lord, when shall we be done growing? As long as we have anything more to do, we have done nothing," said Melville back in Chapter 4.1. By now you have everything you need to write overdetermined action-packed three-dimensional hooked/voiced/saturated/big-idea'd poems, be they long or short, fat or skinny, comical or tragical or somewhere in between.

But there's always more to say. A brief addition to the end of a book is usually called an appendix, a word whose connotations of uselessness and potential infection have always given me the creeps. So don't call them appendices, but do see if you can find something that will make your poems better and your poetical journey even more enjoyable in these seven little chapter-ettes.

Dr. Dave's Guide to Pyrotechnic Punctuation and Sensational Syntax

All writers know how to use a period: as you learned in the first grade, you just stick it on the end of a sentence. But only half of them use commas correctly, and few writers use semicolons, dashes, and colons anymore. When a writer uses only two marks of punctuation (and one of them incorrectly), the result is boring, repetitive syntax. Instead of a variety of combinations of words and phrases, the reader sees the same old subject + verb + object pattern again and again, not to mention lots of run-on sentences.

Now as I say, everybody's doing it, so you have two choices: you can join the blissfully ignorant or you can be one of the elite. If you choose the second option, here's how you use those underrated punctuation marks I just mentioned.

The Semicolon

The main use of the semicolon is to link two independent clauses; usually they're related in content. E.g., "My hair stood on end when I stuck my finger in the socket; apparently I'd forgotten to turn the power off."

The semicolon is also used to attach a series of complex dependent clauses to the independent clause. E.g., "We went up there to meet new people, hoping they'd be as different as possible from the ones we already knew; to party day and night, regardless of the expense or the consequences; and to avoid law enforcement, whose reputation for hostility toward the young was legendary."

The Dash

The dash has just one use—to provide drama. You can substitute it for a comma or a period to give your writing more flair. E.g., "He sank his teeth into my leg and wouldn't let go—man, you wouldn't believe how hard that sucker could bite." (If you don't use the "Symbols" function on your computer, note that a dash is made with two hyphens, not one.)

The Colon

Often the colon is used the same way as the dash: to provide variety by taking the place of a comma. Usually the colon conveys a slightly more formal sense than the dash, though. For example, "The spreadsheet has just two functions: to collate data and display it."

The main use of the colon is to introduce a list that is attached to an independent sentence. E.g., "There was every kind of food imaginable on that table: deviled eggs, collard greens, meat loaf, salmon croquettes, coleslaw, sweet potatoes, pecan pie."

Now that you've mastered these three punctuation marks, measure your prowess by means of the following quiz. In each case, the sentence is correct except for the missing punctuation you'll supply.

1. Punctuate the following sentence correctly by inserting a colon.

   Here's why you're in this class to learn how to write better poems and, if the gods are smiling that day, to get published.

2. Punctuate the following sentence correctly by inserting two semicolons.

   The guys from the other fraternity took over our whole house, first turning on all the taps and causing a huge flood then painting all our cars purple, which really annoyed some people and, finally, shaving our mascot, a treatment Rascal did not enjoy.

3. Punctuate the following sentence by inserting a colon.

   Three people walk into this bar a lawyer, an accountant, and a poet.

4. Punctuate the following sentence correctly by inserting a dash.

   Jennifer opened the door you should have seen how big her eyes got.

5. Punctuate the following sentence correctly by inserting a semicolon.

   The attorney said he hoped his client could get on with his life he'd had quite enough media attention for now, thank you.

A word on syntax. Often people say "grammar" when they're talking about syntax and other mechanical aspects of writing, and usually they're not even talking about that. Syntax is simply the arrangement of words, but it also means long and supple sentences and then short, crisp ones when you need them. So many poems are choppy and monotonous. Remember that Pound said "poetry should be at least as well-written as prose."

That means exquisite sentences, which means a mastery of syntax. Kim Addonizio told me she had students imitate syntactically complex poems like Ginsberg's "Howl," literally writing out "I saw the best minds of my generation destroyed by madness, starving hysterical naked," and then mimicking that syntax but plugging in their own words for Ginsberg's. Is that a marvelous idea or what?

Everything you write is a self-introduction. Your syntax tells anyone who reads it what kind of person you are. As the poet Li-Young Lee says, "Syntax is identity."

And so are punctuation and grammar and margins and line breaks and everything else about poetry that we sometimes write off as merely mechanical. If anyone ever tells you that poetry is all lofty ideas and airy fantasy that shouldn't be brought to earth by mundane mechanical matters, you can shut them up like that by quoting the words of Isaac Babel, who said that "no iron spike can pierce a human heart as icily as a period in the right place."

How a Poet Reads

In the foreword, I quoted Thomas Hobbes as saying a writer shouldn't read too much. I have no idea what he meant by that. But I will say that reading is like anything else in that you can do it right or do it wrong. The wrong way is to read obsequiously and cap in hand, kowtowing to the masters and thinking you have to do what they do. The right way is to read ruthlessly, cannibalizing other texts and making new ones from them like a welder in a chop shop slapping stolen parts together and making new cars out of old. In Chapter 3.5 I quote Henry Fielding as saying that other writers are as wealthy squire from whom we should take "whatever we can come at." Now there's a guy who knew how to read.

Once the city laid a sidewalk that intersected my driveway. I've always felt there's something wrong with a person, even a grownup, who doesn't want to write in wet concrete, but I must have telegraphed my desires—too many how-you-guys-doing visits, too many furtive glances out the den window—because the workers delayed the pouring.

Then one night we came home from a party, and sure enough, the bastards had poured, even though there'd been only an empty frame in the ground when we'd left. In fact, I'm sure they waited until we backed out of the driveway and then dragged their equipment out of the bushes, because the concrete was almost dry. Still, while Barbara held a flashlight, I went to work.

I ruined a perfectly good True Value screwdriver and had to hold the light in my teeth after Barbara got tired and went in, but in forty-five minutes or so, I managed to scratch JOHN KEATS in one corner where sidewalk and driveway intersected, LITTLE RICHARD opposite it, and then, in the two corners that remained, WALT WHITMAN and JANE AUSTEN (though I have to confess that I was thinking as much of the film version of *Pride and Prejudice* I'd just seen as I was the author).

When people ask me what my favorite book is, which they do frequently, I tell them this story. There are two points I'm trying to make: one is that no writer loves just one book above all others. Only Playboy bunnies claim to read *Antigone* over and over. The second point is that the list has got to be a little odd, in terms of both strange bedfellows (Whitman and Austen) and the unexpected (Little Richard). Just as original thinkers tend to be a little off kilter, so a good reading list is asymmetrical. Otherwise, you might as well just photocopy the table of contents of the Norton Anthology.

Does this sound a little like that soul sibling assignment I discuss in Chapter 3.5? It should, because the point is the same. Our relatives, be they biological or literary, should be a little peculiar. You want some solid types in there, but you want a couple of froot loops as well. If we handpicked our ancestors from the ranks of the nobility, we'd all be boring and we'd all be the same.

After I tell the story of the sidewalk, sometimes my questioner will say, "So those are your favorite artists, huh?" I tell them that I'm not trying to say "these are my favorite artists" but "this is the way a writer's mind works." And if someone ever asks me if I like Little Richard better than I like Keats, I'll answer with Montaigne's observation that raisins are the best part of a cake, though raisins aren't as good as a cake.

Sometime after my wet-concrete adventure, an editor asked me to send him a list of the five to ten books that I'd regard as essential reading for young poets. So I gave him these titles:

1. William Blake, *The Marriage of Heaven and Hell*

2. Walt Whitman, *Leaves of Grass*

3. Allen Ginsberg, *Howl and Other Poems*

4. Dante, *The Inferno* (the Ciaran Carson translation, though John Ciardi's is just as good)

5. Shakespeare, *Complete Works*, especially *Macbeth* and *Twelfth Night*

6. John Keats, *Odes*

7. Little Richard, *The Essential Little Richard*

8. Barbara Hamby, *On the Street of Divine Love*

9. Herman Melville, *Moby-Dick*

10. Primo Levi, *If This Is a Man* and *The Truce* (in one volume; also published as *Survival in Auschwitz* and *The Reawakening*)

In compiling my list of ten essential works, I begin with the three great dithyrambic poets of Western literature, Blake, Whitman, and Ginsberg, because that's the tradition I write in, for the most part. Next, I list Dante and Shakespeare, because I try to incorporate their majesty and rough humor. Keats is there because I want to borrow as much lushness from him as I can.

Little Richard is next on my list because I need him for rhythm. In Chapter 3.2, I quote from Virginia Woolf on how rhythm works; briefly, Woolf says that "style is a very simple matter; it is all rhythm. Once you get that, you can't use the wrong words." All the heavy furniture I get from Ginsberg and Dante and Shakespeare and Keats will get up and fly around the room if I can just get the right rhythm going. I also like Little Richard's speed and, even though we're in different branches of showbiz, his crowd appeal.

Having lit so many candles at the feet of what Keats calls "the mighty dead," I have to say that the poet I read the most is my wife, Barbara Hamby, author of *Delirium* and *The Alphabet of Desire* as well as *Babel*. Just as Barbara reads everything I write, so I read everything of hers. I've never known anyone to spend as much time as she does on a poem. Nothing leaves her desk until every word, every mark of punctuation, every margin and space has been weighed in the balance as if it were platinum. Barbara's writing practices bring mine up to a higher level, though I can't imagine anyone being as meticulous as she is.

So if I had to pack light for a desert island, these eight choices would be the ones I'd make. But if I had a little more room in my knapsack, I'd take the works by Melville and Primo Levi, an Auschwitz prisoner and the best chronicler of the Holocaust. These writers, too, hit the same notes of grandeur and joy that Dante and Shakespeare do. To a supple mind, laughter can be heard even in a death camp.

Now I'll have no respect at all for you, reader, if you merely copy my list and begin to read it. But I'll love you forever if you come up with a lopsided list of your own.

Barbara's Ten-Point Scale

In Chapter 4.3 I gave you a list of points to discuss with someone when they're making comments on your poems and vice versa. Barbara takes it one step further. When she teaches a workshop, she uses a ten-point scale to grade each poem, starting with the most rudimentary of criteria and concluding with the sublime. Here it is, directly from Barbara's syllabus.

- The poem is written in English.

- The poem is written in complete sentences. If fragments are used, they are for special effect or emphasis.

- The poem is grammatical. This includes standard punctuation, spelling, and capitalization. Ezra Pound said that a poem should at the very least be as well written as prose. Also, e.e.

cummings owns the typographical thing, so don't go there.

- The poem is clear. The reader knows what the poet is talking about.

- The poem uses images and concrete language instead of relying on abstractions, ideas, and the other techniques of analytical writing.

- The poet has control of the poetic line.

- The poem uses repetition of language for poetic effect (rhyme, assonance, alliteration, anaphora, images, etc.).

- The poem makes full use of the poetic line (enjambment, end stops, versification).

- The poem uses language in extraordinary ways (for example: sustained and complex use of metaphors throughout a poem; mix of popular and high culture; rich vocabulary; leaping; duende).

- The poem marries form and content in such a manner that, as Emily Dickinson put it, the poem takes the top off your head when you read it or gives you a chill no fire can warm.

"The first four points are concerned with basic control of the English language," says Barbara. "Points five through ten are an escalating scale of poetic complexity."

Boot Camp

Right now there are three other poets on our faculty besides Barbara and me, and part of our job is training teaching assistants who handle the junior-level technique classes that students take before they apply to our senior-level workshops. We usually start our TA boot camp by distributing a handout that serves as both a script for the first day of class and one that can be used all semester long.

This is an example of such a handout. The most important items are ones I've emphasized in *The Knowledge*. You should feel free to chase down the others and add them to your already-bulging toolbox.

WHAT YOU'LL NEED TO KNOW TO DO WELL IN THIS COURSE

This is information that poets use every day. Any poet publishing today is going to have a solid working knowledge of the following terms and concepts. And, yes, you do want to publish: if not in journals and books, at least you want others to appreciate what you've written. If you write "just for myself," you're not writing poems; you're making diary entries. Diaries are fine, but if you're in this class, it's assumed that you want eventually to write poems that will dazzle other people and leave them calling for more.

THE BASICS

You may have been taught that poetry is self-expression. It isn't: it's communication. A poem is a gift. You're not writing it for yourself; you're giving it to someone else.

All things being equal, you need to write in **full sentences**: fragments are sloppy, and they say you don't care. (Sometimes you want to be sloppy, though.)

Similarly, you need to use **standard punctuation**; absence of periods and commas suggests you can't be bothered. Use **concrete language**—appeal to the five senses. And whereas abstractions are meaningless, **images** will enter your reader's mind and heart.

THE DIFFERENT TYPES OF POEMS

When most people say the word "poetry," they mean **lyric poetry**. But there's also **narrative poetry**. You also need to be familiar with these types: **dramatic monologue**, **elegy**, **epic**, **found poem**, and **ode**.

LINE AND STANZA

Is your **line** under control—does it break off arbitrarily or does it end purposefully, usually on strong parts of speech (nouns and verbs)? Are you using **end-stopped lines** or **enjambment**?

Now for the **stanza** (literally "room" in Italian): are you using irregular lengths or are you using the **couplet**, **tercet**, **quatrain**, or some other regular stanza length?

THE MUSIC OF POETRY

You make your poetry more musical through **alliteration** (which includes both **assonance** and **consonance**) and such devices as **anaphora**. If you rhyme, be aware that **end rhyme** can give your poetry a tick-tock rhythm, whereas **run-on rhyme** is more fluid. **Half rhyme** (sometimes called **slant rhyme**) can also make your poetry flow smoothly.

FORM

You may wish to experiment with **accentual-syllabic poetry**, which means you'll have to know something about **prosody**, to perform **scansion** as you count **feet** (**spondee**, **iamb**, **trochee**, **anapest**, **dactyl**) and **meter** (**trimeter**, **tetrameter**, **pentameter**, and so on). Accentual-syllabic poetry includes such forms as the **sonnet**, but there are other types of formal poetry based on line repetition, syllable count, and so on; these include the **sestina**, the **pantoum**, the **acrostic**, the **abecedarian poem**, the **ghazal**, the **villanelle**, and **syllabic poetry**.

THE WORLD OF POETRY

Whether you know it or not, you're writing within a particular tradition, so you need to be aware of it. Let's begin with the easy distinction: **formal poetry** versus **free verse**. Within the first, though, you could be a lush and word-drunk formalist like Gerard Manley Hopkins or a plainspoken one like Marilyn Hacker.

And you free-versers: are you pithy and gnomic like Stephen Crane or loose and "prophetic" in the Old Testament/Whitman/Ginsberg way? If you think you haven't been influenced by anyone, usually that means you're being influenced by poets you can't name. You should be able to identify three or four poets you're like and say why.

Locally, you'll want to go to the **readings** sponsored by schools and poetry groups. And it's easy to access **online poetry** at such websites as www.poems.com. Additionally, you should read and subscribe to

poetry journals you'll find online, in the library, and in bookstores.

As far as individual poets go, you'll want to be acquainted at least with **poets of the ancient world** (Catullus, Martial, Sappho), **poets of the English and American canon** (Keats, Browning, Dickinson), **living classics** (Strand, Brooks, Kumin), **African American poets** (Alexander, Hayes, Komunyakaa, Moss), **Hispanic poets** (Cofer, Ríos, Soto), **Asian poets** (Basho, Li T'ai-Po, Tu Fu), **Asian American poets** (Lee, Song, Sze), **Russian poets** (Akhmatova, Mandelstam, Tsvaeteva), and **European poets** (Rilke, Lorca, Milosz, Szymborska).

MORE, MORE, MORE

You can find out more about all these terms and concepts and the poets who use them in books of **poetics** (such as Kim Addonizio and Dorianne Laux, *The Poet's Companion*; Alfred Corn, *The Poem's Heartbeat*; Philip Dacey and David Jauss, *Strong Measures*; Mary Kinzie, *A Poet's Guide to Poetry*; John Hollander, *Rhyme's Reason*; Mark Strand and Eavan Boland, *The Making of a Poem*; Lewis Turco, *The New Book of Forms*) and **theory** (such as Robert Bly, *Leaping Poetry*; T. S. Eliot, *The Sacred Wood*; Louise Glück, *Proofs and Theories*; Robert Hass, *Twentieth Century Pleasures*; Richard Hugo, *Triggering Town*; Robert McDowell, ed., *Poetry After Modernism*; Molly McQuade, ed., *By Herself*; Robert Pinsky, *The Situation of Poetry*; Ezra Pound, *ABC of Reading*; any book in the University of Michigan Poets on Poetry series).

THE OUTCOME

Anyone who masters these terms and concepts and readings, puts them to use, and works hard can write at least One Good Poem. Of course, writing a great poem is another matter; if it were easy to follow a recipe for greatness, then we'd all be getting the Nobel Prize every year. But everyone has the potential to write at least One Great Poem as well. Which would you rather hear, "Hmm, you've got some language organized intelligently here" or "Wow! This is fabulous!"? So study hard, write a lot, show your work to smart readers, and enjoy yourself. If you do, your luck will be good luck, but that'll be because you yourself have made it so.

Working with Editors

In Chapter 4.4, I go over the basics of submitting your poems to a magazine. But what happens when one (or more) of your poems is accepted? Usually the editor who writes you will simply say that they're taking the poem and that you should expect proofs when it gets close to publication time.

But occasionally the editor will ask for changes in your poem. Now don't get upset. You're a pro now, so act like one. That means slamming your laptop shut, stomping around the room and calling the editor every name in the book, then coming back and looking at the editor's suggestions and see if they make sense. Often they do. Which makes your job easy, because at this point, your loyalty, like the editor's, is to the poem. I've been edited many, many times, and usually the poem has gotten better as a result.

But that doesn't mean you have to salute and do exactly what the editor says. Let me tell you about an exchange I had with an editor not long ago.

This is the poem the editor took for her magazine. It recounts a true story told to me by my brother and one too good to ignore.

Not Easy to Believe

My brother's colleague is on trial for murder. He had a pulley
in his bedroom that he used to lower his wife out the window

in the hours before dawn, and then he'd go outside and have sex
with her, though my brother never got the details on that.

One morning, the rope breaks, and the next thing he knows,
my brother's colleague is in jail. He says it was consensual,

that his wife asked for it that way, but the state says he killed her,
that it was a deliberate act, he wanted her dead. "All truths

are easy to understand once they are discovered," says Galileo;
"the point is to discover them." Once I was having a drink with

a friend, and he told me that his marriage was over, that he
and his wife barely spoke to each other, and then his wife

joined us and began to talk about the trips they had planned
and the vacation home they were thinking of buying.

If we knew what we liked, why would we ever do anything?
Many thought Bobby Fisher the greatest chess player of all time,

but when asked if he enjoyed himself after a visit to a brothel
in Curaçao, he said, "Chess is better." In the end,

my brother's colleague got off. The defense had a witness.
It was the paperboy; he'd peddled by many times on his route,

saw them loving each other, said of the two, the wife took
the most pleasure, filling the darkness with her silent cries.

Now here's the letter of acceptance I got.

Dear David Kirby,

Thank you for sending us your poetry packet. We are pleased to inform you that we would like to publish "Not Easy to Believe" in the next issue of ______. We loved the way the poem weaved together so many narratives. And we thought you managed to make observations on life that felt new and refreshing. I particularly enjoyed the line "If we knew what we liked, why would we ever do anything."

We have a few small changes we would like to suggest. We would like to put the first line into the past tense in order to keep the tense consistent. So it would read "My brother's colleague was on trial" rather than "is." We also wanted to change "my brother's colleague is" in line 6 to just "he's." We didn't think there was any confusion on who the subject was, and thought that read a little cleaner. Finally, we wanted to change the conjunction in the third to last stanza from "but" to "and," and remove the word "silent" from the final line. Let us know what you think of these changes.

We are looking forward to publishing this piece, and we are excited to take the next steps with you. Our managing editor, ______, will be in touch shortly with a more formal letter and details.

Thanks!

All the best,

______

Poetry Editor

_______ Magazine

The day I received this acceptance, I worked my way through my poem again and replied, saying I wanted to keep the poem as is and addressed each of the suggested changes separately, explaining why I didn't think it improved the poem. To begin with, "is" is better than "was" because, as Berry Gordy Jr. says, the present tense gives a sense of immediacy (Chapter 3.3). I also wanted to keep line 6 as is because it seemed to me there would be pronoun confusion otherwise.

But the main thing is that I absolutely insisted on keeping the word "silent" in the last lines. For a woman in a state of ecstasy to "fill the night with her cries" is simple physics. But for her to "fill the night with her silent cries"? That's poetry.

Within a couple of hours of sending my reply, the editor with whom I'd been corresponding said that the changes to the poem were suggestions only and that "we very much want to publish it."

Point: Editing is part of the acceptance process. You should expect it, but you should also remember that, except for factual errors, you don't have to change anything.

When to Hold and When to Fold

Remember the ring-toss experiment in Chapter 1.2, not to mention my several references to Goldilocks throughout? The idea in both cases is to not make your poem too explicit or too mysterious but to find some middle ground that makes the reader want to play along with you rather than being bored or baffled. Here are two poems of mine that grapple with the issue of saying too little or too much. In each case, I've bolded short passages that I'll follow up on when I comment on the poems.

The Cottingley Fairy Hoax

A jockey who was on a strict diet had a single almond
for dessert, but he was going on a trip, so he took the almond
on the plane with him. I wonder if he ever ate it. **Isn't it better**
to want something than to have it? In 1917, two young cousins

go down to a stream at the bottom of a garden and take photographs
of fairies which are actually cut-outs which Elsie Wright, age 16,
had copied from a children's book. She and 10-year-old Frances
Griffiths take turns posing with the sprites, then develop
the photographs in Elsie's father's darkroom and show them to
their parents. The father doesn't believe the fairies are real.
The mother does. She brings the pictures to a meeting
of the Theosophical Society, and then all of England sees them,
and then the world. The war had just ended. A grieving public
wanted to believe in an invisible realm that revealed itself
from time to time, and the language used to describe the fairies
shows that: one enthusiast said of the fairies that the girls
were able "to materialise them at a density sufficient
for their images to be recorded," and Arthur Conan Doyle
himself believed that "a visible sign was coming through."
Before long, Elsie and Frances had grown tired of their prank,
but they were embarrassed to say so, and by then it was too late.
In a 1985 interview, Elsie said, "Two village kids and a brilliant
man like Conan Doyle—well, we could only keep quiet."
Frances said millions believed in the fairies because they wanted
to believe, and today, in the dark corners of the internet,
some still do. But the fairies aren't the miracle. The miracle
is that the girls made up the fairies. And that for so long they lied.

You've probably figured out by now that I'm not much on one-note poems. It's like eating a whole fish or a plate of fries by itself: yeah, that would fill you up, but isn't it better to have both on one plate? I've always been taken with the Cottingley Fairy Hoax and what it tells us about our need to believe (even Conan Doyle was fooled) and the requirements of art (it was a hoax, but it sure lasted a long time). It took me a while to frame the fairy story the way I wanted, but when I heard about the jockey, I thought, this is what my poem needs. But would readers make the connection? Why not make the connection myself, I figured. The bolded sentence in lines three and four is a lot more overt than what you usually see in a poem, but I'm hoping the charm of the story will allow the reader to forgive me.

This second poem is the opposite of the first in that it illustrates a case of saying too much.

The House at the Bend in the River

Omero is the foreman of the crew who are replacing
our roof, and he's shaking his head as the young men
pack their tools and head home for the evening,
and when I ask him why, he says, "These guys—
when they go back to Mexico, all they do is party
and spend all their money. Why not buy a piece
of land, I tell them?" and I'm just about to say
that's good advice when Barbara says, "But they
have to party to meet the girl they buy the land for,"
and Omero and I look at each other like, hmm.
And the girl? What do young women want?
As she watches a movie called *War of the Wildcats*,
Joan Didion hears John Wayne tell a girl that
he will build her a house "at the bend in the river
where the cottonwoods grow." Later, she thinks
of all the men she has loved and how none of them
have been John Wayne and have never taken her
to that bend in the river where the cottonwoods grow.
Young man, go to the party. Find the girl. Ask her
to the movies. Take her to the bend in the river
where the cottonwoods grow. It doesn't have to be
an actual river. Or actual cottonwoods. Put your arm
around her waist. Sweep your other hand from one side
to the other, and say, "Here is where I will build you
a house." Barbara and I have a house, though I didn't
build it, and it isn't on a bend in the river, and the trees
around it are pines and live oaks, not cottonwoods.
And we met at a party, though I don't remember
the party or much of what happened in the days

and months that followed it. But here we are,
right we're supposed to be. Someone said marriage
means dealing every day with the intractable
otherness of someone else, which makes marriage
a matter of finding someone whose otherness
you want to deal with. **We do that.** Sometimes
Barbara wants one thing for dinner and I want
another. She wants to go to a movie, I have
a game to watch, we both decide to read.
We get in bed at the same time, though sometimes
she stays up later, sometimes I do. She sleeps soundly,
I'm like a man on a bicycle with square wheels.
We wake when the sun is at the window or earlier, maybe,
if an owl cries or a cat paws at the door, and lie
in each other's arms and wait as the day comes to us.

I mentioned earlier that when a poem is accepted, usually the editor doesn't want any changes. By the same token, the poet's usually pretty happy with what he's written and doesn't change anything, either. But a day or two after "The House at the Bend in the River" was accepted, I had an uneasy feeling that something was not quite right about it. After a reread, I saw the problem. The three words in bold above say too much; they don't give the reader credit for figuring things out on her own. So I wrote my editor and said I'd like to take them out, and of course she said yes.

Paganini's Kickshaw

Thirteenth-century Franciscan friar Roger Bacon said that "every point on the earth is the apex of a pyramid filled with the fires of heaven." I'm not quite sure what this holy man had in mind when he said that, but I'm guessing that he means there's all this power under our feet and that it's up to us to figure out how to unlock it, which, for you writers, means to write as though your life depends on it, because it does.

Niccolò Paganini was the most celebrated violin virtuoso of the early nineteenth century. His performances left audiences gasping, and he played so furiously that it was rumored he had made a deal with the devil. In fact, he was denied burial in a Catholic cemetery for years because of his supposed dealings with the Prince of Darkness. If Paganini strikes you as the kind of guy I wouldn't write a poem about, then you don't know me very well.

Actually, the poem I wrote is about Paganini's violin. A violin is not exactly a Fender Stratocaster. Violins collapse when you sit on them, and they're always out of tune. Yet Paganini had a nickname for his favorite instrument that suggests how powerful art can be. We poets traffic in words, than which there is nothing flimsier, yet words can change the world.

Thank you for reading *The Knowledge*, and may this closing tribute to poets and poetry speed you on your way.

Paganini's Kickshaw, the Violin Known as "The Cannon"

My physical therapist always says "Do you watch sports
on TV, David?" and I always say "No,"
and he always says, "Did you see last night's game?"
and I always say "No," and he always says,
"Do you think the Knicks (or the Sox or the Browns)
have a chance this year?" and I always say,
"Tom, if they can avoid injury" or "if they can just
move the damned ball" or "if they can keep it together,
then I think they stand a halfway decent chance,"

and he always says "But what about Hardaway
(or Arroyo or Wells)?" and I always say,
"Tom, it comes down to the coaching, doesn't it?"
and we go on like this for hours as he swings my arm
back and forth like a metronome,
and when he's through, my arm feels so good,
and we've said so much, and there was no more sense to what
we said than there is to music or sports or poetry,
and therefore no wonder the old Greeks loved all three.

Well, four: they liked wine, too. Greek or not, someone said,
"Wine is sunlight held together by water."
Lovely expression, don't you think? Makes wine sound
so fragile, which it is, as are words sometimes,
and here are three illustrations to support that

assertion:
sometimes I call myself "Mr. Wonderful"
when I bring Barbara her coffee, saying,
"Here's Mr. Wonderful with your coffee,"
and sometimes she says, "Thank you, Mr. Wonderful!"

though an hour later we could be blackguarding
each other with language that would scour the hide
off an alligator! On a somewhat classier level,
consider that, in 642, when Islamic armies captured
Alexandria, a Greek scholar asked if he might
take possession of the famous library, and the caliph said
that if the writings agreed with the Holy Qu'ran,
they are useless and need not be preserved,
and if they disagree, they are wicked and must be destroyed,

and that was it for the library. Talk about fragile!
A final example, this on the lowest level possible,
at least in the present poem: we are standing in front
of The Assembly Rooms in Bath, and our guide Tony,
who has a slight stutter, is saying, "This is where
you'd come to meet someone if you were a lonely cunt,
a lonely cunt, a lonely country parson who wants to get married."
That's it in a nutshell, folks; language is indeed
delicate,
weak, watery, frail. Yet also hardy, shellproof, burly,

unassailable! "With twenty-six soldiers I have conquered
the world," said the great Johannes Gutenberg.
So which is it, reader, candy-assed or perdurable, gossamer
or rock-hard? The song is beautiful, but it ends.
The athlete looks like a god to us, yet her knees are
shot,
and she will die before we do. And poetry, which we love
more than anything, baffles us, aggravates, makes us want

to pull off our clothes and run out into traffic.
Virgil's biographer Donatus wrote that the poet

used to dictate his poetry in the morning and spend
the afternoon working it over "as a she-bear does
her cubs: licking it gradually into shape."
That's quoted in Harriet Rubin's *Dante in Love*,
where Rubin herself states that the real challenge
for a mythic hero is not to slay the dragon
but to tell the story to those who have never *seen* a dragon.
You nailed that one on the head, Harriet!
We must be as brave before a blank sheet of paper

as we are in the face of a fire-breathing lizard.
We must summon great powers to our aid.
We must speak our minds, even if our voices shake.
Humiliation, sorrow, the contempt of our enemies:
this is the food of heroes! The things given us
to transform, that they may be eternal. We must arm ourselves
like warriors, which is why Niccolò Paganini (1782–1840)
gave the greatest name ever to his favorite violin,
his darling, his kickshaw, calling it—wait,

what do you think he called it? Dainty Lace Doily? No.
Spoonful of Pudding Spit Up By A Pouty Baby?
I don't think so. How about Tattered Antimacassar From
A Run-Down Venetian Palazzo or Leaky Sieve Bailing
A Battered Whale Boat or Papyrus Found In A Cave
By A Goatherd Starting a Fire? No? Self Of Steam?
Dog Bark, Cat Cry, Owl Hoot Fading Into The Dawn, Chimera,
Willow-The-Wisp, Flash In The Pan Of The Day's
Blunderbuss? No, Paganini called his violin The Cannon.

FURTHER READING

These are the principal texts I drew on in writing *The Knowledge*.

"Against Interpretation." *Wikipedia*, 17 May 2021. https://en.wikipedia.org/wiki/Against_Interpretation.

"Pro Tools." *Wikipedia*, 31 May 2021. https://en.wikipedia.org/wiki/Pro_Tools.

Adams, John. *Hallelujah Junction: Composing an American Life*. Picador; Farrar, Straus, and Giroux, 2009.

Ali, Taha Muhammad. Quoted in "A Merchant of Trinkets and Memories" by Garner, Dwight. *The New York Times*, 5 May 2009. https://www.nytimes.com/2009/05/06/books/06garn.html.

Alighieri, Dante. *The Divine Comedy*. Penguin Books, 2006.

Ammons, A. R. "A Poem Is a Walk." *Epoch* 18 (1968): 115–19.

Anastasio, Trey. *Between Me and My Mind*. Directed by Steve Cantor. Trafalgar Releasing, 2019.

Anderson, Sam. "New Sentences: From Morgan Parker's *There Are More Beautiful Things Than Beyoncé*." *The New York Times*, 21 Mar. 2018. https://www.nytimes.com/2018/03/20/magazine/new-sentences-from-morgan-parkers-there-are-more-beautiful-things-than-beyonce.html.

Anonymous. "Pangur Bán." Translated by Seamus Heaney. *Poetry*, April, 2006, Poetry Foundation. https://www.poetryfoundation.org/poetrymagazine/poems/48267/pangur-ban.

Ashbery, John, and Kenneth Koch. "Crone Rhapsody." *Locus Solus 2*, 1961, pp. 157-62.

Babel, Ísaak, and Cynthia Ozick. *The Complete Works of Isaac Babel*. Edited by Nathalie Babel, translated by Peter Constantine, W. W. Norton, 2002.

Bakewell, Sarah. *How to Live: Or Life of Montaigne: In One Question and Twenty Attempts at an Answer*. Other Press, 2010.

Bakhtin, Mikhail. *Rabelais and His World*. Translated by Hélène Iswolsky, MIT Press, 1971.

Barth, John. "An interview with John Barth." *Prism*, Spring, 1968, p. 57.

———. *The Sot-Weed Factor*. Anchor Books ed., Doubleday, 1987.

Baudelaire, Charles. *The Painter of Modern Life and Other Essays*. Edited by Jonathan Mayne, Phaidon, 1995.

The Beach Boys. "Good Vibrations." *Good Vibrations (Single)*, Capital, 1966.

Benjamin, Walter. *The Writer of Modern Life: Essays on Charles Baudelaire*. Edited by Michael William Jennings, translated by Howard Eliand et al., Harvard University Press, 2006.

Benjaminson, Peter. *Mary Wells: The Tumultuous Life of Motown's First Superstar*. Chicago Review Press, 2012.

Betts, Reginald Dwayne. "Blood History." *Felon*, W. W. Norton & Company, 2019.

The Bible. Authorized King James Version, Oxford UP, 1998.

Blake, William. "The Book of Los." *The Complete Poetry and Prose of William Blake*, edited by David V. Erdman and Harold Bloom, Anchor Books, 1982, pp. 67–69.

The Blues Brothers. Directed by John Landis, written by John Landis and Dan Aykroyd. Universal Pictures, 1980.

Bly, Robert. "Looking for Dragon Smoke." *Leaping Poetry: An Idea with Poems and Translations.* Beacon Press, pp 1-13.

———. "Poetry and The Three Brains." In *The New Naked Poetry*, edited by Stephen Berg and Robert Mezey, Bobbs-Merrill, 1976.

Bök, Christian. Quoted in "Poets: Really, They're the Laziest, Stupidest People I Know." By Kenneth Goldsmith. *The Poetry Foundation.* https://www.poetryfoundation.org, December 2009.

Bourdain, Anthony. *Anthony Bourdain: Parts Unknown.* CNN, 2013-2018.

Brady, Frank. *Endgame: Bobby Fischer's Remarkable Rise and Fall: from America's Brightest Prodigy to the Edge of Madness.* Broadway Paperbacks, 2012.

Brooks, David. "Opinion | The Creative Climate." *The New York Times*, 8 July 2014. https://www.nytimes.com/2014/07/08/opinion/david-brooks-the-creative-climate.html.

Browne, Thomas. *Hydriotaphia Urne-Buriall, or, A Brief Discourse of the Sepulchrall Urnes Lately Found in Norfolk.* New Directions, 2010.

Browning, Elizabeth Barrett. "How do I love thee? Sonnet 43." *Elizabeth Barrett Browning: Selected Poems*, edited by Margaret Forster, Johns Hopkins University Press, 1988.

Browning, Robert. "How They Brought the Good News from Ghent to Aix." *Selected Poems*, edited by Daniel Karlin, Penguin Books, 2000, p. 39.

Burke, Edmund. *A Philosophical Enquiry into the Origin of Our Ideas of the Sublime and Beautiful.* Oxford University Press, 2015.

Carson, Ciaran. Interview by Aida Edemariam. "A Life in Poetry: Ciaran Carson," *The Guardian*, 16 Jan. 2009. https://www.theguardian.com/books/2009/jan/17/poetry-ciaran-carson-belfast-ireland.

Chekhov, Anton P. *The Cherry Orchard.* Dover Publications, 1991.

Chesterton, G. K, and Neil Gaiman. Epigraph, misquoted by Neil Gaiman. *Coraline.* HarperCollins, 2002.

The Chiffons. "He's So Fine." *He's So Fine,* Laurie Records, 1963.

Coleridge, Samuel Taylor. "The Rime of the Ancient Mariner (1834)." *The Complete Poems*, edited by William Keach, Penguin Books, 1997, pp. 167–86.

Collins, Billy. "Discovering the Subject." *Billy Collins Teaches Reading and Writing Poetry*. MasterClass. https://www.masterclass.com/classes/billy-collins-teaches-reading-and-writing-poetry/chapters/discovering-the-subject#.

———. "The Lanyard." *The Trouble With Poetry: and Other Poems,* Random House, 2005.

Cortázar, Julio. "Weekend." *Complete Short Stories Vol. 1*, Alfaguara, 1997.

The Crystals. "Da Doo Ron Ron." *Sing the Greatest Hits Vol. 1*, Philles Records, 1963.

Csikszentmihalyi, Mihaly. *Flow: The Psychology of Optimal Experience*. HarperCollins, 1991.

Davie, Donald. *Trying to Explain: Poets on Poetry.* University of Michigan Press, 1979.

Davis, Clive, and Anthony DeCurtis. *The Soundtrack of My Life*. Simon and Schuster, 2013.

Dennis, John. *Appius and Virginia: A Tragedy.* Lintott, 1700, The Bavarian State Library.

Diamond, Neil. "Solitary Man." *The Feel of Neil Diamond,* BANG, 1966.

Diaz, Natalie. "Abecedarian Requiring Further Examination of Anglikan Seraphym Subjugation of a Wild Indian Rezervation." *When My Brother Was an Aztec,* Copper Canyon Press, 2012.

Dickinson, Emily. "L342a, 1870." *The Letters of Emily Dickinson*, edited by Thomas H. Johnson and Theodora Ward, The Belknap Press of Harvard University Press, 1958, p. 208.

———. "315 Untitled [He Fumbles at your Soul]." *The Complete Poems of Emily Dickinson*, edited by Thomas Herbert Johnson, Back Bay Books, Little, Brown and Co, 1997, pp. 223-24.

———. "465 Untitled [I heard a Fly buzz when I died]." *The Complete Poems of Emily Dickinson*, edited by Thomas Herbert Johnson, Back Bay Books, Little, Brown and Co, 1997, p. 148.

———. "1035 Untitled [Bee! I'm expecting you!]." *The Complete Poems of Emily Dickinson*, edited by Thomas Herbert Johnson, Back Bay Books, Little, Brown and Co, 1997, p. 474.

———. "1355 Untitled [The Mind lives on the Heart]." *The Complete Poems of Emily Dickinson*, edited by Thomas Herbert Johnson, Back Bay Books, Little, Brown and Co, 1997, p. 585.

———. "1463 Untitled [A Route of Evanescence]." *The Complete Poems of Emily Dickinson*, edited by Thomas Herbert Johnson, Back Bay Books, Little, Brown and Co, 1997, p. 619.

Dickman, Matthew. "Slow Dance." *All-American Poem*, American Poetry Review, 2008, pp. 6–7.

Dinerstein, Joel. *The Origins of Cool in Postwar America*. University of Chicago Press, 2018.

Dinesen, Isak. Quoted in "Talk With Isak Dinesen." By Bent Mohn, *The New York Times,* 3 Nov. 1957. NYTimes.com, https://www.nytimes.com/1957/11/03/archives/talk-with-isak-dinesen.html.

Doctorow, E. L. Interviewed by George Plimpton. "The Art of Fiction No. 94." *The Paris Review*, vol. Winter 1986, no. 101, 1986.

The Doors. "Hello, I Love You." *Waiting for the Sun*, Elektra, 1968.

The Doors. "Light My Fire." *The Doors*, Elektra, 1967.

Downton Abbey. Directed by Engler, Michael. Focus Features, 2019.

Eliot, T. S. "Tradition and the Individual Talent." *The Sacred Wood: Essays on Poetry and Criticism*. Alfred A. Knopf, 1921, pp. 42-53.

Emerson, Ralph Waldo. "Divinity School Address." *The Portable Emerson*, edited by Carl Bode and Malcolm Cowley, Penguin, 1981.

———. "Montaigne." *Selected Essays.* Penguin, 1982.

———. "The Poet." *Selected Essays*, Penguin, 1982.

———. "Self-Reliance." *Selected Essays.* Penguin, 1982.

Epictetus. *Discourses and Selected Writings,* translated and edited by Robert Dobbins, Penguin Books, 2008.

Freud, Sigmund. *A General Introduction to Psychoanalysis.* Translated by Joan Riviere, Pocket Books. 1953, pp. 384-85.

Fielding, Henry. *The History of Tom Jones, a Foundling.* Edited by Alice Wakely, New Penguin Classics ed., Penguin, 2005.

Flaubert, Gustave. "To Louis Bouilhet." December, 8 1853. *The Letters of Gustave Flaubert*, translated by Francis Steegmuller, Harvard University Press, 1980, p 203.

Flynn, Nick. "Bag of Mice." *Some Ether*, Graywolf Press, 2000.

Frishman, Elyse D. *Mishkan Tefilah: Mishkan T'filah: a Reform Siddur: Weekdays, Shabbat, Festivals, and Other Occasions of Public Worship*. Central Conference of American Rabbis, 2007.

Frost, Robert. "Provide, Provide." *Collected Poems, Prose & Plays*, Library of America, 1995, p. 280.

Gillespie, Dizzy. Interviewed. *Notes and Tones: Musician-to-Musician Interviews*, edited by Art Taylor, Da Capo Press, 1993, p. 125.

Ginsberg, Allen. "America." *Collected Poems, 1947-1997*, 1st ed., HarperCollins Publishers, 2006.

Giraldi, William. "Jack My Heart: On Obsession and the Artist." *Oxford American*, Summer 2014.

Hall, Donald. Quoted in "Donald Hall's Poetry." *Essays on Poetry* by Ralph J. Mills, Dalkey Archive Press, 2003.

Halliday, Mark. "The Arrogance of Poetry." *Georgia Review* 57, Summer 2003, pp. 214-237.

Harrison, George. "My Sweet Lord."*All Things Must Pass,* Apple, 1970.

Harryhausen, Ray, and Tony Dalton. *Ray Harryhausen: An Animated life*. Aurum, 2009.

Harvey, Matthea. "The Backyard Mermaid." *If the Tabloids Are True What Are You? Poems & Images*, Graywolf Press, 2014.

Helm, Levon. *This Wheel's on Fire: Levon Helm and the Story of The Band*. Chicago Review Press, 2013.

Hendrix, Jimi. "Purple Haze." *Purple Haze (Single)*, Track; Reprise, 1967.

Hoagland, Tony, and Kay Cosgrove. *The Art of Voice: Poetic Principles and Practice*. W.W. Norton & Company, 2019.

Hooker, John Lee. "Tupelo, Mississippi," also known as "Tupelo." *Folk Lore Of John Lee Hooker,* Vee-Jay, 1961.

Hopkins, Gerard Manley "Pied Beauty." *Poems and Prose of Gerard Manley Hopkins*, edited by William Henry Gardner, Penguin Books, 2000. p. 30.

Hughes, Ted. Introduction. *The Essential Shakespeare*, HarperCollins,

2000.

Iser, Wolfgang. *The Act of Reading: A Theory of Aesthetic Response.* Johns Hopkins University Press, 1978.

Ishiguro, Kazu. Quoted in "Lost Toys and Flying Machines: A Talk with Kazuo Ishiguro." By Cody Delistraty, *The New Yorker,* 20 March 2015. https://www.newyorker.com/books/page-turner/lost-toys-and-flying-machines-a-talk-with-kazuo-ishiguro.

James, Etta, et al. "The Blues is My Business." *Let's Roll,* Private Music, 2003.

James, Henry. *The Complete Notebooks of Henry James.* Edited by Leon Edel, et al., Oxford University Press, 1987.

———. "The Middle Years." *Complete Stories, 1892-1898,* edited by John Hollander, et al., Library of America, 1996.

———. "The Turning of the Screw." *Complete Stories, 1892-1898,* edited by John Hollander, et al., Library of America, 1996.

Jarrell, Randall. "The Death of the Ball Turret Gunner." *The Complete Poems,* Farrar, Straus and Giroux, 1996, p. 144.

The Jaynetts. "Sally Go Round the Roses." *Sally Go Round the Roses,* Tuff, 1963.

Joplin, Janis. "Piece of My Heart." *Live in Europe 1969,* Aliveville, 1969.

Joyce, James. Quoted in "Further Recollections of James Joyce." By Frank Budgen, *Partisan Review,* xxm, Fall 1956, p. 533.

Kaufman, Andy. Quoted in "Was This Man a Genius?" By Julie Hecht, *The New Yorker,* 22 Nov. 1999, https://www.newyorker.com/magazine/1999/11/22/was-this-man-a-genius.

Keats, John. "Letter to George and Tom Keats." 21, ?27 December 1817, *Selections from Keats's Letters,* Poetry Foundation, 13 Oct. 2009. https://www.poetryfoundation.org/articles/69384/selections-from-keatss-letters.

———. "Ode on a Grecian Urn." *The Complete Poems,* edited by John Barnard, Penguin Books, 1988, p 344.

———. "Ode to a Nightingale." *The Complete Poems,* edited by John Barnard, Penguin Books, 1988, p 346.

Kermode, Frank. *The Genesis of Secrecy: On the Interpretation of Narrative.* Harvard University Press, 1979.

———. *The Sense of an Ending: Studies in the Theory of Fiction*. Oxford University Press, 1968.

Kerry, John. "Death of Robin Williams." *US Department of State*. 12 Aug. 2014. Bureau of Public Affairs. Press Statement.

Keynes, John Maynard. *The General Theory of Employment, Interest, and Money*. Springer International Publishing, 2018.

Kilmer, Joyce. "Trees." *Poetry* Aug. 1913, *The Poetry Foundation*, https://www.poetryfoundation.org/poetrymagazine/poems/12744/trees.

Kirby, David. "Broken Promises." *Big-Leg Music*, Orchises Press, 1995, p. 13.

———. "Fallen Bodies." *Saving the Young Men of Vienna*, University of Wisconsin Press, 1987.

———. "The Cottingley Fairy Hoax." *Copper Nickel*, no. 31/32, Fall 2020, p. 137.

———. "The House at the Bend in the River." *River Styx*, no. 103/104, 2020, pp. 39-40.

———. "How to Use This Body." *The Opera Lover*, Anhinga Press, 1977.

———. "I Had a Girl." *Get up, Please: Poems*, Louisiana State University Press, 2016.

———. "More than This." *More than This: Poems*, Louisiana State University Press, 2019.

———. "Not Easy To Believe." *More than This: Poems*, Louisiana State University Press, 2019.

———. "Paganini's Kickshaw, The Violin Known As The Cannon." *Talking about Movies with Jesus: Poems*, Louisiana State University Press, 2011.

Koestler, Arthur. *The Ghost in the Machine*. Arkana, 1989, p. 288.

Komunyakaa, Yusef. "'You and I Were Disappearing.'" *Dien Cai Dau*, Wesleyan University Press, 1988, p. 17.

Kuhn, Thomas S. *The Structure of Scientific Revolutions*. University of Chicago Press, 1962.

Kumin, Maxine. "Closing the Door." *To Make a Prairie: Essays on Poets, Poetry, and Country Living*, University of Michigan Press, 1979.

La Rochefoucauld, François. *Maxims of La Rochefoucauld*. Translated by John Heard, Dover Publications, 2006.

Lamar, Kendrick. "Wanna Be Heard." *Kendrick Lamar (EP),* Top Dawg Entertainment (TDE), 2009.

Laux, Dorianne. "Fast Gas." *What We Carry: Poems*, BOA Editions, 1994.

Lehane, Dennis. Talk at Nantucket Book Festival, Nantucket, MA, 22 June 2013.

Lerman, Eleanor. "Ode to Joy." *The Sensual World Re-Emerges*, Sarabande Books, 2010.

Levine, Philip. *Don't Ask*. University of Michigan Press, 1981.

Lil' Wayne. Quoted in *The Carter.* Directed by Adam Bhala Lough, QD3 Entertainment, 2009.

Lindsay, Jeff. "Only One Person Could Write That." *Wall Street Journal*, 19 Nov. 2011.

Little Richard, and Dorothy LaBostrie. "Tutti Frutti" (1955). *Here's Little Richard,* Speciality, 1957.

Luscombe, Belinda. "10 Questions for Sting." *Time*, 21 Nov. 2011.

MacLean, Paul D. *Journal of Nervous and Mental Diseases,* vol. CXXXV, no. 4, Oct. 1962.

Marcus, Greil. *The Shape of Things to Come: Prophecy and the American Voice*. Farrar, Straus and Giroux, 2006.

Marlantes, Karl. *Matterhorn*. Atlantic Monthly Press, 2010.

Márquez, Gabriel García. Quoted on *The Writer's Almanac*. Commentary by Garrison Keillor. http://www.garrisonkeillor.com/radio/twa-the-writers-almanac-for-march-6-2020/.

McCarthy, Mary. *The Stones of Florence*. Harvest; Harcourt, 1959.

Melville, Herman. *Moby-Dick, or, The Whale*. Penguin Books, 2003.

Miller, Steve. *Detroit Rock City: The Uncensored History of Five Decades of Rock 'n' Roll in America's Loudest City.* Da Capo, 2013.

Mitchell, Adrian. Preface. *Poems (1964),* Jonathan Cape, 1964.

Mitchell, Joseph. *My Ears Are Bent*. Vintage Books, 2008.

Moss, Thylias. "Lunchcounter Freedom." *Gargoyle Magazine,* 37/38.

Mould, Bob, and Michael Azerrad. *See a Little Light: The Trail of Rage and Melody*. Little, Brown and Co, 2011.

Mouton, Todd. "BackTalk with Cosimo Matassa." *Offbeat*, 2007.

Mustich, James. "John Barth: The Development." Barnes & Noble Review, 17 Nov. 2008.

Nemerov, Howard. *Contemporary American Poetry*. United States Information Agency, 1965.

———. "Bottom's Dream: The Likeness of Poems and Jokes." *The Virginia Quarterly Review*, vol. 42, no. 4, 1966, pp. 555–573.

———. "Poetry and Meaning." *Figures of Thought: Speculations on the Meaning of Poetry and Other Essays*, Little, Brown, 1975.

Oldenburg, Claes. "I Am for an Art (1961)." *Claes Oldenburg: Writing on the Side, 1956-1969*, edited by Achim Hochdörfer et al., Museum of Modern Art, 2013.

Paul, Annie Murphy. "Your Brain on Fiction." *The New York Times*, 17 Mar. 2012. https://www.nytimes.com/2012/03/18/opinion/sunday/the-neuroscience-of-your-brain-on-fiction.html.

Paz, Octavio. "The and This and This." *The Collected Poems of Octavio Paz, 1957-1987*, edited by Eliot Weinberger, translated by Elizabeth Bishop, et al., New Directions, 1987, p. 517.

Petty, Tom. Quoted in "Tom Petty Originally Wrote 'Free Fallin'' Just to Make Jeff Lynne Laugh." By Cathy Applefeld Olson, *Billboard*, 7 June 2016.

Pound, Ezra. "Hugh Selwyn Mauberley." *Selected Poems*, New Directions, 1957.

Proust, Marcel. *Swann's Way: In Search of Lost Time*. Vol. 1.1913, Penguin, 2004.

Redding, Otis, et al. "I've Got Dreams to Remember." *The Immortal Otis Redding,* 1968.

Rich, Adrienne. "2006 Acceptance Speech for Distinguished Contribution to American Letters." National Book Awards presented by National Book Foundation. Speech.

Richardson, Robert D., Jr. *Emerson: The Mind on Fire*. University of California Press, 1995.

Robinson, Edwin Arlington. "Richard Cory." *Poetry Foundation*, https://www.poetryfoundation.org/poems/44982/richard-cory.

The Rolling Stones. *According to the Rolling Stones.* Edited by Phillip Dodd, et al., Chronicle Books, 2003.

———. "Gimme Shelter." *Let It Bleed,* Decca; ABKCO, 1969.

Scott, James. *The Kept.* Harper, 2014.

Shaffer, Eric Paul. "Officer, I Saw the Whole Thing." *Rattle,* 1 Nov. 2010.

Shakespeare, William. *A Midsummer Night's Dream (1595). The Oxford Shakespeare: The Complete Works*, edited by Stanley Wells and Gary Taylor, Clarendon Press; Oxford University Press, 2005, pp. 401–24.

———. *The Tragedy of King Richard II. The Oxford Shakespeare: The Complete Works*, edited by Stanley Wells and Gary Taylor, Clarendon Press; Oxford University Press, 2005, pp. 369–98.

———. *The Tragedy of Hamlet, Prince of Denmark. The Oxford Shakespeare: The Complete Works*, edited by Stanley Wells and Gary Taylor, Clarendon Press; Oxford University Press, 2005, pp. 681-718.

———. *The Tragedy of Macbeth. The Oxford Shakespeare: The Complete Works*, edited by Stanley Wells and Gary Taylor, Clarendon Press; Oxford University Press, 2005, pp. 969–94.

Shalamov, Varlam. "Cherry Brandy." *Kolyma Tales.* Penguin, 1995, pp 68-75.

Shields, David. *Reality Hunger: A Manifesto.* Alfred A. Knopf, 2010.

Smart, Christopher. *The Poetical Works of Christopher Smart, Vol. 1: Jubilate Agno.* Edited by Karina Williamson, Oxford University Press, 1980.

Smith, Paul. Quoted in "Paul Smith, Jazz Pianist, Is Dead at 91." By Peter Keepnews, *The New York Times*, 3 July 2013. https://www.nytimes.com/2013/07/04/arts/music/paul-smith-jazz-pianist-is-dead-at-91.html.

Solotaroff, Ted. *A Few Good Voices in My Head: Occasional Pieces on Writing, Editing, and Reading My Contemporaries.* Harper & Row, 1987.

Sontag, Susan. "Against Interpretation." *Against Interpretation and Other Essays*, Farrar, Straus and Giroux, 1966.

Stafford, Kim. Interviewed by Stuart Tomlinson. KATU News, Portland, 28 May 2018, Sinclair Broadcast Group.

Stevens, Wallace. "The Emperor of Ice Cream." *The Collected Poems of Wallace Stevens*, Vintage Books, 1990, p. 64.

Sugar Boy and His Cane Cutters. "Iko Iko," originally "Jock-A-Mo." Checker Records, 1953.

Sunshine. Directed by_István Szabó. Alliance Atlantis, 1999.

Swift, Taylor, and Liz Rose. "All Too Well." *Red,* Big Machine, 2012.

Tannenbaum, Rob. "Jarvis Cocker Keeps Hearing That Voice." *New York Times*, 6 July 2020. https://www.nytimes.com/2020/07/06/arts/music/jarvis-cocker-jarv-is.html.

Taylor, James. "Sweet Baby James." *Sweet Baby James,* Warner Bro, 1970.

Teresa of Avila. *The Life of Saint Teresa of Avila by Herself.* Translated by J. M. Cohen, Penguin Books, 1988.

Tiomkin, Dimitri. "Acceptance Speech for Best Music Score of a Dramatic or Comedy Picture." 1954 (27th) Academy Award, Academy of Motion Picture Arts and Sciences, 30 Mar. 1955, RKO Pantages Theatre, Hollywood; NBC Century Theatre, New York City. Speech.

Toto. "Africa." *Toto IV,* Columbia, 1982.

Vaughan, Brendan and Esquire, inc, editors. *Esquire-- the Meaning of Life: Wit, Wisdom, and Wonder from 65 Extraordinary People.* Hearst Books, 2004.

Voltaire. *Discours en vers sur l'homme*, 1737.

Wahmanholm, Claire. "O | About This Poem." *Poets.org*, Academy of American Poets.

Wald, Elijah. *How the Beatles Destroyed Rock 'n' Roll: An Alternative History of American Popular Music.* Oxford University Press, 2009.

Walker, Cody. "Trades I Would Make." *Poetry Northwest*, 6 Oct. 2015.

Walsh, Joe. Interviewed by Angie Martoccio. "RS Interview: Special Edition with Joe Walsh," *Rolling Stones.* Penske Business Media, 3 Dec 2020.

Wells, Mary. "Two Lovers." *Two Lovers,* Motown, 1962.

Westen, Drew. "Opinion | What Happened to Obama?" *The New York*

Times, 6 Aug. 2011. https://www.nytimes.com/2011/08/07/opinion/sunday/what-happened-to-obamas-passion.html.

Whitman, Walt. "Song of Myself." *Poetry and Prose*, 1st Library of America College ed., Library of America, 1996, pp. 27–88.

———. "To a Common Prostitute." *Poetry and Prose*, 1st Library of America College ed., Library of America, 1996, p. 512.

Williams, Robin. Live Performance. 5 Dec. 1987. London Palladium, London, UK.

Williams, William Carlos. "Asphodel, That Greeny Flower." *The Collected Poems of William Carlos Williams. Vol. 2: 1939 - 1962*, 4th ed., New Directions Books, 1991, pp. 310–38.

Willis, Ellen, and Nona Willis Aronowitz. "The Feminist." *Out of the Vinyl Deeps: Ellen Willis on Rock Music*, University of Minnesota Press, 2011, pp. 136–39.

Wittgenstein, Ludwig. *Philosophical Occasions, 1912-1951.* Edited by James Carl Klagge and Alfred Nordmann, Hacket Publishing Co, 1993.

Woolf, Virginia. *The Collected Letters of Virginia Woolf.* Harcourt Brace Jovanovich, 1975.

Wordsworth, William. "Nuns Fret Not at Their Convent's Narrow Room." *Selected Poems.* Edited by Stephen Charles Gill, Penguin, 2004, p. 151.

———. "The World Is Too Much with Us." *Selected Poems.* Edited by Stephen Charles Gill, Penguin, 2004, p. 144.

Wright, Charles. *Halflife: Improvisations and Interviews, 1977–87.* University of Michigan Press, 1988.

Wright, James Arlington. "Lying in a Hammock at William Duffy's Farm in Pine Island, Minnesota." *Above the River: The Complete Poems*, Wesleyan Univ. Press; Noonday Press, 1994, p. 122.

Wright, Jay. Interviewed by Charles H. Rowell. "The Unraveling of the Egg: An Interview with Jay Wright," *Callaloo*, 19, Autumn 1983, pp. 3-15.

Yeats, W. B. "The Second Coming." *The Collected Poems of W.B. Yeats*, edited by Richard J. Finneran, Scribner Paperback Poetry; Simon and Schuster, 1996, p. 158.

Young, Charles M. "Eagles: Peaceful, Uneasy Feeling." *Rolling Stone*, May 29, 2008.

Young, Neil. "After the Gold Rush." *After the Gold Rush*, Reprise, 1970.

Zagajewski, Adam. "Try to Praise the Mutilated World." *Without End: New and Selected Poems*. Farrar, Straus & Giroux, 2002.

CREDITS

Special thanks to the students whose poems I have included here: Dorothy Chan, Yeney Echevarria, Landis Grenville, Nicholas Holt, Rita Mookerjee, and Sarah Morrison. Inexpressible thanks to Landis Grenville for her editorial assistance, without which *The Knowledge* would be a whole lot less knowledgeable.

Sandra Beasley, "Sestina Inviting My Sister to Become a Pirate." Copyright © 2005 by Sandra Beasley (originally published in *Cimarron Review*). Reprinted by permission of the author.

Tara Betts, "Hip Hop Analogies," Copyright © 2015 by Tara Betts (originally appeared in *Poetry*, April 2015). Reprinted by permission of the author.

Hera Lindsay Bird, "Jealousy.' Copyright © 2018 by Hera Lindsay Bird, from *Pamper me to Hell & Back*, Reprinted with permission of The Poetry Business.

"At the Sunny Ridge Retirement Center" and "Thinking About What You Wanted Her to Say," by Peg Bresnahan, from *In a Country None of Us Called Home*, published by Press 53. Copyright © 2014 by Peg Bresnahan. Used by permission of the publisher.

Dorothy Chan, "Triple Sonnet for Studmuffins Wrapped in Bacon." Copyright © 2019 by Dorothy Chan (originally published in Waxwing Literary Journal Issue XVIII, Summer 2019). Reprinted by permission of the author.

Franny Choi, "Bedtime Story." Copyright © 2015 by Franny Choi (originally published in *The Journal*, Issue 39.1 Winter). Reprinted by permission of the author.

Julie Danho; "The Best Chocolate Chip Cookie in New York City" from *Those Who Keep Arriving* (Copyright © 2020 by Silverfish Review Press). Reprinted by permission of Silverfish Review Press.

Mark Doty, "Charlie Howard's Descent" from *Paragon Park*. Copyright © 2012 by Mark Doty. Reprinted with the permission of The Permissions Company, LLC on behalf of David R.Godine, Publisher, Inc., www.godine.com.

Sean Thomas Dougherty, "Dear Editor Who Apologized for Taking Six Months to Reject my Poems and Said they Came Close" (originally published in *Birmingham Poetry Review)*. Reprinted by permission of the author.

Yeney Echevarria, "The Learning Channel, or Why I Take the Long Way." Copyright © 2021 by Yeney Echevarria. Reprinted by permission of the author.

Alejandro Escudé, "Bed Sheets (Moving Out After Separation)." Copyright © 2020 by Alejandro Escudé (originally published in *Rattle*, August 2020). Reprinted with the permission of the author.

Maggie Estep, "The Stupid Jerk I'm Obsessed With" from *No More Mr. Nice Girl*. Copyright © 1994 by Maggie Estep, Imago Records. Reprinted with permission of the estate of Maggie Estep.

Molly Fisk, "Cancer Again." Copyright © 2018 by Molly Fisk (originally published in *Vox Populi*). Reprinted by permission of the author.

"Will You" from *The Life* by Carrie Fountain, copyright © 2021 by Carrie Fountain. Used by permission of Penguin Books, an imprint of

Penguin Publishing Group, a division of Penguin Random House LLC. All rights reserved.

Yolanda J. Franklin, "Elegy for Shawn: Omega B-Boy Stance" from *Blood Vinyls: Poems.* Copyright © 2018 by Yolanda J. Franklin. Reprinted with the permission of Anhinga Press.

Landis Grenville, "Ode to the Swamp Monster." Copyright © 2015 by Landis Grenville (originally published in *Hanging Loose* Issue 105, January 2015). Reprinted by permission of the author.

"Mambo Cadillac" from *All-Night Lingo Tango* by Barbara Hamby. Copyright © 2009. Reprinted with the permission of the University of Pittsburgh press.

"An American Sunrise," from *An American Sunrise: Poems* by Joy Harjo. Copyright © 2019 by Joy Harjo. Used by permission of W. W. Norton & Company, Inc.

Terrance Hayes, "I Want To Be Fat," from *Muscular Music.* Copyright © 1999 by Terrance Hayes. Reprinted by permission of the author.

Nicholas Holt, "Half of a Pizza in the Nuclear Apocalypse." Copyright © 2020 by Nicholas Holt (originally published on Poets.org). Reprinted by permission of the author.

Nicholas Holt, "My Cows." Copyright © 2020 by Nicholas Holt (originally published in *Peatsmoke*). Reprinted by permission of the author.

Julie Kane, "Kissing the Bartender" from *Rhythm & Booze: Poems.* Copyright 2003 by Julie Kane. Used with permission of the University of Illinois Press.

Caroline Knox, "The Crybaby at the Library" from The House Party by Caroline Knox. Copyright © 1984 by Caroline Knox. Reprinted with the permission of The University of Georgia Press.

Jennifer Knox, "Hot Ass Poem." Copyright by Jennifer Knox (originally appeared in *Shout Magazine).* Reprinted with permission of the author.

"Ode to the Maggot" from *Everyday Mojo Songs of Earth: New and Selected Poems, 2001-2021* by Yusef Komunyakaa. Copyright © 2021 by *Yusef Komunyakaa.* Reprinted by permission of Farrar, Straus and Giroux.

Danusha Laméris, "Fictional Characters," from *The Moons of August.* Copyright © 2014 by Danusha Laméris. Reprinted with the permission of The Permissions Company, LLC on behalf of Autumn House Press, www.autumnhous.org

Ada Limón, "Crush" from Sharks in the Rivers. Copyright © 2010 by Ada Limón. Reprinted with the permission of The Permissions Company LLC on behalf of Milkweed Editions, milkweed.org.

"(SLANG)UAGE," Kyle Carrero Lopez, from *Muscle Memory,* [PANK] Books, 2021. Copyright © 2020 by Kyle Carrero Lopez. Originally published in Poetry, May 2020, as "(slang)uage." Reprinted by permission of the author.

Adrian Matejka, "Understanding Al Green" from *The Devil's Garden.* Copyright © 2003 by Adrian Matejka. Reprinted with the permission of The Permissions Company, LLC, on behalf of the author and Alice James Books, alicejamesbooks.org.

Arthur McMaster, "Mortgage." Copyright © 2016 by Arthur McMaster (originally published in *Poetry East,* Vol. 88/89, Autumn 2016). Reprinted with the permission of the author.

Rita Mookerjee, "Umbrella Girl Diamond Street." Copyright © 2018 by Rita Mookerjee (originally published in *Lavender Review: Lesbian Poetry & Art).* Reprinted by permission of the author.

Sarah Morrison, "Motel 666." Copyright © 2021 by Sarah Morrison. Reprinted by permission of the author.

John Murillo, "Upon Reading that Eric Dolphy Transcribed Even the Calls of Certain Species of Birds" from *Kontemporary Amerikan Poetry.* Copyright © 2020 by John Murillo. Used with the permission of The Permissions Company, LLC on behalf of Four Way Books, fourwaybooks.com.

Peter E. Murphy, "Doing Time." Copyright © 2020 by Peter E. Murphy (originally published in *Rattle* Fall 2020). Reprinted by permission of the author.

Marilyn Nelson, "How I Discovered Poetry" from The Fields of Praise: New and Selected Poems. Copyright © 1997. Reprinted with the permission of Louisiana State University Press.

Amy Newman, "20 November, Dear Editor" and "The Letting Go"

from *Dear Editor.* Copyright © 2011 by Amy Newman. Reprinted with the permission of Persea Books, Inc (New York), www.perseabooks.com. All rights reserved.

Chessy Normile, "And Send a Bird" from *Great Exodus, Great Wall, Great Party.* Copyright © 2020 by Chessy Normile. Reprinted with the permission of the author and The American Poetry Review.

Dzvinia Orlowsky, "Fack You" from *Bad Harvest.* Copyright © 2018 by Dzvinia Orlowsky. Reprinted with the permission of The Permissions Company, LLC on behalf of Carnegie Mellon University Press, www.cmu.edu/universitypress.Katsyriana Papouskaya, "Welcome to the Office." Copyright © 2021 by Katsyriana Papouskaya. Reprinted by permission of the author.

Morgan Parker, "The Book of Negroes" from There are More Beautiful Things Than Beyoncé, Tin House Books. Copyright © 2017 by Morgan Parker. Reprinted by permission of ICM Partners

"Please Let It Be Aliens" from *Danger Days.* Copyright © 2020 by Catherine Pierce. Used by the permission of Saturnalia Books.

"Permanence" from *The Probable World* by Lawrence Raab, copyright © 2000 by Lawrence Raab. Used by permission of Penguin Books, an imprint of Penguin Publishing Group, a division of Penguin Random House LLC. All rights reserved.

Betsy Rupp, "We Don't Believe in That." Copyright © 2021 by Betsy Rupp. Reprinted with the permission of the au*t*hor.

"Hate Poem," from *Orient Point* by Julie Sheehan. Copyright © 2006 by Julie Sheehan. Used by permission of W. W. Norton & Company, Inc.

Patricia Smith, "Hip-Hop Ghazal." Copyright © 2012 by Patricia Smith. Reprinted with permission of the author.

Jessica Sorenson, "My Dad's Name is D.K. Sorenson, Jr." Copyright © 2018 by Jessica Sorenson (originally published in *The Kudzu Review*, No. 60 Spring 2018). Reprinted by permission of the author.

Michael Steffen, "Which of These is Not Like the Others?" Copyright © 2019 by Michael Steffen (originally published in *The Comstock Review* Spring/Summer 2020 Volume 34.1) Reprinted by permission of the author.

Terry Ann Thaxton, "Getaway Girl" from *Getaway Girl*. Copyright © 2011 by Terry Anne Thaxton. Reprinted with permission of Salt Publishing and the author.

Laurie Uttich, "To My Student With the Dime-Sized Bruises on the Back of Her Arm Who's Still on Her Cellphone," Copyright © 2015 by Laurie Uttich (originally published in *Rattle*, November 23, 2020). Reprinted by permission of the author.

Claire Wahmanholm, "O." Copyright © 2020 by Claire Wahmanholm (originally published in Poem-a-Day on May 2, 2020 by the Academy of American Poets). Reprinted by permission of the author.

Amy Woolard, "Things Go South," from *Neck Of The Woods*. Copyright © 2020 by Amy Woolard. Reprinted with the permission of The Permissions Company, LLC, on behalf of Alice James Books, alicejamesbooks.org.

Josephine Yu, "The Thing You Might Not Understand" from *Prayer Book of the Anxious*. Copyright © 2016 by Josephine Yu. Elixir Press. Reprinted by permission of the author.

INDEX

A

E

F

G

H

I

J

K

L

M

N

O

P

R

S

T

U

V

W

Y

Z

Made in the USA
Monee, IL
13 May 2024